Presented To

St. Mary's

College of Maryland

Library

By ..GUY..T...STEUART..FOUNDATION..

....

Date ....JULY 1980

*Industrialization
in a Latin American
Common Market*

A study undertaken as part of a program of
Joint Studies on Latin American Economic Integration
Estudios Conjuntos sobre Integración Económica Latinoamericana
(ECIEL)
PREPARED BY MARTIN CARNOY

Industrialization in a Latin American Common Market

COLLABORATING INSTITUTIONS

ARGENTINA
Centro de Investigaciones Económicas, Instituto Torcuato Di Tella
Fundación de Investigaciones Económicas Latinoamericanas

BRAZIL
Instituto de Pesquisas Econômicas, Universidade de São Paulo

CHILE
Instituto de Economía, Universidad de Chile

COLOMBIA
Centro de Estudios sobre Desarrollo Económico, Universidad de los Andes

ECUADOR
Centro de Desarrollo

MEXICO
Nacional Financiera, S.A.

PARAGUAY
Centro Paraguayo de Estudios de Desarrollo Económico y Social

PERU
Instituto de Investigaciones Económicas, Universidad Nacional Mayor de San Marcos

URUGUAY
Instituto de Economía, Universidad de la República

VENEZUELA
Centro de Estudios del Desarrollo, Universidad Central de Venezuela

THE BROOKINGS INSTITUTION
Washington, D.C.

THE BROOKINGS INSTITUTION is an independent organization devoted to nonpartisan research, education, and publication in economics, government, foreign policy, and the social sciences generally. Its principal purposes are to aid in the development of sound public policies and to promote public understanding of issues of national importance.

The Institution was founded on December 8, 1927, to merge the activities of the Institute for Government Research, founded in 1916, the Institute of Economics, founded in 1922, and the Robert Brookings Graduate School of Economics and Government, founded in 1924.

The general administration of the Institution is the responsibility of a Board of Trustees charged with maintaining the independence of the staff and fostering the most favorable conditions for creative research and education. The immediate direction of the policies, program, and staff of the Institution is vested in the President, assisted by an advisory committee of the officers and staff.

In publishing a study, the Institution presents it as a competent treatment of a subject worthy of public consideration. The interpretations and conclusions in such publications are those of the author or authors and do not necessarily reflect the views of the other staff members, officers, or trustees of the Brookings Institution.

Foreword

THE EUPHORIA that accompanied the establishment of the Latin American Free Trade Association in the early 1960s arose from little more than broad visions of the benefits to be expected from a Latin American common market, and soon gave way to disillusionment as the region's economic integration proceeded at a discouragingly slow pace. Latin American governments, restrained in part by business interests, in part by political considerations, moved timidly toward the removal of trade barriers. A basic reason for their hesitation was—and remains—lack of knowledge about what to expect from a common market. Ignorance bred fears of economic losses that eventually overshadowed the earlier vision of the benefits of economic cooperation.

In an effort to provide at least part of the requisite knowledge, a group of eleven Latin American economic institutes undertook a collaborative research program coordinated by members of the Brookings Institution's staff and known as ECIEL, the acronym for its Spanish name, Estudios Conjuntos sobre Integración Económica Latinoamericana. The objective of the first study in this program was to analyze the effects of a common market on six industries; the results of the analysis and an account of the methodology by which they were obtained form the substance of this book.

The ECIEL program, conceived and principally coordinated by Brookings Senior Fellow Joseph Grunwald, is supported by grants from the Ford Foundation and the Inter-American Development Bank. The following preface describes the program, the collaborators, and their contributions in greater detail.

Martin Carnoy, who was directly responsible for the technical coordination of the study, prepared this volume on the basis of the work done by the participating ECIEL institutes. Various Latin American collaborators reviewed drafts, and the ECIEL program participants listed in the preface assume responsibility for technical content. The study was completed as part of the Brookings Foreign Policy Studies Program, which is directed by Henry Owen.

A former Brookings research associate and now a member of the faculty of Stanford University, Martin Carnoy is a co-author of two other Brookings books: *Latin American Trade Patterns* (with Donald W. Baerresen and Joseph Grunwald, 1965) and *Latin American Economic Integration and U.S. Policy* (with Joseph Grunwald and Miguel S. Wionczek, 1971).

The Brookings Institution is grateful to the members of the ECIEL Visiting Committee—Carlos Díaz Alejandro of Yale University, Charles Frank of Princeton University, and Gustav Ranis of Yale University, the Committee's chairman—for their comments on an earlier draft. The manuscript was edited by Mendelle T. Berenson. Joy Dunkerley verified the accuracy of the data; Joan C. Culver prepared the index; and Catita Edward supervised the typing of drafts.

The interpretations and conclusions expressed in this book are, of course, those of the author and the participating members of the ECIEL institutes. They should not be attributed to the Ford Foundation, the Inter-American Development Bank, or the trustees, officers, or other staff members of the Brookings Institution.

KERMIT GORDON
President

September 1971
Washington, D.C.

Preface

In 1963 SEVERAL major economic research institutions in Latin America joined forces in a common research program, called the Program of Joint Studies on Latin American Economic Integration, and known as ECIEL, the acronym formed from its Spanish name, Estudios Conjuntos sobre Integración Económica Latinoamericana. While the program's major objective is to prepare useful, professionally competent studies, important by-products have been the strengthening of the economics profession in Latin America through this cooperative effort and support for the development of the participating institutions.

ECIEL: Background and Organization

Institutional research is always difficult to organize. Even where research institutions in economics exist, team research is the exception rather than the rule. Researchers are almost by definition individualists, so that institutions usually provide simply the abode and administrative framework within which they can carry out their own projects independently. This has been the case in Latin America, with the added factor that empirical research in the social sciences is comparatively new in the region.

For a joint research effort to be successful, the area to be investigated must capture the imagination of the participants. Studies on the economic integration of the region meet the test because of the intense interest in this problem in Latin America.

Several attempts were initiated toward the end of the 1950s to establish contact among the research institutions in Latin America. At first, these efforts met with little success, primarily because only a few institutes had personnel sufficiently well trained to carry out research at a professional level. In January 1963 a large-scale conference was held in Rio de Janeiro on the theme of inflation and growth, under the auspices of the Economic Growth Center of Yale University, the National Planning Association, and three major Latin American economic research institutions: the Institute of Economics of the University of Chile, the Institute of Economics of the Vargas Foundation of Brazil, and the Center of Economic Research of the Di Tella Institute of Argentina. A number of economists from the United States, Europe, and Asia attended, but more significant was the participation of many able Latin American economists from governmental and private institutions as well as universities. The conference gathered together most of the professional talent in the region. It also provided a propitious setting for renewing efforts toward collaboration among Latin American research institutions.

At an informal meeting during the conference, it was decided in principle that the Latin American institutions would join together to undertake research on the economic integration of the region. This work would be coordinated under a special program of the Brookings Institution, which I, as the former director of the Chilean institute and then professor of economics at Yale University, was to establish.

An organizational meeting at the Brookings Institution followed in May 1963, attended by economists from the Institute of Economics of the University of Chile, the Institute of Economics of the Vargas Foundation, and the Center of Economic Research of the Di Tella Institute. These institutions committed themselves to collaborate in comparative cost studies of specific industries in the region. Since that time additional research institutions have joined the study so that ten institutions from ten Latin American countries were involved in the project that this book reports.

It has become apparent to all the participants that joint research provides valuable machinery for scientific collaboration in economics. It was therefore decided not to dismantle the mechanism after completion of this study, and thus several new projects have been undertaken, with wider participation of Latin American economic institutes. There are now twenty collaborating institutions in the eleven countries of the Latin American

Free Trade Association (LAFTA),[1] and Costa Rica, covering all of Latin America except part of Central America and the Caribbean.

Until a few years ago there was very little intercourse among Latin American economists, so that economists of one country had scant knowledge about the workings of other economies in the region. By facilitating broadened contacts within the profession, ECIEL plays a significant part in the integration movement in Latin America.

Scholarship has been very unevenly distributed in Latin America but the joint program has tended to narrow the marked differences in the professional competence of the research institutions through semi-annual seminars and a continuing interchange of information. The quality of the work of some institutions has unquestionably been superior to that of others; as a result they have tended to set the standards that the other participants have tried to emulate. Nevertheless there were individuals in all institutions who had special abilities and were thus able to contribute fruitfully to the elaboration and execution of the present study.

Working together on a common project enables researchers to learn from one another and to make progress together. The study presented here is particularly appropriate for this process because it not only embodies a purpose—the economic integration of Latin America—which is a strong motivating factor for collaboration, but also combines practical as well as theoretical elements. The practical economists gained insights from their more theoretically inclined colleagues and the theoreticians were brought down to earth by those who had practical experience. The use of technical and engineering knowledge, which this project involved, reinforced this broadening process.

Beyond the achievement of their specific research purposes, and the mutual strengthening that their association in them provide, the participating institutions could become a permanent professional alliance to investigate common Latin American economic problems and to lend technical support to policy makers concerned with the welfare of the region as a whole.

The Research Project

The specific aims of this research were to indicate minimum cost locations and sizes of plants in selected industries within a potential regional

1. Argentina, Bolivia, Brazil, Chile, Colombia, Ecuador, Mexico, Paraguay, Peru, Uruguay, and Venezuela.

common market in 1975 and to estimate the benefits to be derived from the regional integration of these industries.

Six product groups were selected for the study but not all of them are strategic for economic integration: some countries that have little possibility of competing in important industries may have an absolute advantage in producing other types of products. In order to include institutes from as many countries as possible in the preparation of cost studies, some products that are less important from an integration point of view were included in the project. The products studied were (1) nitrogenous fertilizers—ammonia, ammonium nitrate, ammonium sulphate, and urea; (2) methanol and formaldehyde; (3) kraft paper, kraft pulp, and newsprint; (4) agricultural tractors; (5) universal parallel lathes; and (6) powdered milk and cheese.

The work was divided into four stages: estimation for each LAFTA member of the demand for the given product in 1975; estimation of costs of production of the selected products in various countries; estimation of the costs of transportation; and combination of the previous three estimates to find the minimum cost location of plants in LAFTA for each product or product group.

Coordination

The project was coordinated mainly through periodic seminars attended by the principal researchers concerned with the project in each participating institution and a number of invited observers. The seminar site rotated among the ECIEL institutions in Latin America. The work of the seminars was to develop methodology and procedures, to present and examine progress reports, to resolve research and coordination problems, and to agree on work schedules. In the inter-seminar periods, coordination was effected through correspondence and periodic consultation with Brookings coordinating staff members, who visited the participating institutions in Latin America.

Participation

Of the twenty institutions now taking part in the ECIEL program, eleven are affiliated with universities, five are private research organizations, and four are autonomous government agencies concerned with data collection, planning, or the promotion of industrialization in their respective countries.

It was decided that in each country only one institution should be responsible for a given study in the program, although other institutions within the country could cooperate. Since ECIEL is carrying out several studies at present, more than one institution may be participating in a country. Eleven Latin American institutions from ten countries (the LAFTA nations except Bolivia, which at the time the research was undertaken was not yet a member of LAFTA), and the Brookings Institution collaborated on the present study. Their roles are indicated in the note on authorship, below.

Among the regular observers invited to the seminars have been representatives from the Latin American Free Trade Association, the Inter-American Development Bank, the Economic Commission for Latin America, the Institute for the Integration of Latin America (INTAL), the Organization of American States, the World Bank, and the European Economic Community.

Observers from other international agencies have also attended and, in addition, the institutions that acted as hosts for the meetings invited representatives of public and private organizations from their own countries. Because the seminars were informal, the observers frequently participated in discussions and made contributions to the project.

Although every institute participated in every step, each was primarily responsible for the study of its own country, with special reference to selecting the industries and products to be studied; making market studies and 1975 demand projections for them; establishing cost structures for various levels of output up to total regional demand in 1975; calculating national transport costs; and estimating cost functions, including economies of scale and exchange rates. The project's coordinator was responsible for calculating regional demand; preparing the model and computer programs; determining from the model the minimum cost locations of production and alternatives to it; estimating welfare benefits and costs; and calculating the international transport costs and cost functions. The institutes and the coordinator were jointly responsible for the elaboration of the methodology and the model.

A Note on Form

One of the problems in a study of this nature is to reduce to manageable form materials provided by eleven research institutions. This required a choice of either (1) summarizing the studies of each institute, presenting the demand and cost projections country by country, and then integrating them in a discussion of the regional model, or (2) presenting the studies by industry. The structure of this book reflects the latter choice. The individual institutes are free to publish the studies of specific industries in their own country, and many of them have already done so.

A Spanish edition of this book is being published and a booklet containing a short Spanish summary is to be given wide circulation in Latin America.

A Note on Authorship

The institutes that participated in this project contributed the country studies that form the basis for this book. While the collaboration derived from a commitment by the institutions, the authorship of the studies rests with the members of their staffs who submitted the drafts from which Martin Carnoy prepared the final manuscript. Carnoy also contributed most of the background and methodological material that forms Part I. Donald W. Baerresen, former research associate at the Brookings Institution, participated in the early discussions on methodology. Jorge Salazar, senior fellow at the Brookings Institution, assisted in the preparation of background material for the case studies in Part II. Peter T. Knight, a Brookings research associate, revised several sections of the manuscript, particularly in Part I, and participated in the final revisions.

The practice in some of the participating Latin American organizations has been to publish studies as an institution, with the authors remaining anonymous, but it was agreed that the individual contributions to this publication would be identified wherever possible.[2] The following list is arranged by country because the principal contribution of the authors has been the preparation of demand projections and industry studies for their own countries. Some of the collaborators also participated in the elaboration of the methodology employed in the international comparisons, and one or more persons from each institute reviewed the drafts of the book. In this sense the responsibility for the book rests with all the authors.

2. In the following list, the affiliation given is that of the participant at the time of his association with the project.

ARGENTINA

Project directors: José María Dagnino Pastore until November 1965, then Mario Brodersohn, both of Centro de Investigaciones Económicas, Instituto Torcuato Di Tella.

Demand projections for tractors, lathes, powdered milk and cheese, and kraft paper and newsprint: José María Dagnino Pastore, assisted by Juan Carlos de Pablo, Centro de Investigaciones Económicas, Instituto Torcuato Di Tella.

Demand projections for ammonia, ammonium nitrate, ammonium sulphate, and urea, and methanol and formaldehyde: Mario Brodersohn, assisted by Adrian Guisarri, both of Centro de Investigaciones Económicas, Instituto Torcuato Di Tella.

Cost analysis for tractors: José María Dagnino Pastore, with Jorge H. Meier, consultant; assisted by Juan Carlos de Pablo and Florencio Ballesteros, Centro de Investigaciones, Instituto Torcuato Di Tella.

Cost analysis for lathes and cheese: Juan Carlos de Pablo, assisted by Fernando H. Ibarra, Fundación de Investigaciones Económicas Latinoamericanas.

Transportation costs for ammonium sulphate and urea, methanol, and pulp and newsprint: Mario Brodersohn, assisted by Florencio Ballesteros.

BRAZIL

Joint project directors: Antonio Delfim Netto and Ruy Aguiar da Silva Leme, both of the Instituto de Pesquisas Económicas, Universidade de São Paulo.

Collaborators: Carlos Rocca, Affonso Pastore, Pedro Cipollari, and Eduardo Carvalho, all of Instituto de Pesquisas Económicas, Universidade de São Paulo.

CHILE

Joint project directors: Carlos Massad until November 1964, then Ivan Yanez and Teresa Jeanneret, all of the Instituto de Economía, Universidad de Chile.

COLOMBIA

Project directors: Jorge Ruiz Lara until June 1965, then Francisco Ortega, both of Centro de Estudios sobre Desarrollo Económico, Universidad de los Andes.

Collaborators: Lucia Cruz de Schlesinger and Marta Fernandez, both of Centro de Estudios sobre Desarrollo Económico, Universidad de los Andes.

ECUADOR

Collaborators: Germánico Espinosa, Alberto Kuri, Hugo Molina, and Fernando Leon, all of Centro de Desarrollo.

MEXICO

Collaborator: Eduardo Colín, Nacional Financiera, S.A.
General supervision: Carlos Quintana, Nacional Financiera, S.A.

PARAGUAY

Collaborators: Leopoldino García Franco, assisted by Digno Martinez Lopez and Sergio Gomez Serrato, all of Centro Paraguayo de Estudios de Desarrollo Económica y Social.

PERU

Collaborators: Adolfo Figueroa Arevalo, assisted by Miguel Chinchayan Sandoval, both of Instituto de Investigaciones Económicas, Universidad Nacional Mayor de San Marcos.

General supervision: Carlos Capunay Mimbela, School of Economics, Universidad Nacional Mayor de San Marcos.

URUGUAY

Collaborators: Mario Buchelli and Raul Vigorito, both of the Instituto de Economía, Universidad de la República.

General supervision: Enrique Iglesias, Instituto Economía de Universidad de la República.

VENEZUELA

Collaborator: John Stone, Centro de Estudios del Desarrollo, Universidad Central de Venezuela.

General supervision: Jorge Ahumada (deceased), Centro de Estudios del Desarrollo, Universidad Central de Venezuela.

JOSEPH GRUNWALD
Coordinator, ECIEL Program

Contents

PART ONE: ISSUES AND ALTERNATIVES

1. *The Setting*   3

Historical Influences *3*
Choosing the Road to Market Expansion *8*
CACM, LAFTA, and the Latin American Economic Integration
  Movement since 1960   *13*

2. *The Object, the Method, and the Results*   29

Design of the Study *31*
The Model: Assumptions and Uses *33*
The Results *39*
Benefits and Costs of Union *49*
The Distribution of Gains from Customs Union and Suboptimum
  Locations *59*
The Role of Exchange Rates *64*
Some Conclusions *68*

PART TWO: INDUSTRIAL CASE STUDIES

3. *Nitrogenous Fertilizers*   73

Production and Consumption   1963 and 1975   *74*
Prices and Costs *77*
Calculation of Optimum Location of Production *88*
Costs of Solutions *89*
Some Qualifications to the Results *104*

xix

Capital Investment Requirements *106*
Welfare Benefits and Costs *109*
Nominal and Effective Tariffs *111*
Summary *111*

4. *Methanol and Formaldehyde*   116

Production and Consumption—1963 and 1975   *116*
Structure of Costs and Economies of Scale *118*
Welfare Benefits and Costs *129*

5. *Tractors*   135

Standardization of Tractor Size *136*
Projected Demand for Tractors *137*
Prices *142*
Optimum Location of Production *143*
Welfare Benefits and Costs *148*
Summary *148*

6. *Lathes*   151

Projections of Demand and Cost Estimates *152*
The Optimum Location of Production *155*
Shadow Prices and Indifference Rates *160*
Welfare Benefits and Costs *164*

7. *Powdered Milk and Cheese*   165

Current and Projected Demand *166*
Costs of Production *169*
Optimum Location of Production *174*
Indifference Exchange Rates *178*
Welfare Benefits and Costs *183*

8. *Paper and Pulp*   184

Projections of Demand *190*
Cost Structure *192*
Optimum Location of Production *193*
The Exchange Rate Influence *199*
Welfare Benefits and Costs *201*
Newsprint: Demand and Costs *207*
Some Conclusions *208*

PART THREE: METHODOLOGY

9. *The Model and Its Applications*   213

The Linearized Programming Model *213*
Demand and Cost Estimates *215*
Distributing Gains and Losses from Locating Optimally *224*
Rates of Exchange *226*

Appendixes 229

A. The Linearized Programming Model *231*
B. Cost of Production and Transportation *236*
C. Benefits and Costs to Individual Countries of Buying from Optimum Locations *243*
D. Standardization of Tractor Size *248*
E. Calculation of Powdered Milk and Cheese Production Costs *253*
F. Comparison of Estimates of Costs of Producing Pulp and Paper *260*

Index 262

Text Tables

1-1. Selected Indicators of Industrial Activity in Latin America, 1950 and 1965   19
1-2. Percentage Change in Selected Indicators of Industrial Activity in Latin America, 1950–65   21
1-3. Selected Data on Latin American Exports and Imports, Selected Years, 1960–65   22
2-1. Average Cost of Production of Ammonia, by Country and by Annual Output   41
2-2. Minimum Cost Locations for Production of Selected Fertilizers in Latin America, for Alternative Assumptions about Transport Costs and Exchange Rates   43
2-3. Average Cost of Production of Methanol, by Country and by Annual Output   44
2-4. Welfare Benefits and Costs of Alternatives to Optimum Location of Selected Products in LAFTA, 1975   52
2-5. Total Value of Output of Selected Product Groups in LAFTA, 1975   55
2-6. Relative Welfare Gains from Buying Selected Products from Optimum Location, by LAFTA Country, 1975   57
2-7. Optimum and Alternative Locations in LAFTA of Production of Fourteen Products, 1975   62
2-8. Prices and Indifference Exchange Rates for Selected Products, Assuming Minimum Transport Costs, 1975   66
3-1. Production and Consumption of Nitrogenous Fertilizers in LAFTA, by Country and Product, 1963   75
3-2. Projected Production and Consumption of Nitrogenous Fertilizers in LAFTA, by Country and Product, 1975   78
3-3. Elements of Ammonia Production as Percent of Total Production Costs, and Cost per Ton of Output in LAFTA, by Country and Capacity of Plant, 1964–65   80

3-4. Elements of Urea Production as Percent of Total Production Costs, and Cost per Ton of Output in LAFTA, by Country and Capacity of Plant, 1964–65   81

3-5. Elements of Ammonium Nitrate Production as Percent of Total Production Costs, and Cost per Ton of Output in LAFTA, by Country and Capacity of Plant, 1964–65   82

3-6. Elements of Ammonium Sulphate Production as Percent of Total Production Costs, and Cost per Ton of Output in LAFTA, by Country and Capacity of Plant, 1964–65   83

3-7. Optimum Location of Production of Selected Nitrogenous Fertilizers in LAFTA, by Selected Assumptions about Transport Costs and Exchange Rates, 1975   90

3-8. Optimum Location of Production of Selected Nigrogenous Fertilizers in LAFTA, and Selected Alternatives, and Their Costs, 1975   91

3-9. Prices of Selected Nitrogenous Fertilizers from Selected Sources in LAFTA, 1975   98

3-10. Prices of Nitrogenous Fertilizers and Implicit Indifference Exchange Rates in LAFTA, 1975   102

3-11. Optimum Location of Production of Selected Nitrogenous Fertilizers in LAFTA, and Selected Alternatives, and Their Costs, Assuming Equal Technology in All Producing Countries, 1975   107

3-12. Prices of Nitrogenous Fertilizers in LAFTA Countries Derived from Optimum Solution, Assuming Equal Technology in All Producing Countries, 1975   108

3-13. Demand for Ammonia and Nitrogenous Fertilizers in LAFTA, Net of 1963 Production, 1975   109

3-14. Total Investment Required in Nitrogenous Fertilizer Production in LAFTA, 1963–75   110

3-15. Welfare Benefits and Costs of Selected Alternatives to Optimum Location of Production of Nitrogenous Fertilizers in LAFTA Countries, Assuming Minimum Transport Costs, 1975   112

3-16. Nominal and Effective Tariffs on Nitrogenous Fertilizers in LAFTA, 1966   114

4-1. Production and Apparent Consumption of Methanol and Formaldehyde, 1963, and Projected Demand, 1975, in LAFTA   117

4-2. Projected Total Market Demand for Methanol in Direct Form and Formaldehyde, by LAFTA Country, 1975   118

4-3. Cost Structure of Methanol and Formaldehyde Production in LAFTA   120

4-4. Optimum Location of Production of Methanol and Formaldehyde in LAFTA, and Selected Alternatives, and Their Costs, 1975   123

4-5. Prices of Methanol and Formaldehyde from Selected Sources in LAFTA, 1975   127

4-6. Prices of Methanol and Formaldehyde and Indifference Exchange Rates in LAFTA, 1975   130

4-7. Total Investment Required in Production of Methanol and
Formaldehyde in LAFTA, 1965–75 132

4-8. Welfare Benefits and Costs of Selected Alternatives to Optimum
Location of Production of Methanol and Formaldehyde in LAFTA
Countries, 1975 133

4-9. Nominal and Effective Tariffs on Methanol and Formaldehyde, by
LAFTA Country, 1966 134

5-1. Purchases of Tractors in 1963 and Projected Demand for Tractors
in 1975, in LAFTA Countries 137

5-2. Structure of Costs of Production of Tractors, Uncorrected for
Horsepower, by Firm, Argentina, 1963 139

5-3. Structure of Costs of Production of Tractors, Uncorrected for
Horsepower, by Firm, Brazil, 1965 140

5-4. Costs of Production and Price per Tractor in Selected Countries 142

5-5. Optimum Location of Production of Tractors in LAFTA, and
Selected Alternatives, and Their Costs, 1975 145

5-6. Tractor Prices Associated with Various Patterns of Production,
for LAFTA Countries, and Selected Exchange Rates, 1975 146

5-7. Comparative Prices of Tractors Produced in Argentina, Brazil, and
the United States, by Consuming Country, 1975, and Indifference
Exchange Rates 147

5-8. Welfare Benefits and Costs of Selected Alternatives to Optimum
Location of Production of Tractors in LAFTA Countries, under
Selected Assumptions about Exchange Rates, 1975 149

5-9. Import Duties on Wheeled, 50-Horsepower Agricultural Tractors
in LAFTA Countries, 1966 150

6-1. Projected Demand for Universal Parallel Lathes in LAFTA, 1975 153

6-2. Cost Structure of Universal Parallel Lathe Production in LAFTA,
1975 154

6-3. Optimum Location of Production of Lathes in LAFTA, and
Selected Alternatives, and Their Costs, 1975, under Selected
Exchange Rate Assumptions, Assuming Unlimited Plant Capacity 156

6-4. Optimum Location of Production of Lathes in LAFTA, and Selected
Alternatives, and Their Costs, 1975, under Selected Exchange Rate
Assumptions, Assuming Plants of 500 Unit Capacity 158

6-5. Shadow Prices for Lathes in LAFTA, 1975 160

6-6. Prices of Lathes and Indifference Exchange Rates in LAFTA, 1975 161

6-7. Tariffs on 1,500 Millimeter Lathes in LAFTA, 1966 162

6-8. Investment Required for Lathe Production in LAFTA, 1963–75 162

6-9. Welfare Benefits and Costs of Selected Alternatives to Optimum
Production of Lathes in LAFTA, 1975 163

7-1. Nominal Tariffs on Powdered Milk and Cheese in LAFTA, 1966 167

7-2. Consumption and Production of Powdered Milk in LAFTA, 1963,
and Projected Demand, 1975 168

7-3. Consumption of Cheese, 1963, and Projected Demand, 1975,
LAFTA   169
7-4. Demand for Cheese in LAFTA, 1975   169
7-5. Cost Structure of Powdered Whole Milk Production in LAFTA,
1975   170
7-6. Structure of Costs of Cheese Production in LAFTA, 1975   172
7-7. Wholesale Prices of Milk for Powdered Whole Milk Production
in LAFTA, 1964–65   173
7-8. Optimum Location of Production of Powdered Milk and Cheese in
LAFTA, and Selected Alternatives, and Their Costs, 1975   176
7-9. Prices of Powdered Milk and Cheese in LAFTA, 1975   179
7-10. Prices and Implicit Indifference Exchange Rates for Selected
Locations of Production of Powdered Milk and Cheese in LAFTA   180
7-11. Welfare Benefits and Costs of Selected Alternatives to Optimum
Location of Production of Powdered Milk and Cheese in
LAFTA, 1975   182
8-1. Paper and Paperboard Apparent Consumption and Production in
LAFTA, Selected Years, 1949–64   185
8-2. Paper Pulp Production in LAFTA, Selected Years, 1949–64   187
8-3. Net Imports of Wood Pulp in LAFTA, Selected Years, 1950–64   188
8-4. Nominal and Effective Tariffs on Pulp and Paper in LAFTA,
1965   188
8-5. Production and Consumption of Kraft Paper in LAFTA, 1963   190
8-6. Projected Demand for Kraft Paper in LAFTA, 1975   191
8-7. Demand for Cellulose for Use in Kraft Paper and in Newsprint
in LAFTA, 1975   191
8-8. Cost Structure of Kraft Cellulose and Kraft Paper Production in
LAFTA, 1975   194
8-9. Optimum Location of Production of Pulp and Paper in LAFTA,
and Selected Alternatives, and Their Costs, 1975   197
8-10. Prices of Kraft Pulp and Kraft Paper in LAFTA, 1975   200
8-11. Prices and Implicit Indifference Rates for Chemical Pulp for
Newsprint Production and for Kraft Paper in LAFTA, 1975   202
8-12. Welfare Benefits and Costs of Selected Alternatives to Optimum
Location of Production of Kraft Pulp for Newsprint Production
and Kraft Paper, 1975   204
8-13. Investment Required for Pulp and Kraft Paper Production in
LAFTA, 1963–75   206
8-14. Projected Demand for and Supply of Newsprint in LAFTA,
1975   208
8-15. Cost Structure of Newsprint Production   209
8-16. Projected Cost of Production and Transportation of Newsprint
in LAFTA, 1975   209

Text Figure

4-1. Cumulative Percentage of Alternative Patterns of Production of Methanol and Formaldehyde in LAFTA, by Annual Cost 126

Appendix Tables

D-1. Percent Distribution of Tractor Sales by Size in Horsepower, in Selected LAFTA Countries, Selected Years 249

D-2. Percentage Equivalents of Tractors of Selected Horsepower to 50-Horsepower Tractors Derived from U.S. Conversion Equation, Selected LAFTA Countries 251

F-1. Comparison of ECLA and ECIEL Estimates of Total Cost Curves for Unbleached Pulp and Kraft Paper 261

F-2. Production Costs for Chilean Pulp and Paper Production 261

Appendix Figures

C-1. Welfare Benefits of Importing from Optimum Regional Location Compared with Autarkic Production 244

C-2. Welfare Benefits of Importing from Optimum Regional Location Compared with Extraregional Importing 246

E-1. Fluid Milk Production of Uniform Density in a Circular Area Centered on a Milk Processing Plant 254

PART ONE

Issues and Alternatives

CHAPTER ONE

The Setting

OVER THE PAST FOUR DECADES Latin American development efforts have gradually shifted away from building individual self-sufficient economies toward developing an economically efficient regional industrial structure. The shift in approach—still incomplete—came after a long period of growth in the manufacturing sectors of almost all the Latin American countries, and only when it became clear that further economic development in many countries was beginning to be seriously constrained by the division of the region into small markets.

This chapter reviews the evolution of thought, especially in Latin America, on the role of international trade in economic development, and outlines the progress through 1968 toward the economic integration of the countries south of the Rio Grande. It provides the setting for the study that the rest of the volume reports and for the conclusions that may be drawn concerning the location of some major industries within a future Latin American common market.

Historical Influences

For many years, the less developed countries of the world have watched the standard of life in the developed countries rise more rapidly than their own. At the same time, the developed countries have maintained that free trade is the most efficient means of promoting growth both in less developed countries and in areas that already have a high degree of industrial and agricultural development. The principle of free trade has seldom been fully adhered to by the developed countries. They continue routinely to use protective tariffs and quotas to insulate domestic producers from foreign competition, including that of the less developed countries.

Before the Great Depression many of the larger countries in Latin America had begun to industrialize. Between 1900 and 1929 Argentina's industrial product rose by 500 percent; in 1930 it accounted for more than 25 percent of the country's total output. Brazil's industrial product rose even more rapidly between 1915 and 1930.[1]

This growth, as well as that of other Latin American countries, took place to a considerable extent in a free trade context, responding to the expansion of local markets for products that could compete with imports, though the interruption of supplies from overseas occasioned by the First World War provided an artificial impetus to the process.[2] Food processing, textiles, and other light consumer products were the principal avenues of industrial expansion. Most income growth, however, continued to rely on exports of primary products.

The collapse of the international trading system during the depression severely damaged many economies in Latin America that had depended on export markets in developed countries to finance imported goods. In reaction, Latin American countries began to encourage industrialization through strong protective measures. Shortages in the United States and the cutting off of imports from Europe during the Second World War accelerated the process. The result was a continuing policy of import-substituting industrialization characterized by various combinations of high tariffs, multiple exchange rates, and quotas. As countries in the region sought to produce domestically more and more goods previously imported, however,

1. United Nations, Economic Commission for Latin America (ECLA), *The Process of Industrial Development in Latin America*, E/CN.12/716/Rev. 1 (1966), Chap. 1. (Documents published in Spanish by this arm of the UN bear its title in that language: Comisión Económica para America Latina, or CEPAL. To avoid confusion, references to the organization in citations in this volume will be to ECLA, whether the document itself is in Spanish or English.)

2. See, for example, Werner Baer, *Industrialization and Economic Development in Brazil* (Richard D. Irwin, 1965).

the very crisis that import substitution was supposed to solve—the dependence on developed countries for imported goods and the decline in export earnings relative to expenditures on imports—became more acute.[3] Now, however, the principal imports were not consumption goods, but raw materials and intermediate goods for existing industries and capital goods for new industries. In view of the chronic shortage of international reserves in the region, fluctuations in export earnings now were liable to be translated directly into fluctuations in the level of domestic industrial production and investment.

Small-scale, inefficient domestic industries, heavily protected from foreign competition, may require imported inputs of greater value than their output at world market prices.[4] In addition, currency overvaluation, combined with import barriers, discriminates against exports relative to import-competing and nontraded goods, especially services, thus restricting the supply of exportable products. Because of the distortion in relative prices, resources are shifted away from the export sector to domestic manufactures and services.[5]

As they attempted to industrialize rapidly, the Latin American countries incurred large debts to foreign governments, international agencies, and private lenders, thus greatly increasing their need for foreign exchange. According to the Economic Commission for Latin America (ECLA), the region had, by the mid-1960s, become a net *supplier* of capital to the world

3. The principal exceptions were Venezuela and Mexico, whose massive sales of oil and tourist services, respectively, spared them the severe shortages of foreign exchange suffered by other major countries in the area.

4. Stephen E. Guisinger, "Negative Value Added and the Theory of Effective Protection," *Quarterly Journal of Economics*, Vol. 83 (August 1969), pp. 415–33.

5. For theoretical treatment of these points, see W. M. Corden, "The Structure of a Tariff System and the Effective Protective Rate," *Journal of Political Economy*, Vol. 74 (June 1966), pp. 221–37; Ronald I. McKinnon, "Intermediate Products and Differential Tariffs: A Generalization of Lerner's Symmetry Theorem," *Quarterly Journal of Economics*, Vol. 80 (November 1966), pp. 584–615; Bela Balassa and Daniel M. Schydlowsky, "Effective Tariffs, Domestic Cost of Foreign Exchange, and the Equilibrium Exchange Rate," *Journal of Political Economy*, Vol. 76 (May–June 1968), pp. 348–60; and Bela Balassa and Associates, *The Structure of Protection in Developing Countries* (Johns Hopkins Press, 1971). An early empirical study in a developing country showing negative value added in several manufacturing activities is Ronald Soligo and Joseph J. Stern, "Tariff Protection, Import Substitution and Investment Efficiency," *Pakistan Development Review*, Vol. 5 (Summer 1965), pp. 249–70.

through the payment of interest and amortization on its foreign debt, the profit remittances of foreign investments in the region, and capital export by private citizens in search of security for their funds.[6]

The types of goods imported changed drastically during the import-substituting process. Import demand shifted from consumer goods, and some simple agricultural machinery, toward industrial capital equipment and intermediate inputs for domestic industries. An increasing share of employment depended on a steady supply of these machines and industrial raw materials. Foreign exchange, in turn, became a much more crucial factor in almost all Latin American economies than it had been before the 1930s. Its significance was magnified by the growing political power of urban populations that depended on the industrial structures erected behind protective barriers.

Revised Theory and Its Applications

In the late forties and fifties, Latin American reformer-economists reacted to the theory of international trade in much the same way that their economies had reacted to the temporary collapse of the international economic system twenty years earlier. Some concluded that, since the doctrines of traditional theory did not seem to apply to the problems of the less developed world, traditional theory itself was to be viewed as a device for rationalizing existing inequalities, and that it conflicted directly with Latin American development aims. Established concepts of the international exchange of goods and the distribution of gains from trade were therefore attacked and alternatives were posed that would increase, rather than diminish, the Latin American share of world output.

The intellectual thrust for Latin American economic development was provided by the Economic Commission for Latin America, an organ of the United Nations directed at that time by Raúl Prebisch, a prominent Argentine economist. A major portion of ECLA's second *Economic Survey*

---

6. ECLA, *Economic Survey of Latin America 1968*, E/CN.12/825, Table 54, p. 99, shows that in 1967 there was a net outflow of $501 million in spite of a gross inflow of $4,150 million.

This, of course, does not measure in full the contribution of foreign capital to Latin America's balance of payments, because the net flow does not take into account increases in export earnings and foreign exchange savings (through decreased imports) which the production induced by foreign capital may provide.

of Latin America in 1949 was devoted to showing why Latin America—and, by implication, all less developed countries—had to industrialize and protect the industrial sector from foreign competition. The early ECLA analysis was based on two fundamental assumptions: "Industrialization is an inevitable feature of economic development," and "a reasonable measure of protection is generally indispensable for industrialization."[7] These assumptions in turn were justified by the allegedly grim prospects for primary product exports and the constraints imposed by development based on such exports.

Spurred by these ideas, import-substituting industrialization progressed rapidly during the 1950s, especially in the larger countries—Brazil, Mexico, and Argentina. However, in the early 1960s, industrial growth rates slackened markedly. Led by Raúl Prebisch himself, ECLA economists were not slow to perceive this phenomenon and its implications. They broadened their analysis to account for it, but at the same time they attacked some of the excesses resulting from overemphasis on industrialization at the expense of agriculture and exports.[8] While industrialization is essential to development, they now argued, it becomes increasingly difficult to substitute domestic production for imports once the stage of light manufacturing is passed. Markets for capital equipment and major consumer durables are too small in any single Latin American economy to allow the production of these goods to be even reasonably competitive with imports. In the case of capital equipment, the high price of domestic production is especially harmful to further development because capital goods enter into both light industry and agriculture as inputs.[9]

The industrialization process is faced by a critical balance-of-payments constraint which arises from the very measures taken to stimulate industrialization, from unfavorable world markets for primary products, from the failure to provide incentives to export comparable with those provided to stimulate production for domestic markets, and not least from the protective policies of the developed countries.

7. ECLA, *International Cooperation in a Latin American Development Policy* (1954), Sales No. 54.II.G.2, p. 60.

8. ECLA, *Towards a Dynamic Development Policy for Latin America*, E/CN.12/680/Rev. 1 (1963).

9. In a well-known study, Santiago Macario assessed the cost to Latin America of the pursuit of autarkic industrialization policies. See his "Protectionism and Industrialization in Latin America," *Economic Bulletin for Latin America*, Vol. 9 (March 1964), pp. 61–101.

For ECLA, economic integration was the principal means to ease the balance-of-payments constraint on both industrial development and overall economic growth. With larger markets and eventually reduced imports from outside the region, Latin America might overcome some of the obstacles to further development.

Choosing the Road to Market Expansion

The economist-reformers recognized that integration was only one means to broaden markets. As an alternative, national markets could expand through rapid population growth, a redistribution of income in favor of groups with a higher propensity to consume domestic goods, or an increase in participation in the market economy. On the other hand, international markets could be found for Latin American industrial goods through a system of tariff preferences in developed countries for manufactures of less developed countries in general or Latin American countries in particular. Real devaluation of Latin American currencies in relation to the dollar or export subsidies for manufactures could also stimulate exports to countries outside the region, if no new barriers to them were erected by the importing countries.

In considering these alternatives to economic integration, the economist-reformers found first that, aside from the undesirable length of time involved, to expand national markets through population growth offered a viable alternative to only a few countries in Latin America. (Only three had a total population of over 20 million in 1965.) The reformers did not believe that major income redistributions (such as the one carried out in Cuba) would be in the best interests of their "constituency," which consisted largely of what John Johnson has labeled the "middle sectors"—small businessmen, white collar workers, professionals, bureaucrats, and elements of the military and the Catholic Church.[10] The third means of national expansion—incorporating the Indian population of the Andean countries, and other marginal groups, into the market economy—offered

10. John J. Johnson, *Political Change in Latin America: The Emergence of the Middle Sectors* (Stanford University Press, 1958). Miguel Teubal points out that the reformers miscalculated the support that integration would get from local business groups. See "El fracaso de la integración económica latinoamericana," *Desarrollo Económico* (Buenos Aires), Vol. 8 (April–June 1968), pp. 61–93.

the reformers no hope of quick benefits because of the great length of time and profound cultural and social changes it would require. Moreover, as long as incomes remained close to subsistence levels, the economic payoff of increased market participation would be small.

Broadening the international markets for Latin American goods, as another means of market expansion, was given secondary priority during the 1950s because one of the major flaws of the international system, according to the ECLA critique, was that it exaggerated the dependence of less developed countries on markets in developed countries. Any expansion of manufacturing capacity undertaken on the basis of preferential access to markets in developed countries would be subject to their business cycles as well as to changes they made in the terms of preference.

Export subsidies and real devaluation of Latin American currencies relative to the dollar were unattractive methods of enlarging the international market for Latin American goods because, compared with tariff preferences, they would entail higher resource costs. Furthermore, real devaluation might reduce foreign exchange receipts for primary products that faced a relatively inelastic demand, assuming an elastic supply and the failure to take offsetting measures such as production controls, export quotas, or export taxes.

Without discarding the national and international approaches to market expansion, and fully aware of the continuing efforts simultaneously to promote all three kinds of expansion, the economist-reformers settled in the 1950s on integration as the primary means to that end.

Traditional Customs Union Theory and Its Modifications

Once the analysis moved from the general assault on the international system to specific arguments for Latin American integration, the reformers confronted the inadequacies in the traditional theory of international trade, especially that dealing with customs unions. In the traditional theory, a customs union is analyzed in terms of its "trade-creating" and "trade-diverting" effects.[11] Both types of effects are the result of the extension of

11. These concepts were first systematically developed by Jacob Viner in *The Customs Union Issue* (Carnegie Endowment for International Peace, 1950). Among the major works that built upon the Viner study are: J. E. Meade, *The Theory of Customs Union* (Amsterdam: North Holland, 1956); F. Gehrels, "Customs Union from a Single Country Viewpoint," *Review of Economic Studies*, Vol. 24 (1956–57), pp. 61–64; R. G. Lipsey,

trade preferences to some countries (the customs union partners) but not to others. In Viner's model, *trade creation* results from a shift from high cost domestic production to lower cost imports from partners in the union. This increases the output of a given amount of resources in the region and so augments economic welfare. *Trade diversion*, because it means a shift from a low cost foreign source of imports to a high cost partner source, leads to a welfare loss. The theory was further developed to take into account not only the welfare effect of a shift in production, but also the effect on consumption of changes in relative prices. The inclusion of the consumption effect of a customs union allows for a possible net increase in welfare of a country that joins a customs union, in spite of a shift to a high cost partner as a source of imports.[12]

If a country usually imports from third countries goods that its potential partner produces, it is generally because the partner is less efficient in producing them. If the partners initially have different economic structures— for example, one is oriented toward the production of primary goods, and imports manufactured goods from third countries, and the other produces manufactured goods—the cost of union would be high for the unindustrialized country. A customs union would divert trade to the high cost partner, which would require the unindustrialized country to spend more real resources than it did before union.[13]

If, however, potential partners produce similar goods, and each imports from third countries goods that the other does not produce, the elimination of barriers would yield benefits from specialization in production with little diversion of trade. Two predominantly industrial—or predominantly agricultural—countries forming a union could expand their trade largely through increased specialization, not through a diversion of trade from lower cost third country suppliers.

"The Theory of Customs Unions: A General Survey," *Economic Journal*, Vol. 70 (September 1960), pp. 496–513; and H. G. Johnson, "The Economic Theory of Customs Union," *Pakistan Economic Journal*, Vol. 10 (March 1960), pp. 14–32. The last article is reproduced as Chap. 3 in Harry G. Johnson, *Money, Trade and Economic Growth* (Harvard University Press, 1962).

12. A diagrammatic partial equilibrium treatment of these concepts is given in Johnson, *Money, Trade*.

13. The consumption effect of union would depend on the level of tariffs in a country. The higher the initial tariff against imports from partners and third countries, the larger the effect on consumption. Since among less developed countries, the unindustrialized usually have lower levels of tariff protection than the more industrialized, the consumption effect of a customs union would be less likely to offset the trade diversion effect in the unindustrialized countries.

From this type of analysis, Johnson suggests that a country is

... more likely to reap a gain from entering on a customs union the more it and its partner country (countries) are initially similar in the products they produce but different in the pattern of relative prices at which they produce them. ... Further, members are more likely to gain the more different they are from the rest of the world, since this implies that the possibility of losses from trade diversion in a country is less. ... To reverse the statement, a country is less likely to gain from entering a customs union, the more different it is from its partners, the more the partners produce close substitutes for goods produced in foreign countries, and the greater the difference in real costs between foreign and partner supplies of such products . . .[14]

The Latin American reformers, together with a number of economists in the developed countries, have viewed this analysis of customs unions as inadequate, even for highly industrialized regions. They point out that, while the traditional theory assumes perfect competition within national markets with production costs unchanged or rising as output increases, costs for many heavy industrial products decline over the relevant range of output.

No matter how low the price of labor, most heavy manufactured goods are virtually impossible to produce more cheaply in small than in large plants. Moreover, it is not economically feasible, given realistic prices, to produce these goods with capital-intensive, advanced techniques for a market that is below some minimum size (market size is, of course, also a function of price). Nor do the economies of scale that usually result from these techniques come into play below a certain level of output.

In many basic industries, such as petroleum refining, primary metals, and electric power, economies of scale are found up to very large plant sizes (often the largest built or contemplated). These economies occur mostly in the initial investment cost and in operating labor cost, with no significant economies observed in raw material cost. Scale economies can also result from learning curve effects, spreading of set-up costs, and certain stochastic processes associated with inventories. With some reservations . . . these general results can also be applied to less developed countries, where limited demand and the resulting inability to realize potential economies of scale can present a barrier to investment.[15]

14. Johnson, *Money, Trade*, pp. 57–58. Besides these conditions that directly affect trade diversion and creation, increases or decreases in the relative prices of a country's imports from third countries and exports to those countries (terms of trade) may occur because of the diversion of trade to partner countries. Terms-of-trade effects are secondary, however, and are omitted from the discussion in this chapter.

15. John Haldi and David Whitcomb, "Economies of Scale in Industrial Plants," *Journal of Political Economy*, Vol. 75 (August 1967, Pt. 1), p. 373. This article contains a description of other factors responsible for returns to scale.

A large plant alone, however, does not guarantee economies of scale, if the high output at which they begin to operate is not called forth by the market. The costs of production are often higher in underutilized plants, however modern their machinery and processes, than in less advanced plants that operate close to capacity. This has been demonstrated in some Latin American countries, in which large plants, embodying advanced technology, have been built, only to operate at low rates of capacity because markets are at best small by U.S. or European standards.

The assumption of competitive equilibrium in the traditional model also precludes gains from increased competition among firms. Greater efficiency results from intensified competition only if distortions due to monopolistic elements exist in the economy before union. Thus, in the absence of perfect competition, the welfare gain from union may be much greater. If production costs within the union fall as a result of expanded markets or increased competition, the difference between the prices of a product in a partner country and a third country diminishes. The trade-diversion effect of a customs union would decrease, and the trade-creation effect increase. Furthermore, it has been argued, the dynamic effects of union on economic growth (other than those resulting from economies of scale) may be much greater than any static effects measurable ex ante by traditional welfare analysis. For example, larger markets may induce greater willingness to invest, especially if they do not depend on policies over which Latin Americans have no control.[16]

Besides Scitovsky, other scholars tried in the 1960s to formalize these arguments in a more dynamic theory of trade and growth.[17] These studies extended the concepts of welfare gain and loss to embrace more than short-

16. On this last point, see Tibor Scitovsky, *Economic Theory and Western European Integration* (London: Allen and Unwin, 1958). Scitovsky stresses that economic integration increases the market facing entrepreneurs; hence, they are more willing to invest in expansion as well as in innovations.

17. See Bela Balassa, *El desarrollo económico y la integración* (Mexico City: Centro de Estudios Monetarios Latinoamericano, 1965); *The Theory of Economic Integration* (London: Allen and Unwin, 1961); "Towards a Theory of Economic Integration," *Kyklos*, Vol. 14 (1961), pp. 1–14; Keith Griffen and Ricardo Ffrench-Davis, "Customs Unions and Latin American Integration," *Journal of Common Market Studies*, Vol. 4 (October 1965), pp. 1–21; C. A. Cooper and B. F. Massell, "Toward a General Theory of Customs Unions for Developing Countries," *Journal of Political Economy*, Vol. 73 (October 1965), pp. 460–76. A fuller discussion of the rationale for economic integration is contained in Joseph Grunwald, Miguel Wionczek, and Martin Carnoy, *Latin American Economic Integration and U.S. Policy* (Brookings Institution, 1971).

term increases in economic efficiency. They define gains and losses as a function of the traditional changes in relative prices, in rates of capital formation, and even in the types of goods produced. Thus a customs union may produce net welfare gains largely through satisfying a societal preference for higher levels of domestic industrial production rather than through lower prices for industrial goods.[18]

CACM, LAFTA, and the Latin American Economic Integration Movement since 1960

A decade of discussion—during which the new perceptions of the improved efficiency and enhanced welfare benefits to be found in union came to influence theorist and policy maker alike—culminated in 1960 in the formation of two separate economic unions in Latin America. The first, the Central American Common Market (CACM), brought into being by the Managua Treaty in 1960, includes Costa Rica, El Salvador, Guatemala, Honduras, and Nicaragua. The second, the Latin American Free Trade Association (LAFTA), was established in mid-1961 by the Montevideo Treaty. It was originally signed in early 1960 by seven Latin American countries—Argentina, Brazil, Chile, Mexico, Paraguay, Peru, and Uruguay; they were later joined by Colombia and Ecuador and then by Venezuela and Bolivia, so that in 1970 LAFTA covered Mexico and all of South America except the Guayanas.

The Central American Common Market

The Managua Treaty provided for the elimination of tariffs on almost all goods except some agricultural products and the formation of a commission on external tariffs on all products. Subsequently, a Central American clearinghouse arrangement and the Central American Bank for Economic Integration (CABEI) were created. A special agreement was signed in 1958 for a Regime of Integration Industries—those that must sell their products in the entire Central American market in order to operate efficiently. These industries were to be distributed throughout the CACM countries to insure that all partners, including the least developed members,

18. See Cooper and Massell, "Toward a General Theory of Customs Unions."

Honduras and Nicaragua, could develop their own dynamic industrial sectors.

The CACM had considerable success, particularly in its early days. Between 1960 and 1965 the volume of intraregional trade increased sevenfold. In 1965 it amounted to more than 20 percent of the area's trade with the rest of the world, compared with 8 percent in 1960. Over 40 percent of intraregional trade in 1965 was in manufactures and semimanufactures, most of them consumer goods. By the end of 1966 about 98 percent of the number of dutiable items in Central America were no longer subject to tariffs. Efforts continued to be made to reduce the number of exceptions, which, as of 1969, still included important commodities, accounting for 20–25 percent of the area's imports. By mid-1966 uniform tariffs had been achieved for more than 80 percent of imports from third countries into the region. The common external tariffs, however, appear to be higher than the average of the individual country tariffs previously in effect.[19] In part as a result of the formation of the common market and in part because of favorable trends in the prices of principal Central American exports to developed countries, the economic development of the region accelerated. The average annual growth rate of gross regional product (GRP) increased from 4.5 percent in the years 1955–60 to 5.5 percent in 1960–65. CACM has had its major effect on the manufacturing sector, according to McClelland.[20] The contribution of intraregional trade to growth is a function of the multiplier effect of growth in manufacturing on the rest of the economy. He concludes that with a "minimum normal" growth of 5 percent for manufacturing and 4 percent for the whole economy and with a 0.2 export multiplier and a 0.5 manufacturing multiplier, 4 percent of the 7 percent rate of growth from mid-1962 to 1965 is due to minimum normal growth, 2 percent to the increased growth of exports, and about 1 percent to CACM.

19. ECLA estimates that the regional nominal duty on consumer goods now averages 82.5 percent; on raw materials and intermediate goods, 34.4 percent; on building materials, 32.2 percent, and on capital goods, 13 percent. Before tariff equalization the corresponding arithmetic averages for the five individual countries were 64 percent, 30 percent, 26 percent, and 12 percent. The apparent increase stems from a shift in the focus of tariff policy from a revenue to an import-substitution orientation. See Roger D. Hansen, *Central America: Regional Integration and Economic Development* (National Planning Association, 1967).

20. Donald McClelland, "The Common Market's Contribution to Central American Economic Integration—A First Approximation," in Ronald Hilton (ed.), *The Movement Toward Latin American Unity* (Frederick A. Praeger, 1969), pp. 508–36.

The clearinghouse system of multilateral payments has also been quite effective in Central America. Between 1961 and 1964, multilateral clearances grew from 10 percent to about 90 percent of total settlements in Central American trade, while dollar payments fell from close to 100 percent to only 14 percent.[21]

The Latin American Free Trade Association

The Treaty of Montevideo established a rather complicated mechanism for trade negotiations aimed at gradually eliminating (over the twelve years to mid-1973) customs duties and other restrictions on substantially all of the area's reciprocal trade. A free trade zone was to be achieved by the end of the period through a commitment by each contracting party to grant annually to other LAFTA members reductions in duties and charges equivalent to 8 percent of the weighted average of duties and charges applicable to third countries. Every three years these concessions, which were to be open in the meantime to withdrawal through renegotiation, were to be consolidated into a common schedule of products on which, by collective agreement, all customs duties and other charges applicable to intrazonal trade were to be eliminated completely before mid-1973. This common schedule was to cover 25 percent of the aggregate value of trade among the member countries by mid-1964, 50 percent by mid-1967, 75 percent by mid-1970, and "substantially all" at the end of the period.

Many of LAFTA's supporters hoped that the free trade area could evolve into a full common market, with a unified external tariff structure; but, because of the great heterogeneity of economic and political interests in the countries concerned, a relatively weak form of free trade area was the most that could be achieved at the time of the system's establishment.

Although trade among LAFTA countries increased from a postwar low of 6 percent of their total foreign trade in 1961 to 12 percent in 1967,[22]

21. Jorge González del Valle, "Monetary Integration in Central America; Achievements and Expectations," *Journal of Common Market Studies*, Vol. 5 (September 1966), pp. 18–19. The transactions of the Central American Clearing House totaled $223 million in 1968, an increase of 44 percent over 1966.

22. The doubling of the proportion, while impressive, merely returned it approximately to the level it had attained during the Korean war (10 percent). Trade among the nine original member republics increased from $300 million in 1961, the year in which the treaty entered into force, to $665 million in 1965. This represents an expansion in intra-LAFTA trade of 125 percent against an increase of only 25 percent in the total

tariff negotiations broke down as items to be put on the common schedule began to include products manufactured by member countries.

New Initiatives and Old Problems

In early 1965, the dissatisfaction of the reformers with the progress of LAFTA prompted a letter from the President of Chile, Eduardo Frei, to Raúl Prebisch, Jose Antonio Mayobre, Felipe Herrera, and Carlos Sanz de Santamaria, four of the prominent "tecnicos" and reformers in Latin America, searching for new means to hasten integration in the region. Their response[23] called for a Latin American Common Market (LACM) and the replacement of the Treaty of Montevideo with an instrument that would assure the rapid attainment of economic integration among Latin American countries.

The report on the LACM in response to Frei's letter recommended the establishment of a regional common market by 1975 through annual across-the-board tariff cuts. It also urged that four closely related commitments by all participating countries should be made and fulfilled within a period of ten years: (1) the definition of quantitative targets for the permissible *maximum* level of customs duties for intrazonal trade to be attained in the subsequent stages of trade liberalization; (2) the gradual elimination of quantitative and other nontariff restrictions on intraregional trade; (3) the setting of a common tariff vis-à-vis the rest of the world; and (4) the establishment of definite preferences in the common external tariff. The gradual elaboration of a common external tariff would commence with aligning existing tariffs for raw materials and intermediate products and with relating that alignment—in case the situation arose—to the regional interests in manufacturing covered by future sectoral agreements or industrial complementarity.[24] These agreements would initially involve a limited

---

value of exports of LAFTA members within the same four-year period. The LAFTA performance is much less impressive when compared with the trade among the nine countries during the years 1952–55, when annual intra-group exports averaged $470 million. Between then and 1965, intra-LAFTA trade increased by only 40 percent, a percentage that also includes increases in world prices.

23. Raúl Prebisch, Jose Antonio Mayobre, Felipe Herrera, and Carlos Sanz de Santamaria, "Proposiciones para la creación del Mercado Común Latinamericano," in *Hacia la integración accelerada de America Latina* (Mexico City: Fondo de Cultura Económica, 1965).

24. A complementarity agreement provides for the production of various parts of a

number of industries, such as iron and steel, some nonferrous metals, certain heavy chemicals and petrochemicals, and the manufacture of motor vehicles, ships, and heavy industrial equipment, in all of which economies of scale and external economies may be particularly important for efficient operations.

The experts' report eventually led to the Meeting of the American Chiefs of State in Punta del Este during April 1967. They agreed that a Latin American Common Market was to be initiated in 1970 and to be substantially in operation no later than 1985. It was to be based on developing LAFTA and CACM, which were to converge by stages through cooperation, closer ties, and integration. This process was to be undertaken with a special view to providing and encouraging access to one of the two systems for those Latin American countries not yet associated with either.

Even the presidents' meeting, however, failed to inject new vitality into the negotiation process and the meetings that followed produced no substantial trade concessions.

The slowdown in the integration movement within LAFTA was formally recognized in the Protocol of Caracas which was signed at the ninth conference in December 1969. The protocol postpones the full operation of the free trade area for an additional seven years, from the end of 1973 to the end of 1980. Furthermore, the minimum annual 8 percent reduction in tariffs was reduced to 2.9 percent in future negotiations, and the system of the common schedule mentioned earlier was suspended until 1974. At the same time the protocol instructed LAFTA's Standing Executive Committee to complete studies before the end of 1973 that would lead to new procedures for the common schedule and create "conditions favorable to the establishment of a Latin American common market."

Andean Integration

Besides the small Central American Common Market, the most encouraging sign of progress in Latin American economic integration is the signing of the Subregional Andean Integration Agreement by Bolivia, Colombia, Chile, Ecuador, and Peru in May 1969. Venezuela, which participated in the lengthy negotiations leading to the treaty, did not sign but

---

final product in several countries and the final assembly of the product in each, or in several of them.

has the option of joining later. The Andean group was created within the LAFTA context and the treaty was approved by the full LAFTA membership. In addition the Andean group established the Andean Development Corporation, of which Venezuela is also a member.

The Andean treaty provides for the automatic and irrevocable reduction of tariff and nontariff barriers, leading to substantially free intra-Andean trade by the end of 1980. By that date, a common external tariff, to be established gradually, is also to go into full effect. Moreover, the treaty provides for the elaboration of sectoral development programs, special treatment of Bolivia and Ecuador as less developed nations within the group, and coordination of economic policies. A complementarity agreement in the petrochemical industry is already in effect within the Andean group.

Including Venezuela, the group accounts for about one-fourth of Latin America's economic base in important aspects (gross national product, population, and area), and if successful, may well provide the stimulus for effective integration not only of the subregion, but also eventually of all of LAFTA and, indeed, of Latin America as a whole.

Obstacles to Integration

Perhaps the major problem confronting LAFTA, and indeed any proposal for a Latin American common market, is the disparity in the level of economic development and in the size of member countries. The countries of LAFTA entered it with highly unequal stocks of natural resources and of physical and human capital. Largely because these differences have existed throughout their recent histories, the industrial process is much further advanced in some countries than in others. The Central American Common Market also faced this problem, but to a much lesser degree. As Table 1-1 shows, in 1965 the gross domestic product (GDP) per capita in all industries in Costa Rica, which had the largest for any of the CACM countries, was only 67 percent greater than that for Honduras, which had the smallest, and the Costa Rican GDP per capita in manufacturing alone was just double the Honduran. By contrast, in the LAFTA group, Venezuela's GDP per capita in all industries, the highest, was almost five times as great as Bolivia's, the lowest, while Argentina's GDP per capita in manufacturing was nearly eighteen times that of Bolivia. Between 1950 and 1965 the disparities had widened. It is natural, then, that the less

Table 1-1. Selected Indicators of Industrial Activity in Latin America, 1950 and 1965

Organization and country	Gross domestic product per capita[a]				Gross domestic product in manufacturing			
	All industries		Manufacturing		Ratio to total national GDP		Ratio to total Latin American GDP in manufacturing	
	1950	1965	1950	1965	1950	1965	1950	1965
LAFTA								
Argentina	$456	$541	$143	$194	29%	34%	40%	30%
Bolivia	178	162	13	11	n.a.	11[b]	*	*
Brazil	135	175	22	42	17	23	19	24
Chile	388	474	64	94	17	18	6	5
Colombia	223	286	24	39	16	18	5	5
Ecuador	158	202	22	30	16	17	*	*
Mexico	280	427	42	78	18[b]	22[b]	18	22
Paraguay	178	200	29	32	17	16	*	*
Peru	170	267	22	43	14	18	3	3
Uruguay	479	503	23	35	18	22	1	1
Venezuela	502	797	26	58	9	13	2	3
CACM								
Costa Rica	287	360	21	34	11	14	*	*
El Salvador	199	280	16	32	12	18[b]	*	*
Guatemala	251	310	15	20	12	15	*	*
Honduras	177	215	9	17	8	14	*	*
Nicaragua	208	332	11	24	10	13	*	*
Panama	247	488	17	49	11	15	*	*

Sources: **GDP per capita in all industries**—U.S. Agency for International Development, *Latin America: Economic Growth Trends* (October 1966), Table 4. **GDP per capita in manufacturing** was calculated by multiplying the total 1960 GDP in local currency, taken from *United Nations Statistical Yearbook 1966*, by the percent of total GDP in manufacturing in the same year, taken from Economic Commission for Latin America (ECLA), *Economic Survey of Latin America 1965*, E/CN.12/752/Rev. 1, Table 11. The resulting figures in local currencies were then translated into cruzeiros, which were used because of the similarity of the parity and free rate between the Brazilian and most other Latin American currencies. The translation was made with parity rates of exchange taken from ECLA, *A Measurement of Price Levels and the Purchasing Power of Currencies in Latin America, 1960–1962*, E/CN.12/653. The resulting data in cruzeiros were then divided by population in 1960 to obtain GDP per capita in manufacturing for that year; the 1950 and 1965 data were calculated using these 1960 data and the indices of growth of per capita manufactured product reported in various issues of ECLA, *Economic Survey of Latin America* (see, for example, *Economic Survey of Latin America 1965*, Table 10). **Ratio of GDP in manufacturing to total national GDP** (except as indicated in note *b*) —UN *Statistical Yearbook 1966*. **Ratio of GDP in manufacturing to total Latin American GDP in manufacturing** was calculated using the same sources and method of translation into cruzeiros noted above for GDP per capita in manufacturing. Using total GDP in manufacturing, the percent of total Latin American GDP in manufacturing produced in each country was estimated for 1950 and 1965. Data are not estimated for countries producing less than 0.5 percent of Latin American manufactured product.

n.a. Not available.

* Less than 0.5 percent.

a. 1962 dollars.

b. Source: ECLA, *Economic Survey of Latin America 1965*, Table 11.

developed countries of LAFTA should fear economic domination by their larger neighbors.

Table 1-1 also shows that the productive structures of Latin American countries differ considerably. In 1965 about three-quarters of all manufactured goods in Latin America were produced in three countries—Argentina, Brazil, and Mexico. Argentina had by far the highest manufacturing product per capita in Latin America, followed by Chile and Mexico. However, the figure for Brazil as a whole masks the relatively high level of development in the southern part of the country. Roughly 60 percent of manufacturing takes place in the southern region of Brazil—the states of São Paulo, Rio Grande do Sul, Santa Catarina, and Paraná, which account for just over 50 percent of Brazil's GDP;[25] the per capita industrial product of that region is more than $70, which is comparable with Mexico's per capita GDP in manufacturing. Bolivia, Ecuador, Paraguay, the CACM countries, and Panama, the least industrialized countries of the region, together produce only 4 percent of the manufactured product. The growth of manufacturing was slowest for the "small" LAFTA countries—those with GNP of less than $1 billion in 1960 (Bolivia, Ecuador, Paraguay, and the Central American countries; see Table 1-2). This development is in contrast with that for the "large" and "middle-sized" countries (grouped, like those listed above, roughly according to both geographic size and total GNP).

In addition to the difference in productive structures between the more developed countries of the region and the poorer ones, the current pattern of trade of Latin American countries is not conducive to union. As Table 1-3 demonstrates, exports of manufactured goods form a relatively small part of total exports, but imports of manufactured goods account for a large proportion of total imports.[26] In addition, only a small percentage

25. "Contas Nacionais do Brasil, Novas Estimativas," *Conjuntura Econômica*, Vol. 23 (October 1969), pp. 55–91.

26. Problems in estimating the manufactures component of trade have led to some misleading figures in Table 1-3. For the purposes here, manufactures are defined as SITC categories 5, 6, 7, and 8, plus category 332 (processed petroleum products). The production of primary metals, which is a semimanufacturing activity, is included under category 6. Its inclusion means a very high figure for exports of manufactured goods from Chile, and to a lesser extent from Peru and Mexico. In 1962, for example, Chilean exports of manufactures as a percent of total exports is 70 percent when manufactures includes SITC categories 5, 6, 7, and 8. Excluding unwrought metal from category 6 reduces this proportion to 3.6 percent. Similarly, the Mexican proportion in 1963 drops from 26 to 13 percent, and the Peruvian percentage in 1962 from 24 to 1 percent. See Joseph Grun-

Table 1-2. Percentage Change in Selected Indicators of Industrial Activity in Latin America, 1950–65

| | Gross domestic product per capita[a] | | Gross domestic product in manufacturing | |
| | | | Ratio to total | Ratio to total Latin American GDP in |
Country	All industries	Manufacturing	national GDP	manufacturing[b]
Large[c]				
Argentina	19	35	17	−26
Brazil	30	94	35	28
Mexico	52	87	22	23
Average	30	65	25[d]	−1
Middle-sized[c]				
Chile	22	47	6	−14
Colombia	28	62	12	2
Peru	57	93	28	13
Uruguay	5	22	22	−36
Venezuela	59	120	44	73
Average	36	66	22[d]	4
Small[c]				
Bolivia	−9	−16	n.a.	−40
Ecuador	28	36	6	−9
Paraguay	12	10	−6	−43
Costa Rica	25	65	27	−25
El Salvador	41	106	50	50
Guatemala	24	32	25	−14
Honduras	22	91	75	0
Nicaragua	60	110	30	0
Panama	98	181	36	100
Average	21	46	32[d]	−9

Sources: Calculations based on data in Table 1-1.
n.a. Not available.
a. 1962 dollars.
b. These data show how the *relative* position in Latin America of the manufactured product of each country has changed in the fifteen-year period. The weighted sum of the data is 0.
c. These terms are explained in the text; see p. 20.
d. Unweighted arithmetic mean.

of each country's total imports comes from Latin America (column 2) and this is largely in primary goods. Column 4 shows that manufactured goods constitute over 50 percent of exports to Latin America only for Chile and

wald and Philip Musgrove, *Natural Resources in Latin American Development* (Johns Hopkins Press for Resources for the Future, 1970), Table A-8. The inclusion of category 332, which comprises some semimanufacturing activities, biases the Venezuelan figure. On the other hand, processed foods are not included as manufactures, and this makes many of the percentages for primary good exports too high.

Table 1-3. Selected Data on Latin American Exports and Imports, Selected Years, 1960–65

Country	Manufactured exports as a percent of total exports, 1962–65 average (1)	Percent of total imports from Latin America, 1960 (2)	Manufactured imports as a percent of total imports — Percent (3)	Manufactured imports as a percent of total imports — Data-years averaged	Manufactured exports — As a percent of total exports to LAFTA, 1959–63 average[a] (4)	Manufactured exports — As a percent of total LAFTA-manufactured exports to LAFTA, 1959–63 average[a,b] (5)	Manufactured exports — Share of intra-Latin American exports[b] (6)	Imports as a percent of GNP, 1960 (7)	Simple arithmetic mean tariff level (8)
Argentina	6	16	76	1963–65	17	32 (18)	24	12	131
Bolivia	8	17	81	1958–61	n.a.	n.a.	1	13	n.a.
Brazil	5	16	70	1962–65	15	15 (8)	13	12	168
Chile	66	17	68	1962–63	42 (74)	20 (20)	7	15	78
Colombia	6	4	85	1961–65	41	4 (2)	2	13	71
Ecuador	1	3	78	1961–64	15	1 (1)	1	13	62
Mexico	23	1	84	1962–65	63 (74)	14 (9)	5	9	50
Paraguay	10	25	85	1959–62	11	2 (1)	2	10	n.a.
Peru	22	8	80	1959–62	17 (38)	8 (11)	7	17	30
Uruguay	4	27	84	1959–62	30	2 (1)	1	18	n.a.
Venezuela	27	2	82	1962–65	2 (26)	3 (29)	28	15	n.a.
Panama	n.a.	2	73	1962–65	...	...	*	27	n.a.
Costa Rica	8	8	83	1959–62	...	...	1	25	n.a.
El Salvador	13	15	75	1962–65	...	...	3	22	n.a.
Guatemala	12	9	78	1962–65	...	...	2	14	n.a.
Honduras	4	10	80	1962–65	...	...	1	19	n.a.
Nicaragua	6	11	81	1961–64	...	...	2	19	n.a.
Total CACM	n.a.	5°	n.a.	...	...	...	n.a.	17°	36

Sources: Column 1—Inter-American Development Bank, unpublished data. Column 2—*UN Yearbook of International Trade Statistics 1962, 1964, 1965*; manufactured goods defined as SITC categories 5–8, and 332. Column 3—LAFTA data from Donald W. Baerresen, Martin Carnoy, and Joseph Grunwald, *Latin American Trade Patterns* (Brookings Institution, 1965), Table V; Central American data from *UN Yearbook of International Trade Statistics 1964*. Columns 4–6—Baerresen and others, *Trade Patterns*, Table VII; Central American data in column 6 from *UN International Trade Statistics 1964*. Column 7—*UN International Trade Statistics 1964* for import statistics, and U.S. Agency for International Development, *Latin America: Economic Growth Trends* (1966) for GNP. Column 8—Santiago Macario, "Protectionism and Industrialization in Latin America," *Economic Bulletin for Latin America*, Vol. 9 (March 1964), Table 5, p. 75. The tariffs used are those presented by Macario as amended in Department of State airgram of Dec. 7, 1966, Capito Circular A-94, Table B. They apply to 1952 for Brazil; 1961 for Ecuador; and 1962 for Argentina, Chile, Colombia, and Mexico. Macario gives no date for the Paraguayan data. The amendments consist of omitting one or more products from the list because their inordinately high tariffs seriously distort the arithmetic mean.

n.a. Not available.

* Less than 0.5 percent.

a. Data in parentheses are percentages including semiprocessed metals and petroleum.

b. Data in this column may not add to 100 percent, due to rounding.

c. Does not include imports of CACM countries from CACM countries.

23

Mexico and in the Chilean case this is true only if the manufactured category is defined to include semiprocessed metals. Argentina is the largest exporter of manufactured goods to the region (column 5), but these goods account for less than 20 percent of Argentina's total exports to Latin America.[27]

The low level of intraregional trade in manufactures is due primarily to higher prices (including transportation) of Latin American manufactures relative to goods from third countries. The important trade among Latin American countries still takes place in those products in which they have an advantage over third country producers, such as wheat and meat (Argentina), timber (Brazil), coffee (Brazil, Colombia, and the CACM countries), bananas (Brazil, Ecuador, and the CACM countries), copper (Chile and Peru), and petroleum (Venezuela). The highest percentage of intraregional trade occurs among the economies of the region's southern cone (Argentina, southern Brazil, Uruguay, Paraguay, Chile, and Bolivia), which are linked by the most highly developed transportation network in Latin America. But even this percentage is low compared with the percentage observed for European countries *before* they joined in the European Economic Community.

Applying the New Theory

Despite their doubts concerning the applicability of the traditional theory on customs unions, the framers of the Treaties of Managua and Montevideo explicitly incorporated the dicta of the existing theory in them. They acknowledged that in the short run the potential losses sustained by the less industrialized countries would be the dominant obstacle to intraregional tariff reductions and a common external tariff. They recognized that the equitable distribution of industrialization and growth was an essential element of economic union. Since, in a region with completely free trade, market forces would tend to concentrate industrial growth around established industrial centers, they accepted the need for compensation to less developed members through concessions on tariff reductions or through regional planning to assure benefits for all members.

27. Assuming that 70 percent of Latin American imports are manufactured goods, their average annual value in 1960–63 was $5.8 billion. The average value of Latin American manufactured exports to Latin America in the same period was $150 million, or 2.5 percent of the total value of manufactured imports.

This "reciprocity" principle was incorporated into the Montevideo Treaty through an impressive number of escape clauses available to member countries with respect to trade in agricultural products and also to partners with intrazonal trade disequilibria or seriously unfavorable global balances of payments. Although the Managua Treaty contains no specific reciprocity provisions, it includes the Integration Industries Scheme, which provides for the equitable geographic distribution of new plants in specified industries.

The frustration of the Regime of Integration Industries by erstwhile opposition from the United States and the Inter-American Bank, both of which had refused to give funds to CABEI for this purpose, did much to create the present problems in CACM. Honduras and Nicaragua, the supposed recipients of net benefits from the Regime, while growing rapidly in recent years, have incurred negative balances of payments with CACM, largely because they export a considerably lower volume of manufactured goods to the region than their three partners.

Some Political Impediments to Union

The difficulties in achieving LAFTA's purposes, however, did not arise solely from the less developed members.

The extent of the market in an economically unified region depends on the willingness of member governments to cooperate with one another. The more global the market, the greater the chance that an unfavorable political situation in one member country could stall the entire movement. Victor Urquidi, a prominent Mexican economist, mentioned this principle in 1962, but unfortunately did not analyze its implications for the probable success of either CACM or LAFTA:

The Latin American free trade area and, ultimately, the common market, will only progress if the member countries are capable of submitting their national interests—which should never be neglected—to the interests of the region as a whole; and to do this by negotiation and mutual confidence, because eventually, the interests of the region will coincide with the interests of the individual countries.[28]

At the time the Montevideo Treaty was signed, these considerations had

28. Victor Urquidi, *Free Trade and Economic Integration in Latin America* (University of California Press, 1962), p. 116.

no immediate relevance. Reformism was at its peak in Latin America, and all the major countries of the region had reformist, elected governments that were sympathetic to the idea of regional cooperation. But soon after LAFTA was formed, both Argentina and Brazil changed governments, and the military regimes that came to power began to follow policies unfavorable to regional development. Their economic strategy has been to rationalize the existing tariff structure, lower the average level of duties, and continue industrialization without regard to its implications for the Latin American integration movement, while at the same time seeking access to the immense markets of the developed countries outside Latin America for exports of manufactures. This approach appears to be motivated in part by Argentine and Brazilian fears of one another's low cost products, and reluctance to lose any industrialization already achieved. Traditional military rivalries have contributed to the tendency toward industrial autarky. The withdrawal of effective Argentine and Brazilian support has played an important role in retarding the movement toward integration.

Besides the traditional competition of the two great South American powers, other problems may account for their failure to lend full support to LAFTA itself, let alone to attempts to push toward more complete economic integration. On the one hand, many industrialists who opposed tariff reduction found integration unpalatable. On the other, the high and differing rates of inflation that characterize the region tend to destabilize trade and balances of payments. Without a common policy for setting exchange rates, the uncertainty exporters experience offsets the incentive to invest that would be expected with the prospect of larger markets. These problems might be resolved in the one case by a development bank for integration projects that could hasten the reality of integration before opposition to it could be mobilized and, in the other, by a payments union that could provide a realistic solution to the problem of transitory deficits in balances of payments. Unlike CACM, however, LAFTA lacks such institutions, and movement toward union has thereby been hampered.

Furthermore, the slowdowns in growth rates of both the economies and exports of a number of countries in LAFTA, including Brazil and Argentina, have heightened the fears associated with import liberalization. By contrast, the tariff reductions in Central America in the early 1960s were carried out under conditions of very high growth of exports to the developed world, and thus of very favorable levels of hard currency reserves.

In the last few years Latin American economic policy makers have become aware of a new problem: Foreign multinational corporations are in the best position to exploit complementarity agreements and, probably, to profit from tariff cuts between Latin American countries as well. In LAFTA the fear is that the gains from integration will accrue almost entirely to dynamic firms that can expand rapidly as tariffs are reduced. Foreign firms already maintain production facilities and marketing organizations in several Latin American countries, have access to large sources of capital from the parent firm, and possess the technology to step up production and take advantage of economies of scale. Thus there is great suspicion that U.S. interest in LAFTA since the Frei letter is prompted by the pressure of U.S. firms on their government. Indeed, the preparation for the Punta del Este meeting in April 1967 showed the U.S. negotiators to be staunch supporters of equal treatment for foreign investors in any Latin American common market.

Central America has seen a flood of new foreign investments which at first glance would appear beneficial to the CACM. Planners in the region have noted, however, that these investments are often in assembly industries with a high import content and very low value added, enjoying substantial tariff protection. Much investment has taken the form of purchases of previously established local enterprises. Such acquisition by large multinational corporations is particularly resented throughout Latin America since it does not necessarily imply new industrial capacity in the region and may result in the displacement of Latin American entrepreneurs.

Against this historical background, Chapter 2 sets out the objectives and design of the study, and some of its results. Part 2, which comprises Chapters 3 through 8, reports individual case studies for, respectively, nitrogenous fertilizers, methanol and formaldehyde, tractors, lathes, dairy products, and paper and pulp. Each of the case studies estimates regional demand for the product in 1975, the projected costs of production in two or more countries in the region, and the costs of transportation from production point to markets. All this is undertaken with a view to determining a configuration of plants that would minimize the total cost of supplying the region. The cost of this pattern is compared with costs of other patterns of plant location, as well as with those of importing from outside the region, and of autarkic production by each would-be producing country.

Part 3 consists of a description of the linearized programming model that has been used to determine minimum cost locations for industrial plants within a potential Latin American common market. It also sets forth the welfare analysis that evaluates the benefits and costs to countries in the region. Its appendixes cover special problems of analysis and measurement in the industries studied, and outline the benefits and costs of union to individual countries.

CHAPTER TWO

The Object, the Method, and the Results

VERY LITTLE of the extensive literature in the field of Latin American integration measures the changes resulting from it or the relationships that affect its course.[1] Most of the treatment has been of a very general nature, aimed at convincing opinion and policy makers in particular that the economic union of the region must pass from dream to reality. The Economic Commission for Latin America (ECLA) and, more recently, the Inter-American Development Bank (IDB) have performed this task with the same competence and zeal with which ECLA had earlier made the region "economic development conscious." ECLA's documents provided not only convincing arguments that integration was now feasible, but also the basis for the negotiations that culminated in the establishment of the Latin American Free Trade Association (LAFTA).

Still there was little knowledge about the effects of economic integration on specific economic sectors and countries. Without guidelines to decisions with region-wide impact, businessmen and policy makers were timid in their approach to integration. Governments, pressed by their business communities, were therefore hesitant to make significant concessions under

1. See Jorge Navarrete, "Latin American Economic Integration: A Survey of Recent Literature," *Journal of Common Market Studies*, Vol. 5 (December 1965), pp. 168–77; and Martin Carnoy, "The Economic Integration of Latin America: A Survey of Research," in Roberto Esquenazi-Mayo and Michael Mayer (eds.), *Latin American Scholarship since World War II* (University of Nebraska Press, 1971).

the LAFTA agreement. This gap in knowledge has aggravated the uncertainty that inevitably surrounds such a major departure from established policies as LAFTA. Fear of losses tends to outweigh expectation of gains. Even relatively sophisticated policy makers have suspected that economic union might accentuate already wide intraregional disparities in income by promoting concentration of integration-inspired industries in the established industrial centers, relegating the less developed countries to the role of "hewers of wood and drawers of water" for their more advanced neighbors. But the extent of possible concentration, and the cost to the region and to individual countries of avoiding it, has remained unexplored. While economies of scale were understood to be a significant feature of many industries, little was known concerning their magnitude and the extent to which they would be offset by transport costs as single plants sought to serve ever more distant markets. Changes in exchange rates between Latin American countries were thought to threaten abrupt shifts in trading patterns, but no studies sought to quantify the relative exchange rates at which such disturbances would affect specific industries and countries.

It has been recognized almost from the outset that, to make a significant contribution to the economic welfare of the region, integration must be more than an arrangement to divert trade from third countries to Latin America. Investment within a regional context must be an integral part of whatever form of economic union evolves, if union is, in fact, to accelerate the economic growth of the area. But, whether they are businessmen, governments, or international agencies, investors require a meaningful orientation of regional investment programs in order to minimize waste and maximize their effectiveness.

This study addresses itself to these empirical questions. A theoretical framework and specific methodologies are developed with the objective of providing at least tentative answers of potential use to policy makers.

The specific aim of the study is to determine, on the basis of economic considerations alone, the optimum location and size of plants in selected industries within a regional common market in 1975 and to estimate the benefits to be derived from the integration of these industries. The difficulties in such an undertaking are apparent, especially since no precedent for it exists, not even in connection with the European Economic Community.

Even if the study could accurately determine what is best from an economic point of view, that still might not constitute the appropriate blueprint for the policy maker. The economic optimum need not coincide with the political or social optimum. The results of the studies are, therefore, intended not as a plan of action but rather as guidelines for policy makers and investors. For this purpose the study presents not only a single economic optimum but also a variety of alternatives that may be politically more acceptable but yet are not much more costly in economic terms. The study also estimates the benefits and losses to each country in acquiring the products from the economically optimum location in a regional common market rather than from alternative sources.

Design of the Study

The study develops a model that uses space location theory[2] to estimate costs of production in Latin America based on 1975 demand projections and free trade among LAFTA members. The model first identifies the location that would minimize the costs of production in the area of fourteen products in six industry groups—nitrogenous fertilizers, methanol and formaldehyde, tractors, lathes, dairy products, and paper and pulp—taking account of economies of scale, cost of transportation, and projected demand. Each product group is considered independently of the cost changes in the others, although, within groups, the model links inputs to outputs—for example, methanol and formaldehyde—to solve the model simultaneously. The model then estimates the delivered cost in Latin American markets of each product from the minimum cost location (henceforth also called, interchangeably, the optimum location). The supply price from the optimum location is taken as the "customs union" price of the good in 1975.

Selection of Products

Choosing the industries for study posed special problems. It was obvious that "industries" as such do not lend themselves to comparative analysis and that the studies had to deal with well-defined products. To be included

2. See, for example, Walter Isard, *Location and Space Economy* (Massachusetts Institute of Technology Press, 1956), and *Methods of Regional Analysis* (Massachusetts Institute of Technology Press, 1963); and Bela Balassa, "Towards a Theory of Economic Integration," *Kyklos*, Vol. 14 (1961), pp. 1–17.

in the study, therefore, a product needed to be relatively homogeneous throughout the region. But other criteria were even more important.

Ideally attention should focus on products that are strategic to the economic integration of Latin America. These would be the products of the capital goods and heavy industries, in which economies of scale and strong interindustry effects could be expected. These industries did not necessarily coincide, however, with the interests of the governments or the industrialists of the individual nations, nor with areas in which the participating institutes believed their countries might have, or could develop, a comparative advantage. The final choice, therefore, was a compromise between national and regional interests: From the products in which the individual countries had special interest were selected those that offered prospects of substantial regional growth.

Because some institutes saw no possibilities of comparative advantage for their countries in any of the regionally strategic goods selected, they studied some products that do not appear to be very important for regional economic integration. In these cases, the integration rationale was satisfied by choosing only commodities that at least two institutes agreed to study, so that intercountry comparisons could be made of their costs of production.

Of the original list of products included in the project, some had to be abandoned or postponed for later study because of time limitations, data problems, lack of resources, or other reasons. For instance, the plate glass industry could not be studied effectively because information about production costs was impossible to obtain. For technical reasons, special steels and electric conductors (wires and cables) also were eliminated from the study.

Demand and Cost Projections

Once the selection of products was made, each institute made demand projections for all products included in the project. This permitted the estimation of both national and regional demand.

In many instances either the complete absence of data or deficiencies in the information that was available precluded the use of advanced techniques to project demand. Since the availability and reliability of data vary from country to country and from product to product, adherence to a common methodology for estimating future demand had to be abandoned. Instead, each institute attempted to attain the best projections possible with the data to which it had access. The seminars and the work of the professionally stronger institutions permitted the less experienced to experiment with different methods so that the most appropriate could be applied.

Unlike demand projections, costs were estimated for only a limited number of products—presumably those each institute considered the likeliest exports for its country. The first stage was the preparation of cost profiles of the selected industries in countries where they already existed. Although the operating size of these firms was generally very small, the profiles served as a starting point for estimating economies of scale at higher levels of output and for the investigations of institutes whose countries had no such plants. In some instances cost projections had to be based on factor combinations and production functions used in developed countries. While the error in transferring United States and European production functions to Latin America is not necessarily great when new industries are to be established, the effort was made to adapt foreign production techniques, whenever they were relevant, to the conditions of the country. To this end technical engineering consultants were of the greatest help and their studies were widely utilized in making the cost projections.

The Model: Assumptions and Uses

The basic unifying analytical tool, which incorporates the demand projections, cost analyses, and assumptions about transportation costs and exchange rates, is a modified linear programming model that is used to calculate the optimum production locations to satisfy projected 1975 demand for the products studied in all countries of the Latin American Free Trade Association. The model finds the cheapest way of supplying the projected demand from within the area, balancing the economies of scale made possible by the expansion of production at any one point against the accompanying increase in transport costs. While in many cases the data utilized in the study left much to be desired, the model is capable of utilizing more accurate, complete, and homogeneous information when it becomes available.

Underlying Assumptions

These are the principal assumptions of the industry studies summarized at the end of this chapter, and presented in detail in Chapters 3 through 8:

(1) The relative prices of various inputs at each location and the relative price of each input at various locations remain unchanged between the base year (1963) and 1975. This implies that lowering tariffs between Latin American countries affects production costs at each location either not at all or in equal proportions. The relative effects of technological change are also implicitly equal.

(2) The relative exchange rates between Latin American currencies will not vary outside the limits imposed by the "indifference rates of exchange,"[3] a concept developed for this study. It is examined on pages 35–36 and, in greater detail, in Chapter 9.

(3) Transport costs will remain within the limits imposed by the maximum and minimum assumptions used. The maximum was taken to be current transport rates; the minimum, the projected 1975 rates. Separate optimum solutions were calculated using maximum and minimum estimates of transport costs.

(4) External economies or diseconomies are equal at all possible locations of production for each product.

(5) The relation between market prices and the competitive equilibrium price will be stable.

Further Uses of the Model

The *welfare gains,* or resources saved, by members of LAFTA as a result of importing the fourteen products from the minimum cost location of production—as compared with importing from the United States or producing in a nationalistically oriented pattern of production—are calculated using the solutions to the model. For purposes of this study, national, or autarkic, production does not carry the usual meaning—that each country produces for itself. Here, because not every country presented data for every product studied, "national production" means that each country that presented data produces for itself, and the country with the lowest costs among those that presented data produces for all the others.

This calculation of welfare gains and costs takes account of economies of scale but otherwise is static in its approach.

The model also determines the cost to the area of producing goods at

3. Alternative locations can be calculated if relative exchange rates do move beyond this range.

suboptimum locations—those requiring outlays higher than the minimum costs of production and transportation. The less developed and middle-sized countries of the region (even if the region is the Central American Common Market or the Andean Common Market) must be assured a share in the gains from the increase in trade realized by eliminating trade barriers. This stricture means that industrialization in countries like Ecuador, Bolivia, Paraguay, those in Central America (including Panama), and Uruguay may have to be subsidized in some form if it is to continue. The model sheds light on the magnitude of the subsidies by determining the costs to the area of locating production in these countries even if they do not constitute optimum locations.

Exchange Rates

An important qualification to any study of this kind is that its results are keyed exclusively to the prevailing rates of exchange for the countries studied. Where it was suspected that official exchange rates highly overvalued the currency, estimates were made using both the official and the free rate of exchange.[4] Since the study deals with only six industry groups, it is clearly impossible to determine new equilibrium exchange rates from the results of the analysis. However, it was possible to estimate the sensitivity of the optimal production pattern for each product to variations in exchange rates at each major location of production in the region by calculating "indifference rates of exchange." The indifference rate of exchange between the currencies of two countries is that rate at which a third, importing, country is indifferent about whether it buys a good from one or the other. If, for example, Chile can buy a good from Argentina for 4 pesos and from Brazil for 10 cruzeiros, and the exchange rates are such that 1 escudo equals 4 pesos or 10 cruzeiros, Chile could purchase, indifferently, from either. Thus the exchange rate of 4 pesos for 10 cruzeiros would be the indifference rate for the Argentine and Brazilian currencies in Chile for this good at these prices. If, however, the rates are such that 1 escudo ex-

4. The use of the "free" rate of exchange as a starting point in the exchange rate problem stems from the results of an ECLA study of purchasing power parities, *A Measurement of Price Levels and the Purchasing Power of Currencies in Latin America, 1960–62*, E/CN.12/653 (1963). The study implies that the free rates are fairly representative of purchasing power parities between Latin American countries in both June 1960 and June 1962.

changes for 4 pesos or 8 cruzeiros, and the price of the good in Chile remains 4 pesos from Argentina and 10 cruzeiros from Brazil, then Chile will purchase from Argentina, for the good will cost it only 1 escudo there, but 1.25 escudos bought from Brazil. On the other hand, if the escudo exchanges for 4 pesos or 12 cruzeiros, again assuming the price of the good is 4 pesos or 10 cruzeiros, then Chile will purchase from Brazil, where the cost will be only 0.83 escudo, rather than Argentina, where it will be 1 escudo.

This exercise may reveal that, given their official rates of exchange, some countries cannot compete in any product studied, while others are consistently low cost producers. In some cases, the minimum cost location may shift in response to a small change in exchange rates; in others, it may be insensitive to alterations in rates.

Some Cautionary Notes

Comparative cost studies aimed at determining an economically optimum location for 1975 may appear naïve for a variety of reasons. First of all, information is limited. Basic data may simply not exist, or, where they do, may be deficient and unreliable. Then there are the problems inherent in making projections, no matter how complete and dependable the data. Attempting to foresee all sorts of changes and indirect effects poses a special problem in developing countries. The relative effect of changes in production processes and technology will not remain the same, relative prices will differ, and other factors will be modified in directions that are difficult to predict.

Furthermore, since it deals with only a few industries, rather than with the economy as a whole, this study suffers from all the limitations inherent in partial equilibrium analysis. Ideally, all industries and segments of the economy should be considered within the framework of a general equilibrium system, so that both the direct and indirect impacts of economic integration could be measured. The partial equilibrium approach used here essentially identifies the countries likely to have an absolute advantage in producing a specified product on given assumptions. If these countries had still greater advantages in producing other goods, they might not be the best locations for production of the good under study. The implication is that the study has identified locations that can more properly be labeled "minimum cost" rather than "optimum." Obtaining the optimum requires a general equilibrium analysis that considers all the interrelations in an economy, including limitations on total resources available in each area and in the region as a whole. To do this in a comprehensive fashion is not yet feasible because of computational problems, not to speak of the impossibility of acquiring all the necessary data. Present economic techniques permit a highly aggregative type of analysis for some developed countries, but such global studies say almost nothing about specific products or industries, and would therefore not serve the purposes of this study, even leaving aside the probability that in developing countries they would abstract from reality more than the partial equilibrium analysis used here.

The importance of the ceteris paribus assumptions about costs, prices, and exchange rates in the model varies from industry to industry, depending on the effect changes in the tariff structure can be expected to have on the price of major inputs. The industries studied here represent a variety of production processes—which is, indeed, one of the reasons for their inclusion—and, consequently, the potential errors in the solutions to the linearized programming model that stem from failure to use a more dynamic analysis are more serious for some case studies than for others.

In four of the six industry groups—nitrogenous fertilizers, methanol and formaldehyde, paper and pulp, and dairy products—the cost of raw materials is crucial in determining the optimum location for production. The transportation cost of their principal raw materials is high relative to that for their products, forcing plants to locate near the source of materials rather than final markets. The prices of natural gas, lumber, and fresh milk—the most costly inputs, respectively, in these industries—are likely to be little affected by alterations in the tariff structure of Latin American countries or by free trade among them. Discoveries of resources and innovations in processing and transportation are the primary sources of changes in costs for raw material-oriented products. The bias that partial equilibrium analysis introduces in the investigation of this type of industry is probably not great except with regard to changes in the equilibrium exchange rate.

On the other hand, for tractors and lathes, economies of scale, and a developed industrial base embodied in skilled labor and parts suppliers, are the most important determinants of production costs. Transportation of the inputs and final products forms a small fraction of cost, allowing location of the industry to be more flexible. Because such products depend on inputs produced by a number of highly protected industries, a change

in the tariff structure could radically influence production costs. Biases
due to a quasi-static analysis, then, would probably be much greater for
them than for the raw material-oriented industries.

In light of these qualifications, the solutions to the minimum cost model
and the estimates derived from these solutions must be interpreted with
great care. The solutions estimate absolute, rather than comparative, advantage. Countries may be able to produce a number of goods more efficiently, relative to other countries in the area, than the goods studied here.
With limited resources, a country may not be able to produce all the goods
in which it has an absolute advantage.

Moreover, the solutions are dynamic only in the sense that demand is
projected to 1975, and the distribution of production for each industry is
estimated for that year; at the same time, cost functions are estimated
using, for the most part, base year (1963) prices of inputs. While transport
costs are also taken in the base year, a dynamic element is introduced by
estimating the minimum cost distribution of production with maximum
and minimum values for transport costs (based, respectively, on 1963 and
1975 costs). No attempt is made to project changes in wages or in the cost
of other inputs that result from changes in the tariff structures of member
countries. In addition, the use of market prices for inputs injects the issue
of distortions that arise when the market price does not equal the socially
optimum price of the input. Besides reflecting tariffs and other barriers to
trade, the market price may include monopoly rent (which could be eliminated by competition from other Latin American producers once barriers
to trade are eliminated) and internal taxes, both of which might also change
over time.

The indifference rates of exchange are an effort to test the sensitivity of
the optimum locations to changes in exchange rates; but no account is
taken of general adjustments in exchange rates, though it is expected that
the trade balances of individual countries will shift with a customs union,
and exchange rates will therefore be altered to achieve new long-run
equilibria.

Even if policy makers were willing to accept the many assumptions
underlying the models used in this study, they would require, to be useful
in guiding specific investment decisions in the future, more timely and
possibly more refined data than those employed in this study, which are
now five to seven years old. This substitution could, however, be accom-

plished quite rapidly now that the methodology has been developed and the necessary computer programs written and tested.

These qualifying points having been made, it may added that no investigation can cover all elements of the real world, nor can the results of any study be accepted unquestioningly. Despite the limitations imposed by the data, by research techniques, and by human and financial resources, they nevertheless provide insight into the process of economic integration in Latin America.

The Results

The following sections summarize the studies of the six industry groups, which are reported in detail in Chapters 3 through 8. The chapter closes with a brief section of conclusions about industrial integration in Latin America in general, which have been drawn from the studies of these industries.

Nitrogenous Fertilizers

Ammonia and the products derived from it form the group called nitrogenous fertilizers. The manufacture of these products in Latin America is characterized by very similar capital costs in various locations, since almost all machinery is imported and technology in the various processes is practically fixed.[5] The most important element of in-plant costs that varies from location to location is raw material cost. Since natural gas, the cheapest material for producing ammonia in large quantities,[6] is expensive to transport, the lowest cost production takes place at the source of the

5. It is possible for various locations to have different capital costs even though they import the same capital equipment at equal prices. The return to capital in alternative uses is probably higher in Venezuela and Mexico than in Chile, for example. In this study, however, the opportunity cost of capital is assumed to be 8 percent per annum in every country. Furthermore, plants in different locations may be able to draw on work forces with skills in operation and maintenance of the equipment and thus may have different depreciation costs. See also App. B.

6. UN Industrial Development Organization, *Fertilizer Manual*, ST/CID/15, 1967, p. 71.

gas.[7] But there are differences in the price of gas even at the source. Because in most areas gas is a joint product with petroleum, its price depends on the demand for it relative to petroleum. Theoretically, if the supply of natural gas at a given well is more than the demand at any price, its price would be zero; in several locations, indeed, gas is burned off at the well. Assuming that gas is priced competitively at all locations, the price will always be lower the nearer to the wellhead. In competitive equilibrium, the delivered price of gas could exceed transport costs if demand is high enough, the difference being the equivalent of a scarcity rent on natural gas resources. On the supply side, if, above certain levels of gas production, petroleum production is correspondingly reduced, the transformation function between the two products together with the demand for both would determine the prices. In view of the partial joint product nature of gas and petroleum production, the oligopolistic nature of the international petroleum market, and the natural monopoly inherent in a gas pipeline, the pricing of natural gas is to some extent arbitrary.

According to the ECLA study of nitrogenous fertilizers in Latin America,[8] the price of natural gas at ammonia plants in Latin America varies considerably. The lowest prices are in Punta Arenas, Chile (Ŝ3.50 per 1,000 cubic meters) and in Maracaibo, Venezuela (Ŝ4.60 per 1,000 cubic meters); the highest are in Bahia, Brazil (Ŝ9.00), and Minatitlan, Mexico (Ŝ8.10).[9] With fixed technology, locating production near the cheapest source of natural gas appears to be an important way to reduce costs. Chapter 3 demonstrates that Chile and Venezuela have a significant advantage in production costs at the plant site almost irrespective of plant size. However, even where a single material input is such an important element in cost, economies of scale are a major factor in lowering production costs (see Table 2-1).[10]

7. Once a pipeline is built, the marginal cost of bringing gas to market is low. However, from the point of view of a firm considering a new investment in a pipeline without any subsidy, prices would have to cover average annual costs including depreciation and opportunity cost of capital. This would drive the delivered price of gas considerably above the price at the source.

8. ECLA, *La Oferta de Fertilizantes en America Latina*, E/CN.12/761, Nov. 3, 1966, Table 8, p. 12.

9. In order to be able to make comparisons between costs and prices at various locations, all estimates have been converted into a common unit of account. It is called the "simón," is defined as equal to the U.S. dollar, and takes the symbol, Ŝ.

10. As is pointed out in Chap. 3, Colombian costs are suspect. Estimated cost per

Table 2-1. Average Cost of Production of Ammonia, by Country and by Annual Output

Simones per metric ton[a]

Annual output (tons)	Chile	Mexico	Venezuela	Colombia	Peru[b]
25,000	76	186	71	70	85
50,000	46	99	41	61	53
100,000	31	55	26	48	37
200,000	23	33	19	56	29
330,000	20	25	16	55	26

Source: Chap. 3.
a. Exchange rates per simón:
   Chile—3.26 escudos.
   Colombia—13.5 pesos.
   Mexico—12.5 pesos.
   Peru—26.8 soles.
   Venezuela—4.5 bolivares.
  b. The cost curve for Peru was based on economies of scale as weighted by larger plants. This leads to a steeper slope here than is implicit in Table 3-3.

The differences in average costs shown in Table 2-1 occur in part because of differences in the price of natural gas. If Colombian costs of ammonia are omitted, Mexican and Peruvian natural gas prices are the highest for ammonia-producing countries. Since engineering estimates are used to establish the costs of ammonia, some differences in technical coefficients used from country to country also affect the cost curves. Mexican estimates include actual operating costs for the two smaller plants producing ammonia. This biases Mexican costs upward at lower plant sizes relative to the engineering estimates using advanced technology applied in Chile, Peru, and Venezuela, and helps to explain the greater slope in Mexican average costs. Engineering estimates may also bias costs downward, since engineers tend to be optimistic with regard to construction costs. In chemicals the bias is probably not large. The costs in Table 2-1 do not include marketing overhead, which is about 25 percent of production cost. The lowest cost f.o.b. of ammonia in the region is in Venezuela at about $20 per ton.

The products of the nitrogenous fertilizer industry, like most chemicals, are expensive to transport. But this turns out to be a much less serious constraint than the transportation of natural gas. Brazil has constructed a plant in Santos to produce ammonia using imported naphtha, an input

---

unit rises for the 200,000-ton plant. It is probable that Colombian costs are overestimated for higher outputs.

much cheaper to ship than gas; nevertheless, its output would not be competitive with ammonia imported from either Venezuela or Chile.[11] The nitrogen content determines the agricultural value of a nitrogenous fertilizer, and the cost of shipping nitrogen content increases as the percentage of nitrogen in a ton of final product decreases. Although fertilizers vary in their nitrogen content, anhydrous ammonia contains more nitrogen (by weight) than any of the fertilizers made with ammonia. The cost of transportation between factory and market therefore influences final product mix more than the location of ammonia plants. The cost of transport of ammonia also makes it difficult to export to developed countries. If the f.o.b. price of ammonia is $20 per ton in Venezuela, the delivered price at U.S. ports would be about $40 per ton under the minimum transport cost assumption and about $75 per ton if published transport rates prevail. Although the lower price is competitive with the minimum U.S. f.o.b. price assumed for 1975, the 1969 U.S. tariff on ammonia was $22.05 per metric ton.

The minimum cost locations of fertilizer production are set out in Table 2-2. In order to determine the sensitivity of the optimum solutions to the differences in production technology among countries under both sets of assumptions about transport costs and exchange rates, a second set of calculations was made based on the assumption that all countries used the same technology as Venezuela. Besides the lower total cost of production and transportation, the primary difference between the results given in Table 2-2 and that assumption is that ammonium sulphate production shifts away from Peru to Mexico and Venezuela. In the minimum cost case, Chile produces much more ammonia and urea than it does when national technical coefficients are allowed to vary.

In this and other studies, it is assumed that existing plants at locations that cannot compete with imports from other Latin American countries will be phased out of fertilizer production. Given this assumption, the total investment required between 1963 and 1975 to build all new plants (net of 1963 capacity) in Venezuela would be $144 million (in 1963 prices). Net of 1963 capacity, the cost of building the more dispersed set of plants would be $184 million in 1963–75 (see Table 3-14).

11. See *Brazilian Bulletin*, Vol. 23 (November 1966). The Grace Company has "pioneered in the use of a new type of tanker which can carry anhydrous ammonia at a temperature of 28 degrees below zero Fahrenheit." As a result, the cost of shipping anhydrous ammonia will probably fall substantially. Alliance for Progress, *Weekly Newsletter*, Sept. 25, 1967.

Table 2-2. Minimum Cost Locations for Production of Selected Fertilizers[a] in Latin America, for Alternative Assumptions about Transport Costs and Exchange Rates

Number of plants

Country	Ammonia	Urea	Ammonium nitrate	Ammonium sulphate
Minimum transport costs—free exchange rates[b]				
Mexico	2	0	0	4
Chile	2	2	2	0
Venezuela	2	3	1	0
Peru	2	0	1	8
Colombia	0	0	1[c]	0
Maximum transport costs—official exchange rates[b]				
Mexico	3	2	1	4
Chile	2	1	2	0
Venezuela	1	1	1	1
Peru	2	0	1	7
Colombia	0	0	1[c]	0

Source: Table 3-7.

a. The production of diammonium phosphate (an increasingly popular high-analysis dry fertilizer containing both nitrogen and phosphorus) was not considered because of the problem of allocating costs between the phosphorus and nitrogen content and estimating demand for phosphatic fertilizers.

b. For a full discussion of these assumptions, see p. 35.

c. The ammonia input for this plant is imported from Venezuela.

Methanol and Formaldehyde

As it is in ammonia production, natural gas is the basic raw material input for the manufacture of methanol and formaldehyde. Plants for methanol, the first-stage product, are generally located close to natural gas supplies. Since formaldehyde, a second-stage product, is more expensive to ship than methanol, its plants are usually located near urban consumption centers, especially if they are coastal cities. Economies of scale in the production of this second-stage product are small, so the output of a plant need not be large for it to be competitive locally.

Assuming both minimum and maximum transport cost, the model singles out Venezuela as the optimum location for the production of both methanol and formaldehyde, except for one formaldehyde plant in Colombia which would buy its methanol from Venezuela. The total investment required to build the three methanol plants and seven formaldehyde plants in Venezuela, plus the formaldehyde plant in Colombia, would be $43 million to 1975. Studies of these chemicals demonstrate the importance of the location of raw material. Venezuela has cheap sources of natural gas near well-developed ports. As a result, as Table 2-3 shows, at high levels of production, Venezuela has the lowest costs of producing methanol, as it did for ammonia. Furthermore, for methanol, as for ammonia, economies of scale have a major influence on production costs, despite the significance of a single raw material in total costs. Transportation costs are relatively low for moving final products to market country ports. Discoveries of natural gas in other locations as advantageous as Venezuela would alter the optimum distribution of production. The solutions also might shift with changes in natural gas pricing and with the development of technical processes that make other inputs as cheap to use as natural gas.

Table 2-3. Average Cost of Production of Methanol, by Country and by Annual Output

Simones per metric ton[a]

Annual output (tons)	Chile	Mexico	Venezuela
5,000	142	179	162
10,000	101	126	106
20,000	80	100	72
40,000	70	87	63

Source: Chap. 4.
a. See note *a*, Table 2-1.

Tractors

Tractor production in Latin America uses few direct raw material inputs. It involves importing finished parts, buying domestically produced semi-finished parts, completing their fabrication, and assembling the finished product. The high value of the parts entering into final assembly makes their transport costs a small fraction of their total cost. Importing parts from various Latin American countries and assembling the tractors in several locations could, therefore, be cheaper than production that depended on domestic output of both parts and final product. To take advantage of the economies of scale that are important in both the production of parts and final assembly, the number of producers of each part or of the entire tractor would probably be limited. In addition, a ready supply of parts, if they are not to be imported from outside the area, is also important.

Tractor manufacturing, then, falls into the category of industries that could be located in almost any large industrial area in Latin America.

It is not unusual, however, for such an industry to locate near its largest markets, possibly even in agricultural areas.

Argentina and Brazil absorbed about two-thirds of the total Latin American tractor production and imports in 1963, and they were the only countries in Latin America producing tractors in that year. If parts were readily available, however, a large-scale operation in Argentina, Brazil, or even Chile or Mexico, could easily have an advantage over the smaller firms recently characterizing the industry in the two large consuming countries. In many ways, the distribution of this kind of industry is the most important for Latin Americans: Since the industry can spread over a number of countries through complementarity agreements, the middle-level countries have been pressing to share in the fruits of integration and insisting that the more highly developed countries not dominate market-oriented industries.[12] The difficulty in complementarity agreements is that little is known of their welfare cost to the area and the individual countries. Tractors are currently being produced on a small scale in both Argentina and Brazil; the average output of an Argentine plant is about 10 percent of that of the largest U.S. plant and 3 percent of that of the largest plant in the world. Benefits could be shared through a system of regional international companies rather than complementarity agreements involving different firms.[13]

The optimum location of tractor production in 1975 is estimated for alternative exchange rates and plant sizes. Whether the plant produces 20,000 or 62,000 units annually (the two maximum sizes considered) does not affect the optimum location. Only Argentina and Brazil are included as possible Latin American production locations. Under both assumptions about relative exchange rates between the currencies of the two countries, Argentina emerges as the lower cost producer. However, the quality of Brazilian cost estimates and the sensitivity of this optimum solution to the exchange rate make it very tentative. Interestingly enough, when it is assumed that its production takes advantage of economies of scale, Argentina is competitive with the United States but not with Europe. It should be

12. See Organization of American States, *Declaration of the Presidents of America*, Meeting of American Chiefs of State, Punta del Este, Uruguay, April 12–14, 1967 (OAS, Ser. C/IX.I).

13. See I. M. D. Little, "Regional International Companies as an Approach to Economic Integration," *Journal of Common Market Studies*, Vol. 5 (December 1966), pp. 181–86.

pointed out again that the analysis does not include (1) changes in the prices of inputs due to changes in the tariff structure; (2) changes due to external economies or diseconomies in production, or (3) the possibility of nonprice competition such as product differentiation by quality of service and for attachments available.

Lathes

The quality control necessary, the variety produced, and the sizable component of skilled labor combine to make competition possible between small- and large-scale producers of lathes. Like tractors, the machine tool industry is oriented toward markets rather than materials, and plants can be located in a number of industrial areas in Latin America. The primary factors are the size of the market and the availability of a pool of skilled labor.[14] Of all the industries studied here, machine tool production is most likely to be located near industrial markets, since both production and final use require the same factor—skilled labor. However, the relatively low cost of transporting the final product to market means that plants can be located in less developed countries with smaller markets for machine tools but with cheaper labor. The cost to the area of such a distribution may be quite low.

The minimum cost location for producing parallel lathes in Latin America is highly sensitive to the exchange rate. There is also some doubt about whether the costs of production for different countries are comparable because of differences in the metal content of the lathes.[15] No cost estimates are available for Mexico, a large lathe producer and consumer. Furthermore, cost curves used are for single plants, and so probably yield a biased estimate of large-scale production costs and perhaps of the optimum location. With these important reservations in mind, Chile is estimated to be the optimum location when free rates of exchange are assumed. With the higher, official, rates, Argentina becomes the optimum location.

14. The market for machine tools is considerably different from that for consumer durables like automobiles and refrigerators or for agriculturally oriented producer durables like tractors. Even in primarily agricultural countries, such as Argentina before 1910, consumer durables can face large markets.

15. An attempt was made to obtain U.S. lathe prices in order to adjust these different metal contents to a constant content; however, U.S. lathe producers do not supply price or cost estimates unless the inquiry concerns the purchase of a specific machine.

Since the Argentine lathe is approximately the same weight as the Brazilian lathe, costs for these two are comparable. Argentina appears to have an advantage over Brazil whether the official or free Argentine-Brazilian exchange rate is used.

Powdered Milk and Cheese

Processing of perishable foods has some of the characteristics of mineral- and forest-based industries. The most important similarity is in the limitation imposed on plant size by the cost of transportation of the raw material, which is usually an even more important element of cost here than it is in the forest- or mineral-based industries. This limitation is reinforced by the perishability of the raw material, but moderated by the possibility of rapidly increasing the density of raw material available in a given area. Raw milk is not very expensive to transport over short distances, but once it must be refrigerated for shipment over long distances, transportation costs rise steeply. Powdered milk and cheese plants avoid the high cost of refrigeration by locating in milk-producing areas.

Since the yield of agricultural products is not fixed by nature, the output of raw milk per hectare can be rapidly increased in most areas of Latin America by applying modern technology. Not only can the intensity of production of raw agricultural goods be increased, but the location of their production can be varied. Perishable agricultural goods have usually been grown close to final markets; however, processing plants could conceivably move much farther from urban areas to take advantage of lower costs. Compared with the raw materials, the final products are not expensive to ship relative to their value unless they have to be refrigerated, as in the case of cheese.

The results of the processed food analysis are particularly interesting because of the importance of the industry in Latin American economies and its export potential. The limitation imposed on plant size by the transport of perishable raw materials has resulted in a large number of plants; furthermore, they are widely dispersed because of the small range of output subject to economics of scale (diseconomies appear at levels of output much lower than domestic consumption) and the large number of products being produced. In the four products studied in detail—powdered milk, and hard, semihard, and soft (bland) paste cheese—Uruguay and Argentina generally have an advantage within Latin America. The costs of production of soft paste cheese, the most popular domestic cheese, vary considerably less than those of the other products. In all but powdered milk, Latin American products have an advantage compared with imports from outside the region. The diseconomies of scale at output levels that are low relative to regional demand dictate a large number of plants to meet 1975 demand (ranging from 100 to 460, depending on the product). An important distortion may have been introduced in the estimates of optimum location because the cost curves for dairy products, except for Uruguayan hard and semihard paste cheese, are for the short run. The effect may be to lower costs in Uruguay relative to those in other countries and to inflate the shadow prices derived from the optimum location cost curves.

Paper and Pulp

Paper plants are almost always located next to the forests that are their sources of pulp. In recent years, the use of sugar cane (bagasse pulp) or used paper has enabled many countries without extensive suitable long-fibered (coniferous) woodland to produce paper. Although bagasse pulp does not have the broad range of paper production possibilities of long-fibered pulp, the costs for both are analyzed in this study.

Unlike gas for chemicals, the cost of the wood for pulp production is likely to be affected by the size of the pulp plant. As the output of pulp or paper increases, so does the distance the plant must go to get its trees. The density of planting varies greatly from place to place, and economies of scale are limited by the total forest area available for paper production. Therefore it may be expected that in regions where paper is competing with lumber for limited forest resources, the price of wood will be higher than otherwise. Raw material costs will also rise with the number of paper plants in an area.

Both pulp (in dried form) and paper are relatively inexpensive to transport to markets. Transportation charges are a much smaller percentage of total cost than they are in the case of ammonia, finished fertilizers, methanol, or formaldehyde. For this reason, paper plants are usually built near the source of raw materials and also tend to be located with pulp plants to avoid the additional cost of drying the pulp for transport. Pulp and paper manufacturing is therefore representative of many industries that process a bulky nonperishable raw material, expensive to transport and available only over a large area.

Newsprint, which is made from kraft pulp, is included in estimates of final demand for pulp. No optimum location study is made for newsprint, however, because production cost data are available only for Chile.

Assuming the free rate of exchange for the Chilean escudo and minimum transport costs, the optimum location of kraft pulp and paper production in 1975 is in Chile, with one exception: Mexico would import Chilean cellulose to produce kraft paper to meet domestic demand. If maximum transport costs and the official rate of exchange for the Chilean escudo (which overvalues it) are assumed, the optimum location shifts quite radically: With the exception of Brazil, which would meet its own substantial demand for both products, Latin America would import its kraft pulp and Mexico would produce all kraft paper. If production of pulp is protected from extraregional imports, the economic optimum would be autarkic production of pulp and paper in Mexico, Ecuador, and Brazil, plus Mexican production of kraft paper for the rest of Latin America. Chile would produce kraft pulp for its own and Argentine newsprint production.

The Chilean costs of paper and pulp are engineering estimates, which may somewhat understate operating costs, and the size of the paper plants used to estimate the long-run cost curves of kraft paper production is much smaller for Brazil than for Chile, Colombia, or Mexico. Furthermore, Mexican costs of producing kraft paper (value added to pulp) may be seriously understated. All these biases raise doubts as to the validity of the minimum cost locations presented in Chapter 8. Nevertheless, the shadow prices of pulp and paper derived from the Chilean estimates are probably realistic, and the study does indicate the role of exchange rates and transport costs in the distribution of paper production in a Latin American customs union.

Benefits and Costs of Union

An estimate of the annual welfare benefits and costs to LAFTA countries in 1975 can be derived from the optimum location studies. An estimate of the total cost to the region of locating production in some way other than the optimum manner is provided directly by the linearized programming model (see Chapter 9). For political reasons, other patterns of production may be preferable to those identified as optimal in this study, and some of these are discussed in the next section. Here the concern is with the cost to the region and to each country of two specific alternatives to the optimum: (1) imports from third countries (which are represented by the United States); and (2) autarkic production by countries that presented cost studies, and imports from the lowest cost source within LAFTA (except where noted) by those that did not.[16] The estimates made here deal not with the diversion or creation of trade caused by union, but rather with the gains or losses to LAFTA countries from using one of these alternatives. It is also assumed that the region will export negligible quanties of manufactured goods. Given the tariff policies of both developed and less developed countries, this is not an unreasonable assumption; it does, however, tend to bias upward the estimates of welfare costs of national production.

These gains and losses are a function of total market demand for the product in 1975, the differences at any one market among the delivered prices from alternative production points, and the elasticity of demand, which is taken as unity over the range of prices considered. Table 2-4, pages 52–53, gives the welfare gains and losses by country and by product group and the gain or loss from the alternative compared with the optimum location based on (1) the minimum transport cost and free exchange rate, and (2) maximum transport costs and official exchange rates. In the first case, delivered prices of products to markets are at the minimum, which may bias upward both gains and costs; the second case may result in downward bias on gains and costs.

Table 2-4 gives first the estimated annual gains for each product group of buying from the optimum location within the region rather than importing from the United States. The import price is the 1965 New York, San Francisco, or Laredo f.o.b. price plus transport costs to Latin American markets. Possible changes in world market prices between 1965 and 1975 are accounted for only in the case of nitrogenous fertilizers.[17] It should also be pointed out that European prices for a 50 horsepower

16. App. C explains the derivation of the formulas used to calculate welfare benefits and costs. For a general welfare analysis, see James E. Meade, *Trade and Welfare* (London: Oxford University Press, 1960).

17. In the minimum transport cost-free exchange rate case, the f.o.b. prices at U.S. ports for nitrogenous fertilizers are reduced to a projected 1975 price; 1965 prices are used in the maximum transport cost case.

tractor are considerably lower than the price of a U.S. tractor, so estimates of welfare gains of producing tractors in Latin America versus importing from the United States are biased upward. In all other goods considered here the United States is competitive in the world market. The table then sets out the annual welfare costs of autarkic development as compared with union. The difference in the national price and the optimum location price reflects differences in scale of production as well as in input prices.[18] In the table are given the total welfare gains and losses, and the component that is attributable to the resource saving on the amount purchased in the base year, called the production effect. The difference between the total and the production effect is the consumption effect, which results from the increase in the quantity of the product consumed when its price falls. This division is made in order to compare the production effect with the total value of output of the fourteen products and to estimate the contribution of economies of scale to growth rates.

Gains from Regional Production versus U.S. Imports

The welfare gain of producing the fourteen products studied in Latin America rather than importing from the United States is $230 million to $250 million annually under both sets of assumptions about transport costs and exchange rates. The use of official rates of exchange would be

---

18. It is also possible to estimate the annual welfare cost to consumers of the present tariff structure in LAFTA countries. This estimate can be taken as the maximum welfare cost of national production in 1975, since existing (1965) tariffs are assumed to reflect maximum price differentials between domestic, nationally oriented production in Latin America and imports in 1975. It implies that the internal expansion of national markets will not narrow the differential between domestic and import prices. However, the estimate of welfare cost made in this way is subject to upward bias on several other counts. First, the assumption is made that cost differences are equal to the tariff although domestic competition often reduces the domestic price below the sum of the world market price and the (prohibitive) tariff. Second, the elimination of tariffs would entail a devaluation to maintain balance-of-payments equilibrium. The "proper" protected domestic good price to use as an alternative to the foreign price, therefore, should be lower in simones (dollars) than (1 + tariff rate) times the foreign price. Third, in some countries, the tariffs are revenue rather than protective tariffs. They are not designed to protect domestic production, because usually there is none. In the revenue tariff case, it would be necessary to deduct customs receipts from the estimated welfare cost of the tariff. Most revenue tariffs are low, however, and the resulting welfare cost estimates are small. If welfare costs are calculated from the 1965 tariff structure, the total welfare cost for the fourteen products and ten countries is Ŝ500 million, half of which is in dairy products.

Table 2-4. Welfare Benefits and Costs of Alternatives to Optimum Location of Selected Products in LAFTA, 1975

Thousands of simones

Consuming country	Nitrogenous fertilizers		Methanol and formaldehyde		Tractors		Lathes		Powdered milk and cheese		Paper and pulp		Total	
	Production effect	Total	Production effect	Total	Production effect	Total	Production effect	Total	Production effect	Total	Production effect	Total	Production effect	Total
Buying from optimum location versus U.S. imports—minimum transport costs and free exchange rates														
Argentina	5,988	7,633	293	319	13,281	15,008	2,398	3,069	24,568	32,798	2,516	2,908	49,044	61,725
Brazil	26,804	32,082	3,065	3,343	22,368	25,499	2,780	3,586	4,541	10,316	16,385	18,732	75,943	93,557
Chile	687	949	119	125	2,458	2,802	207	271	-4,769	-4,729	5,364	6,659	4,066	6,078
Colombia	2,969	3,888	202	227	2,302	2,509	932	1,146	-2,020	-2,222	6,254	7,192	10,639	12,740
Ecuador	366	500	...	...	71	77	...	...	-694	-763	15,006	17,407	14,749	17,221
Mexico	15,805	18,490	325	356	3,618	3,758	2,050	2,377	...	...	14,418	15,981	36,216	40,962
Paraguay	...	...	...	...	327	370	...	...	-212	-215	29	34	144	189
Peru	7,429	10,662	148	161	604	670	...	...	1,102	1,421	3,547	4,221	12,830	17,135
Uruguay	2,083	2,996	11	12	2,040	2,284	...	...	2,013	2,646	424	491	6,571	8,429
Venezuela	1,497	1,933	43	54	...	...	...	...	-23,708	-27,027	...	...	-22,168	-25,040
Total	63,628	79,133	4,206	4,597	47,069	52,977	8,367	10,449	821	12,225	63,943	73,625	188,034	233,006
Buying from optimum location versus U.S. imports—maximum transport costs and official exchange rates														
Argentina	9,155	12,433	583	660	6,852	7,195	2,275	2,798	24,568	32,798	791	822	44,224	56,706
Brazil	44,119	56,828	5,173	5,914	12,171	12,901	2,628	3,259	4,541	10,316	13,811	15,446	82,443	104,664
Chile	1,104	1,561	277	310	1,406	1,490	193	237	-4,769	-4,729	2,079	2,245	290	1,114
Colombia	4,969	7,171	349	415	559	571	818	956	-2,020	-2,222	4,127	4,457	8,802	11,348
Ecuador	474	707	...	...	20	20	...	...	-694	-763	10,601	11,555	10,401	11,519
Mexico	31,230	42,446	680	758	...	...	1,671	1,854	...	...	12,268	13,372	48,012	60,626
Paraguay	...	...	...	...	169	177	...	...	-212	-215	9	10	-34	-28
Peru	10,252	19,103	245	273	242	249	...	...	1,102	1,421	2,542	2,796	14,383	23,842

Uruguay	2,059	2,676	18	20	983	1,022	...	...	2,013	2,646	152	158	5,225	6,522
Venezuela	2,457	3,884	92	100	...	...	...	...	−23,708	−27,027	...	...	−21,161	−23,043
Total	105,819	146,809	7,417	8,450	22,402	23,625	7,585	9,104	821	12,225	46,380	50,861	192,584	253,268
National production versus production at optimum location—minimum transport costs and free exchange rates														
Argentina	−1,576	−1,666	−293	−319	...	...	−466	−485	−9,117	−9,917	−412	−423	−11,864	−12,810
Brazil	−10,100	−11,355	−3,065	−3,343	−24,498	−28,173	−2,162	−2,573	−68,683	−95,271	−2,312	−2,381	−110,820	−143,095
Chile	−1,300	−1,904	−470	−627	...	...	−16	−17	−196	−198	−876	−906	−2,561	−3,652
Colombia	−1,232	−1,350	−127	−137	...	...	−90	−92	−113	−118	−8,157	−9,870	−9,719	−11,567
Ecuador	−192	−229	...	...	...	...	...	...	−35	−37	−8,754	−9,454	−8,981	−9,720
Mexico	−3,438	−3,706	−617	−675	...	...	−2,477	−2,987	...	...	−17,717	−20,147	−24,248	−27,526
Paraguay	...	...	...	...	...	...	...	...	...	...	−5	−5	−5	−5
Peru	−702	−722	−217	−247	...	...	...	...	−716	−802	−4,466	−5,628	−6,101	−7,398
Uruguay	−260	−276	−17	−20	...	...	...	...	...	...	−70	−73	−347	−368
Venezuela	−1,578	−2,257	−39	−45	...	...	...	...	...	...	...	...	−1,617	−2,302
Total	−20,078	−23,465	−4,845	−5,413	−24,498	−28,173	−5,211	−6,154	−78,860	−106,343	−42,769	−48,887	−176,262	−218,444
National production versus production at optimum location—maximum transport costs and official exchange rates														
Argentina	2,825	3,101	−583	−660	...	...	−711	−754	−9,117	−9,917	−2,226	−2,461	−9,812	−10,691
Brazil	12,000	12,925	−5,173	−5,914	−14,605	−15,628	−1,889	−2,172	−68,683	−95,271	...	...	−78,349	−106,060
Chile	−1,306	−2,304	−516	−665	...	...	−151	−176	−196	−198	−1,858	−1,939	−4,027	−5,282
Colombia	−2,306	−2,327	−205	−227	...	...	−294	−309	−113	−118	−12,064	−15,804	−14,982	−18,785
Ecuador	−123	−135	...	...	...	...	...	...	−35	−37	−2,120	−2,162	−2,279	−2,334
Mexico	...	...	−506	−577	...	...	−2,135	−2,455	...	...	−15,021	−16,740	−19,621	−21,770
Paraguay	...	...	...	...	...	...	...	...	...	...	−28	−31	−28	−31
Peru	−325	−334	−220	−244	...	...	...	...	−716	−802	−5,532	−7,191	−6,793	−8,571
Uruguay	−199	−217	−16	−18	...	...	...	...	...	...	−391	−438	−606	−673
Venezuela	−1,145	−1,581	−38	−43	...	...	...	...	...	...	...	...	−1,183	−1,624
Total	9,421	9,128	−7,256	−8,348	−14,605	−15,628	−5,180	−5,866	−78,860	−106,343	−39,240	−46,766	−137,680	−175,821

Sources: Tables 3-8, 4-4, 5-5, 6-4, 7-7, and 8-9.
Note: Details may not add to totals due to rounding.

expected to lower the welfare gains of producing in the region; and for products in which the optimum regional production point is in a country for which a free exchange rate is also used in the study, such as Argentina, Chile, or Colombia, the welfare gain does fall. Tractors, lathes, and paper and pulp are such products (only a single estimate is made for dairy products). But chemicals are produced largely in Mexico, Peru, and Venezuela in the optimum solution, and their exchange rates remain constant in the model. Furthermore, in the maximum transport cost case, U.S. prices of nitrogenous fertilizers are taken equal to the 1965 price, which greatly raises the welfare gain of producing fertilizers in Latin America. If the lowest estimates of gain for each product group are combined, the low estimate of total gain is $182 million annually, of which $147 million is the production effect and $35 million the consumption effect. The high estimate of total gain, constructed similarly, is $304 million, of which $233 million is the production effect and $71 million the consumption effect.

In relative terms, the production effect is between 10 and 15 percent of the projected total value of production of the six product groups in 1975.[19] Table 2-5 shows the value of output (including transportation charges) supplied from the minimum cost locations for the six groups. The values equal the cost of filling 1975 projected physical demand for each product for all or most LAFTA countries. To make it correspond to the data in Table 2-4, the data in Table 2-5 are shown for both sets of transport cost and exchange rate assumptions. The total value of production and transportation of the six groups in 1975 is only slightly different for the two cases—$1.5 billion and $1.6 billion, respectively.[20] Assuming (a) that the manufacturing sector accounts for 25 percent of gross domestic product in 1975;[21] (b) that the six industries, producing approximately 4 percent of

19. The production gain, which measures the resources saved by buying the amounts of a commodity consumed in a base year from the optimum location in Latin America rather than importing it from the United States, should be compared with the value of the amount consumed in the base year. Under the assumption of unitary elasticity of demand, the value of the amount consumed in the base year at base year prices is equal to the value of the projected 1975 consumption at 1975 prices.

20. The projected value of production of the six groups represents approximately 1 percent of the projected value of LAFTA gross national product for 1975. The GNP estimate is based on Hollis B. Chenery, "Towards a More Effective Alliance for Progress" (Agency for International Development, Discussion Paper No. 13, March 1967; processed).

21. See ECLA, *Economic Survey of Latin America 1964* (1966), Table 23. Manufacturing accounted for 23 percent of the gross domestic product of Latin America in 1964. This percentage has been steadily increasing from 18 percent in 1950.

Table 2-5. Total Value of Output of Selected Product Groups in LAFTA, 1975

Millions of simones

Product	Minimum cost[a]	Maximum cost[b]
Nitrogenous fertilizers	239	279
Methanol and formaldehyde	32	39
Tractors	263	300
Lathes	24	29
Powdered milk and cheese[c]	643	643
Paper and pulp	292	321
Total	1,493	1,611

Sources: Tables 3-8, 4-4, 5-5, 6-4, 7-8, and 8-9.
a. Minimum transport costs and free exchange rate.
b. Maximum transport costs and official exchange rate.
c. As explained in Chap. 7, the assumptions about transport costs and exchange rates were not varied for the milk products group.

Latin American gross domestic product in manufacturing in 1975, are representative of the manufacturing sector in the region; and (c) that only the manufacturing sector is affected by the formation of a customs union, the gains from producing at the optimum locations rather than importing would imply an expansion of between 2.5 and 3.8 percent of gross domestic product (GDP) in real resources for Latin America (0.10 and 0.15 times 0.25). Assuming a 15 percent average rate of return to capital, the 2.5 and 3.8 percent gains translate into increases of 0.4 to 0.6 percent in the growth rate of the region, if the maximum gains were used to increase production capacity. The increases in the growth rate would be smaller to the extent that the gains were used to expand current consumption rather than investment.

Thus even if none of these Latin American products can now compete with U.S. imports, the optimum location and welfare analyses summarized above suggest that formation of a customs union not only would allow Latin America to compete in the production of manufactured goods, but would also free 3 to 4 percent of GDP each year to be used for further investment. Even under the assumptions of maximum transport cost and the official rate of exchange, only powdered milk and kraft pulp would be imported from the United States.[22] For many products, then, market expansion and specialization appear to offer opportunities for making Latin American producers competitive in world markets.

22. With completely free trade, Argentine tractors would not be able to compete with English imports even under the more favorable assumptions.

Assessing the relative welfare gains involves using the lowest production effect for each product (see Table 2-4), whether obtained under the minimum transport costs and free exchange rates, or the maximum transport costs and official exchange rates. With this procedure, the largest gains to the region are in nitrogenous fertilizers, lathes, and paper and pulp. For these products, the minimum production gain would be 27, 36, and 22 percent, respectively, of the minimum total production and transportation costs in 1975. These substantial gains occur in paper and pulp and nitrogenous fertilizers in part because of the weight of transport cost in the U.S. import price and in part because these products use a high proportion of inputs—natural gas and wood—that are relatively cheap at least somewhere in Latin America. In addition, production costs in the optimum location from which regional shadow prices are derived for both products are engineering estimates. For this reason they are probably biased downward. The case of lathes is more difficult to explain. One explanation might be that lathes use a high proportion of labor; and although it could be argued that skilled labor is expensive even in Latin America, it is still relatively cheap compared with its cost in the United States. The comparable U.S. lathe may be of higher quality. It should be noted that the cost curves used in estimating shadow prices for lathes at the optimum location are for the short run and are based on operating plants, and thus tend to underestimate gains of producing in the region over importing from the United States.

Table 2-6 reflects the results of using a similar procedure to assess relative gains for the countries. Peru and Uruguay gain relatively the most from regional production of all goods rather than importing from the United States.[23] Chile and Paraguay lose slightly due to the unfavorable effect of milk products; Venezuela is also a net loser, but the results are incomplete because studies were not made for a number of products. The highest relative gains from regional purchase rather than national production are garnered by Colombia and Peru, followed by Brazil and Ecuador.

Gains from Regional versus Domestic Production

Data in Table 2-4 can be used to calculate the low estimate of cost (the total of the lowest values for each product group) to the area of national

23. Peru's gain is almost entirely from nitrogenous fertilizers and pulp and paper, while Uruguay's is spread over all the products.

Table 2-6. Relative Welfare Gains from Buying Selected Products from Optimum Location, by LAFTA Country, 1975

Lowest total production gain as percentage of minimum value of consumption

Consuming country	Buying from optimum location versus importing from United States	Buying from optimum location versus autarkic production
Argentina	13	3
Brazil	10	13
Chile	*	4
Colombia	13	25
Ecuador	14	13
Mexico	14	8
Paraguay	−1	0ᵃ
Peru	25	16
Uruguay	18	4
Venezuela	−15	1
Average	10	9

Source: Minimum total gain for each country from Table 2-4 divided by minimum value of these products produced by each country (Table 2-5 figures disaggregated).
* Negative; less than 0.5 percent.
a. Paraguay did not present cost studies for one or more of the products, and is assumed to import them. Thus the relative gain of buying from the optimum location rather than national production will be zero for such products.

production rather than producing at the minimum cost location: about $170 million, of which $133 million is the production effect. The high estimate is $221 million, $178 million of which is the production effect. It should be remembered that, in the framework of this study, national production is not available to every country for all products. Since tractor production costs, for example, are presented in this analysis only for Brazil and Argentina (Mexico began production in 1965), only those countries can choose national production as the alternative to the minimum cost location in Argentina. Thus Brazil is the sole country that could supply its own 1975 demand with its ow tnractors, while all other countries of the region buy Argentine tractors.[24] Similarly, production costs for hard and semihard paste cheese and powdered milk are available only for two countries.

The estimates of $133 million to $178 million are 9 and 11 percent of the total minimum and maximum projected value of production of the six product groups in 1975. Under the assumptions about the importance of

24. The limitation of plant size to 20,000 units annually removes any scale effect of eliminating Brazilian markets for Argentine production.

the manufacturing sector in the domestic economy, of these products in the sector, and of the exclusive impact of union on the sector, outlined on pages 54–55, the welfare benefits of producing at the optimum location rather than nationally imply a gain of 2.2 to 2.8 percent of GDP in real resources of the area. This translates into an increase in the regional growth rate of 0.3 to 0.4 percent annually.

Since it is assumed that countries for which production costs are not available buy from the optimum location, the estimate of welfare costs of producing nationally is biased downward. The failure to include the cost of production of chemicals in Argentina and Brazil, paper and pulp in Argentina, and dairy products in Mexico and Venezuela as alternatives to the optimum location price reduces the total welfare cost of national production. Countries that did not provide costs of production are generally those that have no possibility of being competitive in that product with other Latin American producers.

These estimates suggest that, as a result of union, costs of production of manufactured goods could fall significantly in the region. But they also imply that reducing tariffs alone would not stimulate growth rates much more than national production, especially if tariff policies are such as to assure internal price reductions conforming to cost reductions. It should be noted, however, that in the shadow price estimates for national production, nonproducing countries in the region are assumed to buy from low cost regional producers except where noted. Therefore, the estimates do not measure the effect of complete autarky. Even though trade would be diverted by union to initially high cost production, the resulting expansion of markets (combined with specialization within the area) would lead to consumer benefits if the real resource cost of regional production falls below the real cost of imports.

The welfare benefits to consumers in the region that are reaped from economies of scale, and the trade diversion effects, accrue gradually rather than at any one point in time. Thus, trade would not be diverted to higher cost regional producers all at once, especially since trade among Latin American countries is currently quite small. Gradually, Latin American consumers would shift to Latin American goods that, with the elimination of duties, appear cheaper to them. The rigidity of habit and the sensitivity of consumers to price differentials would affect the speed of the process from country to country. At the same time, the growth of demand and the specialization of production would lower prices in industries characterized by economies of scale. The gains from union would also increase over time as prices from plants at optimum locations fell compared with those of autarkic plants (assuming that output of the former would increase relative to that of the latter) and those of third country imports net of tariffs.

The Distribution of Gains from Customs Union and Suboptimum Locations

The analysis thus far has indicated that with free trade among them, under most of the assumptions made here, the distribution of manufacturing in a Latin American customs union could be expected to benefit, if unequally, all the large and middle-sized Latin American economies. The analysis is based on the distribution of natural resources used in industry since it is their availability and price that largely determine the location of many industries.

Given this probably unequal distribution of the benefits of union, prospective member countries would find it in their own interest, whether or not in the interest of the region as a whole, to obtain concessions to enhance their own gains. They might lower tariffs more gradually than other members, subsidize certain industries, arrange complementarity agreements in monopolies, or devise a gain-shifting pattern of social investment in roads, schools, power facilities, and so forth.[25]

Perhaps the most important feature of the model is that it can establish alternative distributions of plants producing the projected output that result in higher cost to the region than the minimum cost solution.[26] Anal-

25. Whether lowering tariffs more gradually results in gains to the less developed members depends in part on their production-consumption preferences. Thus the continued existence of tariffs may be a burden to the country's consumers, but might maintain the country's desired level of industrialization. The other means of "forcing" the geographic pattern of industrialization might also result in a cost to the region's consumers, but would satisfy long-run industrialization goals. See C. A. Cooper and B. F. Massell, "Toward a General Theory of Customs Union for Developing Countries," *Journal of Political Economy*, Vol. 73 (October 1965), pp. 460–76.

26. The solutions to the model are a series of minimum cost solutions on the assumption that certain production locations are "allowed" to exist; the higher the number of possible plant locations, the higher the number of possible solutions. Also, the more numerous the possible locations, the more numerous the combinations of locations that could be close to the optimum. For example, even though the best location for production of a product might be in a single country, other combinations of locations

ysis of the alternative distributions shows how much it would cost Latin America to depart from the optimum, and thus the welfare cost of locating production, at least for local markets, in countries not included in the optimum pattern. The alternative distributions also identify costs to the region of meeting its projected demand by importing, and the costs if each country manufactures the good purely for its domestic market.

The optimum solutions indicate that no country has an absolute advantage in production in more than two of the six groups. In four of the groups studied—nitrogenous fertilizers, methanol and formaldehyde, paper and pulp, and dairy products—the costs of a number of suboptimum solutions are within a few percent of the minimum cost solution itself. Table 2-7 summarizes the optimum plant location for each product and alternatives to the optimum with their costs to the area. These alternatives are presented for both sets of assumptions about transport costs and exchange rates.

The policy implications of the narrowness of the range of costs of various alternatives are quite clear. Under the assumption of minimum transport costs and free rates of exchange, the cost of the difference between widely dispersed production and production concentrated in one or two countries is quite small. Table 2-7 shows that for some products—for example, nitrogenous fertilizers—the optimum location using minimum transport costs provides a greater dispersion than the next alternative; and for several others—methanol, formaldehyde, and hard and bland paste cheese—the cost of greater dispersion than that provided by the optimum solution is small. For maximum transport costs and official rates of exchange, the optimum location of production in Latin America changes for several goods, and the cost of scattered production deviates even less from the optimum. Since the error in estimating production and transport costs could be large, the small differences between the costs of the optimum and of its alternatives imply that a number of plants in the region for each good is almost as economical as a single or double production site for the whole area. Furthermore, there are alternatives for nitrogenous fertilizers, methanol and formaldehyde, and pulp and paper that are not shown in Table 2-7 but whose costs are within 10 percent of that of the minimum

---

could yield total costs to the area very close to the one-country solutions. Furthermore, since maximum plant size is usually smaller than the total demand of the region, economies of scale are technically limited, and this would also tend to disperse production. Even in the one-country solution, at least several plants are required to fulfill demand for each product.

cost solutions. Of the 256 possible "local optima" identified in the methanol-formaldehyde study, over half meet this criterion.[27] Given the range of errors in costs, such alternatives may in fact constitute the optima, and the elimination of trade barriers could result in the larger number of plant locations even without subsidies.

Even assuming that the errors in costs are smaller than their deviation from the alternatives, solutions with a higher number of plant locations are close enough to the optimum to keep subsidized, "forced" locations of plants from being very costly for the region. On the other hand, a number of patterns of plant distribution deviate greatly from the minimum cost solutions. The welfare costs of autarkic production patterns are high for some products, as Table 2-4 shows. Furthermore, except for Uruguay in the case of dairy products, the smaller countries do not figure in the optimum or near-optimum locations (see Table 2-7). This is partly a statistical problem, stemming from the absence of production cost data for Ecuador and Paraguay for many products.[28] However, it is also true that those two countries, as well as Bolivia and Central America, which were not included in the studies, will find it difficult to compete in heavy industries, lacking as they do the skilled labor and similar factors that create external economies in production.

A particularly cogent example is the relationship between northeastern and southern Brazil, in which the Northeast has traditionally supplied foreign exchange from its long-established exports to further the already advanced industrialization of the South. Until recently, little effort has been made in the Northeast to build the physical and human infrastructure that would attract industry—a typical case of unequal partnership between an industrialized and an agricultural area. There is evidence, however, that the partnership is not so inequitable as it might appear. Stefan Robock has shown that the Northeast has maintained its relative position in income

27. See Fig. 4-1.
28. Cost data are presented for bagasse-based paper production in Ecuador. No cost data are shown for Paraguay, largely because the Paraguayan institute (CEPADES) entered the project when this stage was nearly completed. The cost to Ecuador of having its own bagasse-based paper plant rather than importing from the optimum location would be $2 million annually in 1975 under the assumption of maximum transport costs and the official rate of exchange, and $10 million annually under the assumption of the minimum transport costs and free rate of exchange. These estimates do not take account of possible external economies, benefitting other industries, that could obtain from having such a plant in Ecuador. Such external economies could be quite important (see Chap. 2).

Table 2-7. Optimum and Alternative Locations in LAFTA of Production of Fourteen Products, 1975

	Minimum transport cost, free exchange rate			Maximum transport cost, official exchange rate		
		Alternative to optimum			Alternative to optimum	
Product	Optimum location	Combination of countries[a]	Cost to area[b]	Optimum location	Combination of countries[a]	Cost to area[b]
Ammonia	Venezuela, Mexico, Chile, Peru	Venezuela	2.5%	Chile, Mexico, Peru, Venezuela	Chile, Colombia, Mexico, Peru, Venezuela	*
Ammonium nitrate	Venezuela, Chile, Peru, Colombia	Venezuela	2.5	Chile, Colombia, Mexico, Peru, Venezuela	Chile, Colombia, Mexico, Peru, Venezuela	*
Ammonium sulphate	Peru, Mexico	Venezuela	2.5	Mexico, Peru, Venezuela	Mexico, Peru, Venezuela[e]	*
Urea	Venezuela, Chile	Venezuela	2.5	Chile, Mexico, Venezuela	Chile, Mexico, Colombia, Venezuela	*
Methanol	Venezuela	Venezuela, Mexico, Chile	4.1	Venezuela	Chile, Mexico	10.0%
Formaldehyde	Venezuela, Colombia	Venezuela, Chile, Colombia	4.1	Colombia, Venezuela	Chile, Colombia	10.0
Tractors[d]	Argentina	Argentina, Brazil	11.7	Argentina	Argentina, Brazil	5.2

Product	Optimum	Alternative[a]	Percent[b]	Optimum	Alternative[a]	Percent[b]
Lathes[e]	Chile	Argentina	7.4	Argentina	Argentina, Brazil, Chile, Mexico	12.7
Powdered milk[f]	Uruguay	Argentina, Brazil, Uruguay	32.1	Uruguay	Argentina, Brazil, Uruguay	32.1
Hard paste cheese	Uruguay	Argentina, Uruguay	3.6	Uruguay	Argentina, Uruguay	3.6
Semihard paste cheese	Uruguay	Argentina, Uruguay	10.9	Uruguay	Argentina, Uruguay	10.9
Bland (soft) paste cheese[g]	Argentina	Argentina, Brazil, Peru	1.0	Argentina	Argentina, Brazil, Peru	1.0
Kraft pulp	Chile	Brazil, Chile, Mexico	20.4	Chile, Mexico, Brazil[h]	Chile, Mexico, Brazil	5.0
Kraft paper	Chile, Mexico	Brazil, Mexico, Ecuador, Peru, Colombia	20.4	Mexico, Brazil[h]	Brazil, Mexico, Ecuador, Peru, Colombia	5.0

* Less than 0.05 percent.
a. The alternative to the optimum is the next lowest cost alternative that significantly changes the location of production in the region and that does not include the United States as a product on point.
b. Calculated as percent increase of total cost of alternative solution over cost of optimum solution.
c. Note that the optimum location already includes all possible production points.
d. Minimum and maximum transport costs are taken to be equal; plant size limited to 20,000 units.
e. Minimum and maximum transport costs are taken to be equal; plant size limited to 500 units.
f. The optimum locations shown are the minimum cost locations in Latin America. The model identifies the United States as the optimum location.
g. The optimum solution includes production in Argentina and imports from the United States by some Latin American countries.
h. The optimum locations shown are the minimum cost locations in Latin America. The model shows that for some countries, the optimum solution is importing from the United States.

63

per capita in Brazil, although largely by emigration from the area to the South.[29] Migration would be more difficult in a common market than within a country, as was dramatized by the July 1969 hostilities between El Salvador and Honduras. The Central American experience has also contradicted the theoretical prediction about the partnership. Honduras and Nicaragua, the least developed of the countries in the Central American Common Market (CACM), increased their share of CACM's manufactured product from 25.9 percent in 1951 to 27.3 percent in 1965. However, they have suffered negative trade balances with the rest of the common market.

The Role of Exchange Rates

The rate of exchange between the currencies of two countries is crucial in determining the optimum location of production. It has already been pointed out that in the case using maximum transport costs, official rates of exchange are employed to translate local currency costs into simones. The case of minimum transport costs uses an approximate free rate of exchange, which is set equal to the official rate in countries with no active black or gray market and which is, therefore, not a shadow rate reflecting the real price of foreign currency. Although industry studies demonstrate the importance of differences between the two rates, only in Argentina, Chile, and Colombia can the free rate-official rate distinction be made.

In order to go beyond the limited sensitivity analysis possible with two rates of exchange, an estimate was made for each industry of the rate of exchange at which a consuming country would be indifferent to buying from one production location or another. This indifference rate is, in other words, the exchange rate between the currencies that reduces to zero the advantage of one location over another. To estimate indifference rates in each market for various production locations, it is assumed that all production takes place at each point.

Despite the biases in this method, the indifference rates demonstrate approximately how sensitive the optimum location is to the exchange rate.

29. Stefan H. Robock, *Brazil's Developing Northeast: A Study of Regional Planning and Foreign Aid* (Brookings Institution, 1963), p. 35.

Sensitivity varies from product to product. Table 2-8 shows, for example, that in the minimum-transport-cost case of nitrogenous fertilizers, Venezuela is competitive with U.S. imports everywhere in LAFTA at an exchange rate of 3.5 bolivars to the simón except in four instances; this implies that a revaluation of the bolivar of 20 percent would still permit Venezuelan exporters of nitrogenous fertilizers to undersell their U.S. competitors. Similarly, Venezuela is competitive with Chile almost everywhere in Latin America in all nitrogenous fertilizers when the Chilean escudo and the bolivar are equal in value. This means that at the official exchange rate for the escudo, Chile cannot compete with Venezuela in Latin America, but at the free rate of 1.22 escudos to the bolivar it could be highly competitive.

Chile can compete with Argentina and Brazil in lathes at the free rate, but the indifference rate of exchange with Argentina is only slightly below the free rate.[30] Chile cannot compete with either Argentina or Brazil at the respective official rates of exchange. Chile appears as a producer in many of the industry studies, and in all of them the official rate of exchange for the escudo virtually prices Chilean production out of the market. Since these cost studies were made, the escudo has been steadily devalued until its official rate has begun to approach the free rate. However, other LAFTA currencies have also been devalued in the face of domestic inflation—by especially significant proportions in Argentina, Brazil, Colombia, Peru, and Uruguay.

Yet despite rather large fluctuations, the 1963–67 average of real rates of exchange (the rate of exchange at a given date times the wholesale price index) compares favorably with the rates used in this study to convert imported inputs into national currencies and output into simones. Rate of exchange dates vary from country to country, although most are for December 1963 to December 1964. The annual real rate of exchange has been calculated in 1965 prices between 1963 and 1967, averaged over that period, and then compared with the real rate of exchange used for each country in 1965 prices. These real rates for the year used do not differ greatly from the average real rate for the period. In addition, for Argentina, Chile, and Colombia, two sets of rates are used in the study.

---

30. The bias in the Chilean production costs mentioned earlier in this chapter should be noted.

Table 2-8. Prices and Indifference Exchange Rates for Selected Products, Assuming Minimum Transport Costs, 1975

Prices in simones

Producing country and currencies exchanged	Consuming country									
	Argentina	Brazil	Chile	Colombia	Ecuador	Mexico	Paraguay	Peru	Uruguay	Venezuela
Chile[a]										
Nitrogenous fertilizers: Prices per ton										
Ammonia	55.1	65.4	38.4	...	...	51.6	...	...	...	46.4
Urea	114.0	117.7	84.6	106.2	96.1	87.5	...	103.0	86.3	90.2
Ammonium nitrate	169.1	161.8	130.3	151.4	135.9	127.4	...	145.2	...	127.0
Venezuela[b]										
Ammonia	54.2	67.1	40.5	...	...	44.5	...	...	...	31.2
Urea	125.9	216.0	95.0	102.2	99.1	89.0	...	108.8	98.2	83.4
Ammonium nitrate	167.8	166.3	133.4	135.4	132.3	113.9	...	140.5	...	94.3
Ammonium sulphate	235.8	238.8	...	213.8	191.9	158.8	...	204.6	171.9	167.2
United States										
Ammonia	85.2	100.4	88.8	...	...	57.8	...	...	...	73.6
Urea	185.5	187.9	157.0	173.8	170.0	132.9	...	176.0	157.8	149.5
Ammonium nitrate	248.9	252.0	216.0	219.1	206.2	132.3	...	218.7	...	182.1
Ammonium sulphate	296.5	301.1	...	281.9	291.9	171.8	...	299.6	232.6	238.2
Nitrogenous fertilizers: Indifference exchange rates										
Bolivars to escudo[c]										
Ammonia	0.88	0.92	0.94	...	...	0.78	...	...	...	0.60
Urea	0.99	0.96	1.01	0.86	0.93	0.92	...	0.95	1.03	0.83
Ammonium nitrate	0.89	0.93	0.92	0.80	0.87	0.80	...	0.87	...	0.67
Bolivars to simon[d]										
Ammonia	2.88	3.02	2.07	...	...	3.46	...	...	...	1.89
Urea	3.06	3.02	2.70	2.66	2.61	3.02	...	2.79	2.79	2.52
Ammonium nitrate	3.02	2.98	2.79	2.79	2.88	3.87	...	2.88	...	2.34

	3.60	3.56	...	3.42	2.97	4.14	...	3.06	3.33	3.15
Ammonium sulphate	3.60	3.56	...	3.42	2.97	4.14	...	3.06	3.33	3.15
Tractors: Prices per unit[e]										
Argentina[f]	4,671	4,773	4,734	5,040	5,027	5,024	4,687	5,036	4,725	...
Brazil[g]	5,520	5,418	5,596	5,861	5,873	5,853	5,514	5,881	5,489	...
United States	5,117	5,297	5,299	5,196	5,248	4,802	5,131	5,362	5,118	...
Tractors: Indifference exchange rates										
Pesos to cruzeiro[h]	0.062	0.062	0.064	0.063	0.063	0.063	0.062	0.063	0.063	...
Pesos to simón	123	122	122	131	130	140	123	127	124	...
Lathes: Prices per unit										
Argentina[j]	2,962	3,042	3,014	3,270	...	3,315	2,987	...	...	...
Chile[k]	2,775	2,860	2,726	3,006	...	3,050	2,806	...	...	...
Brazil[l]	3,986	3,929	4,042	4,264	...	4,297	3,997	...	...	...
Lathes: Indifference exchange rates										
Pesos to escudo[m]	33.2	32.8	33.8	33.8	...	33.8	32.8	...	...	...
Cruzeiros to escudo[n]	632	602	652	625	...	620	625	...	...	...
Cruzeiros to peso[o]	19.0	18.3	19.0	18.5	...	18.5	19.0	...	...	...

a. Chile does not intend to produce ammonium sulphate. The exchange rate is 5 escudos per simón.
b. The exchange rate is 4.5 bolivars per simón.
c. Calculated as the ratio of Venezuelan to Chilean prices times 0.9 (the number of bolivars per escudo).
d. Calculated as the ratio of Venezuelan to U.S. prices times 4.5 (the number of bolivars per simón).
e. The calculations assume a 20,000 unit limit on plant capacity and that all tractor production takes place at each production point.
f. The exchange rate is 135 pesos per simón.
g. The exchange rate is 1,850 cruzeiros per simón.
h. Calculated as the ratio of Argentine to Brazilian prices times 0.073 (the number of pesos per cruzeiro).
i. Calculated as the ratio of Argentine to U.S. prices times 135 (the number of pesos per simón).
j. The exchange rate is 155 pesos per simón.
k. The exchange rate is 5 escudos per simón.
l. The exchange rate is 2,200 cruzeiros per simón.
m. Calculated as the ratio of Argentine to Chilean prices times 31 (the number of pesos per escudo).
n. Calculated as the ratio of Brazilian to Chilean prices times 440 (the number of cruzeiros per escudo).
o. Calculated as the ratio of Brazilian to Argentine prices times 14.2 (the number of cruzeiros per peso).

	Real rate used (in 1965 prices)	Average real rate, 1963–67 (in 1965 prices)
Argentina	187.9 (1964)	197.0
Brazil	2.2–2.8 (1964–65)	2.0
Chile	4.0 (1964)	4.5
Colombia	14.0 (1964)	14.4
Mexico	12.7 (1964)	12.4
Peru	31.4 (1964)	30.0
Uruguay	43.4 (mid-1965)	46.1
Venezuela	4.7 (1964)	4.6

The indifference rates have the advantage of being adjustable for both inflation and devaluation. An attempt is made to do this in the case of tractors. The rate of inflation of tractor prices in domestic currency is available for Argentina in 1964 and 1965. Data are also available for exchange rates in that same period in both Brazil and Argentina. Comparing inflated tractor costs of June 1965 in Argentina (Argentine tractor costs are taken for December 31, 1963) with measured tractor costs in Brazil at that date shows that at official rates, the optimum location of tractor production in LAFTA switches from Argentina to Brazil.[31] Exchange rates at any point in time therefore play a leading role in projecting the distribution of production in a customs union, especially in a region of rapid price changes.

Some Conclusions

Apart from the determination of the minimum cost location and the welfare gains and costs from integrating the six industry groups studied here, several conclusions emerge that have significant implications for integration policy.

First, while there may be only one set of economically optimum production points for an industry in a regional common market, at least several other combinations for each industry studied would not seriously violate precepts of economic efficiency. Furthermore, given the possibility of error in the estimates of production and transportation costs used in these studies, these industries could be even more dispersed than the optimum

31. See Chap. 5.

solutions and their close competitors would allow. The small differences in the cost to the area of a number of possible patterns of production allows the policy maker a range of choice from which he can make a politically acceptable decision without incurring excessive economic cost.

A related, but distinct, conclusion is that many countries in Latin America—not merely those that already have a large industrial establishment—would benefit directly from economic union. The fear that, because of the historically unequal development in the region, industrial investment will tend to be concentrated in a few larger and richer countries has restrained Latin American governments and businessmen from moving boldly toward a common market. The results of the study can alleviate this fear—at least with respect to the industries examined. Under the assumption of minimum transport costs and free exchange rates, six of the ten countries studied would be producers, and, if maximum transport costs and official exchange rates are assumed, seven countries would share production of the fourteen products.[32] Furthermore, as the first conclusion implies, weaker countries could in some cases be included in regional investment programs without a serious misallocation of resources.

Third, analysis of the six industry groups indicates that economies of scale are significant for a wide range of products in Latin America. Costs of domestically produced goods can therefore be expected to fall in a free trade area or customs union in the region, minimizing the net trade diversion that occurs as a result of union.

Fourth, in most of the industries studied, Latin American production for a regional market in the optimum or near-optimum patterns of location would be competitive with imports from developed countries. Thus there could be a net gain to Latin America even under a narrow definition of welfare benefits from a customs union. The notion that Latin American manufacturing industries could never compete with goods from the United States and other highly industrialized countries has been another deterrent to regional integration. The study suggests that whenever output moves to the levels where economies of scale operate, as it would for many commodities in a Latin American common market, and transportation costs

32. Of the eleven LAFTA countries, Bolivia and Paraguay did not present any cost studies and therefore were not candidates for an optimum location. Ecuador presented a cost study only for paper and pulp, and Uruguay only for powdered milk and cheeses. Other countries are represented by cost studies in at least two product groups.

are significant, production costs would permit competition with developed countries even without tariff protection.

These conclusions are highly relevant for regional integration policies, and should help dispel some of the doubts that public and private officials, as well as businessmen, hold about economic union in Latin America.

Other insights can be gleaned from the joint project. While precise cost comparisons may be faulty, the cost profiles indicate wide differences among countries in the composition of production costs, a fact important to the understanding of the nature of particular industries. Furthermore, the study throws into strong relief the role of transportation costs, economies of scale, and exchange rates. The estimation of welfare costs and benefits, for all its deficiencies, sheds new light on their order of magnitude for individual countries.

PART TWO

Industrial Case Studies

CHAPTER THREE

Nitrogenous Fertilizers

ALONG WITH STEEL AND AUTOMOBILES, chemical fertilizers have been identified as an industry in whose development Latin American economic integration can play a major role.[1] The potential benefits to the region of operating this industry on an area-wide rather than a national scale are quite high. The industry is relatively new; and although a number of plants already exist in Latin America, their 1963 production was only about 12 percent of the area's projected demand in 1975. The production of nitrogenous fertilizers also involves important economies of scale, which might be exploited best by limiting the number of new plants in Latin America through free trade in their products within the region. Because of the high cost of transport per unit of nitrogen between production and consumption centers, the optimum distribution of plants may be more dispersed than it would be if production costs alone were taken into consideration. These cost factors must be evaluated in finding minimum cost answers to the question of plant locations.

The present study attempts to find such answers for nitrogenous fertilizers.[2] Until recent years, output of nitrogen nutrients in Latin America

1. See Organization of American States (OAS), Inter-American Economic and Social Council, Fourth Annual Meeting at the Ministerial Level, *Final Report of the Fourth Annual Meeting* (OEA/Ser.H/X.8, CIES/1070, April 2, 1966). Felipe Herrera, Jose A. Mayobre, Raúl Prebisch, and Carlos Sanz de Santamaria, *Proposals for the Creation of the Latin American Common Market* (Economic Commission for Latin America (ECLA), TD/B/11, 1965).

2. In 1963, nitrogen consumption in the Latin American Free Trade Association

73

was concentrated almost exclusively in the natural forms of Peruvian guano and Chilean nitrates. The location of these sources of nitrogen made those countries two of the largest consumers of fertilizers per hectare in the area. By 1963, the base year chosen for projections in this study, the source of supply of nitrogenous fertilizers had altered considerably. Chile still produced 169,000 nitrogen-equivalent tons of natural nitrates in 1962–63, and Peru 25,000 nitrogen-equivalent tons of guano. But this production constituted only 42 percent of the total consumption of fertilizers, including urea, ammonium nitrate, and ammonium sulphate. Only 11 percent of Chilean exports of natural nitrates in 1962–63 was consumed by other countries in the Latin American Free Trade Association (LAFTA).

Production and Consumption—1963 and 1975

Table 3-1 summarizes the domestic production and consumption of ammonia (for direct use), urea, ammonium nitrate, and ammonium sulphate, in the LAFTA countries in 1963.[3] Paraguay's current and projected consumption is so small that it has been omitted from study.

It is clear that even its small consumption of nitrogenous fertilizers in

---

(LAFTA) (plus Venezuela) was 42.6 percent of total nitrogen, phosphates, and potash fertilizers (in plant nutrients). Nitrogen consumption in 1975 (projected by ECLA) is 46.3 percent of the total. See ECLA, *La Oferta de Fertilizantes en America Latina*, E/CN.12/L.10 (1966), pp. 6–7.

3. These four products are assumed to be the only forms in which nitrogen is consumed. Perhaps the most significant flaw in this assumption is that it ignores the rapid increase in the consumption of diammonium phosphate (DAP) since this study was prepared. DAP is a high analysis fertilizer commonly containing 18 percent nitrogen and 46 percent phosphorous pentoxide equivalent by weight. It has the highest nutrient content per unit weight commonly available as a dry commercial fertilizer, which results in low delivered costs per unit nutrient on the farm, since a minimum of inert material is transported. DAP is also used to prepare other high analysis nitrogen-phosphorus-potassium (NPK) blends by mixing it with urea (46 percent nitrogen content) and potassium chloride (60 percent potassium dioxide equivalent content).

Nitrogen consumption in the form of DAP was not considered in the present study because of (a) the difficulty in allocating joint costs between the nitrogen and phosphorus components and (b) the necessity of forecasting phosphate demand in addition to that for nitrogenous fertilizers. The effect of including DAP in the study would be to push the solution of the linearized programming model toward a more decentralized production pattern in much the same way as does the assumption of minimum as opposed to maximum transport costs, since the principal advantage of DAP is its low transport costs per unit of nutrient.

Table 3-1. Production and Consumption of Nitrogenous Fertilizers in LAFTA, by Country and Product, 1963

Thousands of metric tons

Country	Ammonia for direct use[a]		Urea[b]		Ammonium nitrate[c]		Ammonium sulphate[d]	
	Consumption	Production	Consumption	Production	Consumption	Production	Consumption	Production
Argentina	1.5	1.5	3.4	...	0.5	0.5	35.9	11.7
Brazil	20.3	2.3	17.5	...	34.5	30.2[e]	173.9	8.2
Chile	0.2	0.2	1.2	...	18.5	...	0.4	...
Colombia	...	9.9[f]	20.2	10.7	2.0	13.0	5.0	3.2
Ecuador	...	...	3.1	...	0.1	...	1.5	...
Mexico	75.7	25.4	74.5	39.7	131.9	138.5	204.8	159.6
Peru	...	...	0.5	...	37.7	34.4	59.9	12.1
Uruguay	0.2	...	0.4	...	...	...	3.2	...
Venezuela	2.5	...	4.9	4.6	0.5	17.9	39.3	22.7
Total	100.4	39.3	125.7	55.0	225.8	234.5	524.0	217.5

Sources: Estudios Conjuntos sobre Integración Economica Latinoamericana (ECIEL), *The Demand for Chemical Fertilizers, Tractors, Paper and Pulp, Milk Concentrates, and Lathes in the Latin American Free Trade Association (including Venezuela)* (Brookings Institution, 1966; processed), Pt. 1; ECLA, *La Oferta de Fertilizantes en America Latina*, E/CN.12/L.10 (1966).

a. One ton of ammonia equals 0.82 ton of nitrogen.
b. One ton of urea equals 0.6 ton of ammonia.
c. One ton of ammonium nitrate equals 0.45 ton of ammonia.
d. One ton of ammonium sulphate equals 0.26 ton of ammonia.
e. Includes nitrocalcium in ammonium nitrate equivalent units.
f. Exports.

1963 was not met by the area's own production. The only country that could be considered a major manufacturer of nitrogenous fertilizers is Mexico, which produced 67 percent of the area's total output of nitrogen in the four forms in that year. By 1975, the situation is expected to change radically:

Fertilizer	Demand (tons) 1963	Demand (tons) 1975	Average compound annual increase
Ammonia for industrial uses, other fertilizers, direct application	100,000	590,000	*16.0%*
Urea	126,000	792,000	*16.6*
Ammonium nitrate	226,000	681,000	*9.7*
Ammonium sulphate	524,000	2,307,000	*13.2*

Mexico will remain the major consumer, but its share in the total LAFTA market for ammonia-equivalent units of these products falls from 59 to 48 percent. Brazil maintains its share at 30 percent of the total. The absolute number of ammonia-equivalent units of the four products consumed in 1975 is projected as 1,971,900 tons.[4]

Perhaps of even greater significance, the supply of nitrogenous fertilizers is also expected to increase rapidly. Large supplies of natural gas, the cheapest of the several raw materials that can be used for ammonia synthesis, are readily available.[5] According to an ECLA study, the productive capacity of plants in the planning stages in LAFTA countries (some of which, at this writing, are already under construction or completed) will

4. This is the sum of the midpoints of the maximum and minimum projections for each product. See Estudios Conjuntos sobre Integración Economica Latinoamericana (hereafter referred to as ECIEL), *The Demand for Chemical Fertilizers, Tractors, Paper and Pulp, Milk Concentrates, and Lathes in the Latin American Free Trade Association (including Venezuela)* (Brookings Institution, 1966; processed). Projections made by ECLA, *La Oferta de Fertilizantes*, p. 7, show the maximum hypothesis projection to be strikingly close to the midpoint sum (ECLA maximum projection equals 1,629,000 tons of nitrogen versus 1,630,000 tons as the midpoint projection of this study). However, the similarity is misleading: The ECLA projections include forms of nitrogenous fertilizers other than those products treated here; also, on a country-by-country basis, the projections often differ radically. For example, the ECLA projection has Brazil consuming 191,000 tons of nitrogen in 1975; this study projects 507,000 tons. Chile is projected here to consume 13,000 tons of nitrogen in 1975, and by ECLA, 141,000 tons. Both ECLA projections include natural nitrates as well as chemical fertilizers. On the other hand, projections for Mexico and Argentina in the two studies approximately agree with one another.

5. The principal alternatives, in order of increasing cost at most locations, are naphtha, fuel oil, and coal.

be 2.3 million tons by 1975.[6] This does not include existing capacity in Aruba and Curaçao (400,000 tons of nitrogen), nor possible plants in Central America, which could produce more than 180,000 tons annually.

A slightly more conservative estimate of production in 1975 is shown in Table 3-2. It attempts to divide total production into the four products studied.[7] The total quantity of ammonia produced by 1975 is estimated at 2,316,000 metric tons (1,900,000 tons of nitrogen), which exceeds the midpoint of projected consumption by 344,000 tons annually. This figure is considerably less than the excess shown for LAFTA by the ECLA study. The interesting feature of projected capacity, however, is its distribution, since according to Table 3-2, only Chile, Colombia, and Venezuela would have exportable surpluses. Argentina and Peru would be largely self-sufficient, and the other countries of the area would be net importers. The question posed by such a distribution is whether the three fertilizer exporters can compete in world markets, and whether the other producers— Argentina, Brazil, Mexico, and Peru (Ecuador also intends to produce some ammonium sulphate)—can manufacture fertilizers in free competition with imports either from Latin America or from third countries.

Prices and Costs

Prices of fertilizers to the farmer in 1961 in several countries of the area varied greatly. In U.S. dollars per ton of nitrogen, the prices were the following: Argentina, $390; Chile, $324; Colombia, $380; Mexico, $250; and Peru, $347. These figures are generally above prices to the farmer in developed countries;[8] but, according to an ECLA hypothesis that appeared to be confirmed by 1969, rapidly increased production of ammonia in the rest of the world,[9] as well as in Latin America, could mean a significant

6. ECLA, *La Oferta de Fertilizantes.*

7. For the most part the division is made on the basis of past trends and expected changes in those trends. Because of the increasing use of other nitrogen-containing fertilizers (especially DAP) in the second half of the 1960s, the projection for ammonium nitrate and ammonium sulphate may be too high.

8. From Food and Agriculture Organization, *Fertilizers: An Annual Review, 1961,* Table 28. Bagged prices per ton to farmers in 1960–61 were the following: France, $305; Germany, $250; United Kingdom, $170 (net of subsidy); and United States, $327, all for nitrogen in the form of ammonium sulphate or ammonium nitrate. Bulk prices were somewhat lower.

9. ECLA, *La Oferta de Fertilizantes,* p. 15. Table 4 on that page shows an increase in the supply of nitrogen in the world from 23,184,000 tons of nitrogen in 1964–65 to 43,050,000 tons in 1970–71.

Table 3-2. Projected Production and Consumption of Nitrogenous Fertilizers in LAFTA, by Country and Product, 1975

Thousands of metric tons

Country	Ammonia for direct use		Urea		Ammonium nitrate		Ammonium sulphate	
	Consumption	Production	Consumption	Production	Consumption	Production	Consumption	Production
Argentina	2.6	51.1	155.9	135.0	27.8	35.0	86.8	85.0
Brazil	161.1	16.5	84.0	82.5	273.5	207.6	1,092.6	135.2
Chile	3.3	145.0	4.2	150.0	22.2	200.0	0.6	...
Colombia	...	235.0	85.0	190.0	33.0	16.8	8.0	8.0
Ecuador	...	...	9.4	...	0.3	...	4.6	25.9
Mexico	414.2	236.4	437.8	355.0	190.7	165.0	710.7	474.6
Peru	...	...	0.8	...	126.4	160.0	225.0	180.0
Uruguay	...	...	5.0	...	...	...	94.3	...
Venezuela	9.2	355.0[a]	10.3	115.0	7.4	66.0	84.7	158.4
Total	590.4	1,039.0	792.4	1,027.5	681.3	850.4	2,307.3	1,067.1

Sources: Consumption—ECIEL, *Demand for Chemical Fertilizers*; production—ECLA, *La Oferta de Fertilizantes*.
a. The output of one plant, whose capacity would be 330,000 tons of ammonia annually, could not be divided into the output of final fertilizers.

fall in the world price of nitrogen between 1966 and 1975. A decrease in the world price of fertilizers implies an increase in demand in Latin America probably greater than that projected by either this study or ECLA. It also means a loss in competitive ability of Latin American production both in world markets and within the region. If Latin American countries are quite low cost producers of nitrogenous fertilizers—and the evidence suggests that at least some of them are—then the demand engendered by falling prices quite probably could absorb the excess capacity indicated by the data in Table 3-2. For the purposes of this study, however, optimum production is based on the projected level of consumption in 1975.

As the number of new plants in each country increases, however, the low costs associated with output of fully utilized plants become less likely to prevail.[10] With sufficient protection (which will be a characteristic feature of the growth of domestically oriented fertilizer plants) the price of nitrogen to farmers in many countries may rise despite a falling world price. In those countries in the area with rather small domestic consumption of industrially fixed nitrogen, such as Chile, Colombia, Ecuador, Uruguay, and Venezuela, domestic price (if there are no exports) would be increased significantly because output was limited. The most important economies of scale in the production of these fertilizers come in the production of ammonia,[11] and they taper off only in the range of output higher than 400 tons per day (or 132,000 tons per year). Under a national distribution of fertilizer production, Chile, Colombia, and Venezuela would have to depend almost entirely on markets outside Latin America in order to sell the output of the plants they now intend to build.

Structure of Costs

Projected total costs for ammonia and the other products are shown in Tables 3-3 to 3-6. The cost structures for each product are quite similar from country to country. For example, in the largest size ammonia plants,

10. For an inventory of planned fertilizer plants in Latin America, see U.S. Department of Commerce, Bureau of International Commerce, Office of Commercial and Financial Policy, *Preliminary Inventory of Projects for Increasing Fertilizer Production in Latin America*, prepared by the Agri-business Staff (1968).

11. It should be noted in the following tables that the economies of scale in the production of urea, ammonium nitrate, and ammonium sulphate are very small net of changes in the cost of ammonia.

Table 3-3. Elements of Ammonia Production as Percent of Total Production Costs, and Cost per Ton of Output in LAFTA, by Country and Capacity of Plant, 1964–65

Country and plant capacity in tons per year	Production costs										Cost per ton in national currency
	Materials	Direct labor	Utilities	Mainte-nance	Depre-ciation	Super-vision	Insur-ance	Opportunity cost of capital	Other	Total	
Chile											
165,000	14.2	3.2	2.1	1.9	39.0	a	3.4	24.4	11.8	100.0	99.20
250,000	15.0	2.4	2.2	1.7	40.0	a	3.6	25.4	9.7	100.0	93.20
330,000	17.4	2.1	2.6	1.8	39.2	a	3.5	25.0	8.4	100.0	82.17
Colombia											
16,500	7.5	8.0	18.0	8.8	21.9	0.8	2.2	18.8	14.0	100.0	1,188.42
100,000	20.2	0.9	29.7	7.1	17.8	0.1	1.8	15.7	6.7	100.0	640.93
200,000	18.4	0.6	24.8	8.3	20.8	0.1	2.1	17.5	7.4	100.0	769.15b
Mexico											
60,000	8.4	2.8	23.0	6.5	28.1	0.7	2.8	22.5	5.2	100.0	741.25
66,000	11.1	2.8	24.3	6.1	26.2	0.7	2.6	20.9	5.3	100.0	729.59
132,000	14.3	2.4	30.0	5.2	22.4	0.6	2.2	17.9	5.0	100.0	591.73
229,370	20.3	3.2	16.6	6.1	25.1	0.8	2.5	20.8	4.6	100.0	319.79
Peru											
36,000	36.6	2.1	4.8	8.3	22.1	a	a	22.1	4.0	100.0	1,343.15
108,000	43.7	2.3	5.7	7.3	19.4	a	a	19.4	2.2	100.0	1,123.68
180,000	47.0	1.6	6.2	6.9	18.3	a	a	18.3	1.7	100.0	1,052.45
Venezuela											
100,000	13.1	5.8	19.7	9.8	24.5	0.9	2.9	19.6	3.7	100.0	110.27
132,000	13.7	4.6	20.6	9.8	24.4	0.7	2.9	19.6	3.7	100.0	105.50
200,000	16.8	4.5	12.0	10.8	26.9	0.7	3.3	21.5	3.6	100.0	82.16
330,000	22.0	3.1	10.4	10.4	26.0	0.5	3.2	20.8	3.6	100.0	72.31

a. Included in other.
b. Since Colombian costs were estimated on the basis of plants at different locations, the cost per unit of ammonia happens to increase for the larger plant.

Table 3-4. Elements of Urea Production as Percent of Total Production Costs, and Cost per Ton of Output in LAFTA, by Country and Capacity of Plant, 1964–65

Country and plant capacity in tons per year	Production costs										Cost per ton in national currency
	Materials	Direct labor	Utilities	Maintenance	Depreciation	Supervision	Insurance	Opportunity cost of capital	Other	Total	
Chile											
50,000	30.2	7.9	10.3	2.1	20.4	a	1.7	14.9	12.5	100.0	150.00
100,000	34.6	6.1	11.7	1.2	18.8	a	1.0	13.6	13.0	100.0	131.85
150,000	37.0	5.1	12.5	1.8	17.3	a	1.4	13.0	11.9	100.0	123.08
Colombia											
10,000	56.5	3.7	8.0	4.2	10.5	a	1.0	10.0	6.1	100.0	1,007.00
80,000	66.4	0.8	8.8	3.3	8.2	a	0.8	8.2	3.5	100.0	917.30
150,000	64.6	0.5	9.0	3.7	9.2	a	0.9	8.3	3.8	100.0	943.00
Mexico											
50,000	55.6	1.0	6.6	a	8.9	a	a	7.1	20.8	100.0	1,013.45
85,000	49.4	0.9	6.9	a	10.4	a	a	8.4	24.0	100.0	822.58
170,000	38.3	0.8	6.4	a	13.2	a	a	10.5	30.8	100.0	569.89
Venezuela											
50,000	41.3	6.1	11.2	6.3	15.8	0.7	1.9	12.6	4.1	100.0	181.99
100,000	48.7	4.2	13.2	5.0	12.6	0.4	1.5	10.1	4.2	100.0	154.40
125,000	49.5	3.8	13.4	5.0	12.4	0.4	1.5	9.8	4.2	100.0	151.99
150,000	51.3	3.1	13.9	4.7	11.7	0.3	1.4	9.4	4.2	100.0	146.55

a. Included in other.

81

Table 3-5. Elements of Ammonium Nitrate Production as Percent of Total Production Costs, and Cost per Ton of Output in LAFTA, by Country and Capacity of Plant, 1964–65

Country and plant capacity in tons per year	Production costs										Cost per ton in national currency
	Materials	Direct labor	Utilities	Mainte- nance	Depre- ciation	Super- vision	Insur- ance	Opportunity cost of capital	Other	Total	
Chile											
50,000	22.0	12.6	5.3	2.4	22.6	a	1.9	16.9	16.3	100.0	174.60
100,000	27.6	9.1	6.7	2.3	21.3	a	1.8	16.1	15.1	100.0	139.00
200,000	31.4	5.2	7.6	2.4	22.2	a	1.9	16.2	12.7	100.0	122.20
Colombia											
40,000	85.0	0.6	1.7	1.7	4.2	0.1	0.4	4.4	1.9	100.0	896.48
100,000	88.5	0.3	1.9	1.2	3.0	0.3b	b	3.5	1.3	100.0	810.47
150,000	88.6	0.2	2.0	1.2	3.0	0.3b	b	3.5	1.2	100.0	793.88
Mexico											
99,000	71.6	1.5	3.2	21.3c	c	c	c	2.4	c	100.0	767.22
198,000	72.8	1.3	3.2	20.5c	c	c	c	2.2	c	100.0	754.03
Peru											
36,000	84.7	1.5	2.0	2.0	4.6	a	a	4.6	0.8	100.0	1,104.44
50,000	87.4	1.8	2.1	1.8	4.0	a	a	1.8	1.1	100.0	1,070.69
120,000	90.1	0.7	2.1	1.2	2.7	a	a	2.7	0.5	100.0	1,039.24
160,000	90.4	0.6	2.2	1.1	2.6	a	a	2.6	0.4	100.0	1,034.10
Venezuela											
100,000	68.5	4.6	6.7	2.5	6.2	1.3	0.7	5.0	4.5	10.00	137.19
200,000	70.4	3.8	6.9	2.3	5.7	1.1	0.7	4.6	4.5	100.0	133.48

a. Included in other.
b. Percentage given for supervision also covers insurance.
c. Percentage given for maintenance also covers depreciation, supervision, insurance, and other.

Table 3-6. Elements of Ammonium Sulphate Production as Percent of Total Production Costs, and Cost per Ton of Output in LAFTA, by Country and Capacity of Plant, 1964–65

Country and plant capacity in tons per year	Production costs										Cost per ton in national currency
	Materials	Direct labor	Utilities	Maintenance	Depreciation	Supervision	Insurance	Opportunity cost of capital	Other	Total	
Mexico											
50,000	86.7	1.2	2.0	8.5[a]	[a]	[a]	[a]	1.6	[b]	100.0	458.41
100,000	89.6	0.6	2.1	6.5[a]	[a]	[a]	[a]	1.2	[b]	100.0	443.82
180,000	92.2	0.4	2.1	4.8[a]	[a]	[a]	[a]	0.7	[b]	100.0	431.16
Peru											
24,000	81.4	2.5	6.8	1.2	3.4	[c]	[c]	3.4	1.3	100.0	612.58
50,000	83.7	2.2	6.9	1.0	2.5	[c]	[c]	2.5	1.2	100.0	596.33
100,000	86.3	1.1	7.2	0.8	2.0	[c]	[c]	2.0	0.6	100.0	578.06
180,000	87.7	0.7	7.2	0.6	1.7	[c]	[c]	1.7	0.4	100.0	569.17
Venezuela											
50,000	82.2	2.1	1.9	1.0	2.5	0.9	0.3	4.5	4.5	100.0	131.04
100,000	87.0	1.1	2.0	0.8	2.0	0.5	0.2	4.7	1.6	100.0	123.77
180,000	88.3	0.8	2.0	0.6	1.7	0.2	0.2	4.7	1.4	100.0	122.04

a. Percentage given for maintenance also covers depreciation, supervision, and insurance.
b. Included in maintenance, depreciation, and insurance.
c. Included in other.

materials constitute between 17 and 22 percent of total cost in every country except Peru, which has an inordinately high percentage in this category due both to the high cost of natural gas, and the large amount used per ton of ammonia output.[12] Direct labor is, not surprisingly, a very small percentage of total cost. Utilities form a very small proportion of cost in Chile and Peru in comparison with the other countries in this study. The low percentage is accounted for in the Chilean case because the plant is located in Punta Arenas, where the alternative uses of electricity and water are few. The same could hold true for Chimbote, Peru. On the other hand, the relative cost of capital is somewhat higher in the Chilean location than at others, as is evidenced by the high percentage of cost for depreciation and the opportunity cost of capital. Except for materials, various categories of cost represent percentages of the total that remain fairly constant as plant size increases. Materials are a constant percentage of total output and enter the analysis at a constant price so that, as output increases, so does the value of materials as a percentage of total unit value.

Certain features of the structure of costs for the other products—urea, ammonium nitrate, and ammonium sulphate—are significantly different from what might be expected. In urea production, the percentage of cost accounted for by materials increases with plant size for all countries except Mexico. The reason is that estimated Mexican costs, unlike those for the other countries, are based on prices of ammonia that decline as the size of the urea plant increases. The calculation of the optimum location of urea production is not affected, however, since urea costs (like those for ammonium nitrate and ammonium sulphate) are estimated net of ammonia costs. Otherwise, the structure of costs is quite similar to that for ammonia, except that again the cost of materials is significantly lower, and the cost of capital significantly higher, in Chile. In ammonium nitrate, materials present another problem: Chilean costs are estimated on the basis of production of ammonium nitrate directly from ammonia, without the intermediate production of nitric acid. Costs for other countries are estimated on the basis of ammonia combined with nitric acid manufactured in a previous process. This leads to a much lower proportion of materials in the structure of Chilean costs, and a much higher proportion of utilities, direct labor, depreciation, and the opportunity cost of capital than for other countries. The structure of production costs for ammonium sulphate

12. The plants in Chile use 1,000 cubic meters per ton of ammonia; Mexico, 660; Peru, 1,500; and Venezuela, 950.

is the most similar among producing countries for any of the four products. Again, a rather large variation occurs in the proportion of costs accounted for by utilities. It is interesting to compare the percentages in these tables with those for U.S. plants with the indicated capacities.[13]

Category	Ammonia (*66,000 tons*)	Urea (*40,000 tons*)	Ammonium nitrate (*82,500 tons*)	Ammonium sulphate (*50,000 tons*)
Materials	29.5	39.7	42.5	42.2
Direct labor	5.1	4.6	3.9	6.5
Utilities	3.6	6.3	14.0	1.0
Maintenance	8.5	8.0	6.1	7.7
Depreciation	23.5	18.1	13.9	17.8
Supervision	6.9	6.6	5.8	8.8
Opportunity cost	15.0	11.6	8.9	11.2
Other	7.9	5.0	4.9	4.8
Total	100.0	100.0	100.0	100.0
Cost (dollars per ton)	34.63	50.09	37.44	38.29

Checking these percentages against those for similar size plants in Latin American countries, one finds considerable difference in the relative cost of raw materials and utilities for the various products. For the smallest size ammonia plants, for example, the only country that has close to the U.S. percentage of materials is Peru, and only Chile and Peru have similar percentages of utilities. As might be expected, depreciation and opportunity cost (plus insurance) are generally higher in Latin American than in U.S. ammonia plants, and maintenance is lower. In urea production, the differences are least apparent, but materials are a higher percentage of cost in Latin America, except in Chile and Venezuela, which are the lowest cost ammonia producers. Both ammonium nitrate and ammonium sulphate production in Latin America (except Chile) are marked by much higher percentages in materials and much lower relative capital costs than those in the United States.

Economies of Scale

The unit costs of production for the various size plants of each product in each country describe a long-run average cost curve for that product in

13. The source for these data is United Nations, *Studies in the Economics of Industry, 1. Cement/Nitrogenous Fertilizers Based on Natural Gas*, ST/ECA/75 (1963), Table 7, p. 37. The data in the original table have been broken down: 0.575 times the cost of

that location. If techniques of production were identical for all countries—that is, if there were no difference in the quantity of labor and capital necessary to produce a given output and in changes in output from a given increase in inputs—economies of scale in terms of physical output would be equal. However, changes in unit cost with changes in output would not have to be equal. Since cost is a function of both prices of inputs and characteristics of production, the slope of the average cost curves derived from plants with various capacity outputs could be quite different.[14]

The slope of an average cost curve at any given level of production is equal to the derivative of the average unit cost with respect to the quantity produced (the ratio of the change in average costs to the change in production for an infinitesimal change). It may be shown that given linear total cost curves, it is possible to compare changes in average cost at a given output for different plants operating at the same output if fixed costs alone are known for each plant.[15]

For example, at an annual output of 100,000 metric tons of ammonia, the slope of the average cost curve for the different countries presenting ammonia costs are the following at the exchange rates shown above:

Chile	1.70×10^{-4}/ton
Colombia	5.0×10^{-5}/ton
Mexico	5.48×10^{-4}/ton
Peru	2.0×10^{-4}/ton
Venezuela	1.88×10^{-4}/ton.

The figures show that changes in average costs in the range of output

---

ammonia is included in urea cost; 0.460 times ammonia cost in ammonim nitrate cost; and 0.258 times ammonia cost in ammonium sulphate cost. Insurance is included in opportunity cost.

14. Economies of scale in physical production units should be quite clearly separated from the slope of the average cost curve, which shows the change in cost from increasing output.

15. Mathematically, with a linear total cost curve

$$AC = TC/q$$
$$d(AC)/dq = [qd(TC)/dq - TC]/q^2$$
$$= [q(MC) - FC - (MC)q]/q^2$$
$$= -FC/q^2$$

where

AC = average unit cost
TC = total cost of production
q = output
MC = marginal cost (variable component of the total cost curve)
FC = fixed costs.

for which the linear approximation holds are about three times as great for Mexican ammonia production as for that in Chile, Peru, and Venezuela (which are about the same), and about twelve times that in Colombia. Average Mexican costs fall at a rate of $0.55 per thousand tons; Colombian at a rate of $0.05 per thousand tons, and the others, at about $0.20 per thousand tons. Assuming that the costs presented for the largest Colombian plant are not comparable with those for the two smaller Colombian plants,[16] and using only those two smaller plants to calculate the cost curve, the intercept term becomes 1.0×10^{-6} (at 13.5 pesos per simón), and average cost change is only about one-half that in Chile, Peru, and Venezuela. The Colombian cost estimates clearly leave much to be desired, and with only two, relatively small plants as its basis, the cost curve probably has an upward bias. The intercept term is probably biased downward since marginal cost is relatively high in the lower range of the cost curve, and this explains the relatively low change in average cost for Colombia.

Scale economies appear high for Mexico because a heavy weight was put in the linear approximation on the section of the curve from 132,000 to 299,000 tons of output, and the large plant on which the Mexican cost estimate was based uses a production process different from that of the smaller plants.[17] This acts to augment changes in average cost significantly, and accounts for part of the difference between Mexico and countries for which the process was not changed. Furthermore, the higher price of natural gas in Mexico than in Chile, Venezuela, or Colombia would be another cause for the greater change in Mexican average costs.

Changes in average cost are markedly smaller for the production of final fertilizers net of ammonia cost. The slope of the average cost curve for the other products at 100,000 tons of output (in ammonia equivalent units) is much lower than that for ammonia at every location but Colombia.

	Urea	*Ammonium nitrate*	*Ammonium sulphate*
Chile	5.4×10^{-5}/ton	8.8×10^{-5}/ton	...
Colombia	1.2×10^{-5}/ton	5.2×10^{-5}/ton	...
Mexico	1.0×10^{-4}/ton	0	1.5×10^{-5}/ton
Peru	...	1.2×10^{-5}/ton	6.0×10^{-6}/ton
Venezuela	7.2×10^{-5}/ton	2.1×10^{-5}/ton	1.6×10^{-5}/ton

16. Although the distribution of costs in the largest plant is similar to that in the smaller plants, the total cost of production per unit rises in the larger plant, which makes the estimate suspect.

17. The smaller plant uses reciprocating compressors and the larger plant centrifugal compressors, which are much more economical at high outputs. The centrifugal com-

Calculation of Optimum Location of Production

On the basis of (1) the linear approximations to the curves of total costs of production of the four products, (2) the fixed demand at each of the consumption points, as shown in Table 3-2, and (3) the costs of transportation between production and consumption points of ammonia (both fertilizer plants and final markets), and between production and consumption points of final fertilizers, the distribution of plants that would provide the area with fertilizers at minimum cost can be found using the linear programming model described in Chapter 9. Production cost curves, transport costs, and final demand for the three solid fertilizers—urea, ammonium nitrate, and ammonium sulphate—are all expressed in ammonia-equivalent metric tons, that is, they are standardized on the basis of the ammonia required to produce a metric ton of each. Production costs are also expressed net of ammonia costs, which allows for the cost of locating ammonia plants and final fertilizer plants at separate sites. The production of final fertilizers is related to the ammonia input by constant coefficients that do not depend on the scale of production.[18]

Size of Plant

Although the computed production costs are long-run curves, applicable to the whole range of output, it is more correct to say that the linear production cost curve is likely to overestimate unit and total cost but underestimate economies of scale at low levels of capacity (less than 100,000 metric tons of ammonia annually), and, at high levels of capacity (above 330,000 tons per year), to overestimate both costs *and* economies of scale. Since cost estimates are made only for plants up to 330,000 tons capacity, for purposes of the model, an upper limit is imposed on the size of the plant. This slightly raises estimated costs per unit in comparison with a 500,000-ton-per-year plant, and favors Venezuela and Chile over Mexico because of the greater economies of scale in the Mexican esti-

---

pressors become feasible at 160,000 metric tons of annual output, or 450 metric tons per day.

18. For the linear approximations to the cost curves and costs of transportation (both maximum and minimum) between points, see ECIEL, Martin Carnoy (ed.), *The Optimum Location of Specific Industries in the Latin American Free Trade Association (including Venezuela)*, Vol. 2: *Nitrogenous Fertilizers* (Brookings Institution, 1966; processed).

mates. The technologically maximum size of ammonia plants has been increasing rapidly, but, among Latin American countries, only Venezuela is planning the 1,500-ton-per-day plants now being built in the United States. Fertilizer plants greater than the maximum size available under 1965 technology are unlikely to be built elsewhere in Latin America. Therefore this study assumes that the largest ammonia plant can produce 330,000 metric tons annually; urea, ammonium nitrate, and ammonium sulphate plants are limited to 220,000 tons per year.

This constraint naturally raises costs above what they would be if plants could be of infinite size: In an industry characterized by economies of scale, multiple plants require a greater fixed cost per unit of output than a single plant producing the same output. Although the intercept terms of the linear approximation to the long-run cost curves are not the fixed cost for a single plant, they represent the element of total long-run costs resulting from their linear approximation that must be included every time a plant of *any* capacity is assumed to operate at a given location. The intercept term is the same whether the plant can produce 330,000 tons of ammonia or only 100,000 tons. Thus intercept terms are added into total costs as many times as there are plants in each location, and the number of plants at the location is determined by the minimum cost solutions in terms of multiples of 330,000 or 220,000 tons of output.

Costs of Solutions

The solutions to the linear programming model reveal a number of configurations of plant location whose total costs to the area differ only slightly from one another.[19] Table 3-7 summarizes information about the optimum locations, while Table 3-8 lists a selection of the solutions to the model. The optimum location under both minimum and maximum cost assumptions is a set of integrated plants in Chile, Mexico, Venezuela, and Peru, and a plant in Colombia producing ammonium nitrate (buying ammonia input from Venezuela). Production, however, is somewhat more

19. The solutions presented below are only a sampling of the 2 million-plus possible solutions to the four-product, twenty-one-plant fertilizer problem. As is demonstrated in the methanol-formaldehyde study (256 possible solutions), there are a number of configurations of plants that imply a total cost to the area very close to the lowest cost solution.

Table 3-7. Optimum Location of Production of Selected Nitrogenous Fertilizers in LAFTA, by Selected Assumptions about Transport Costs and Exchange Rates, 1975

Annual output in thousands of metric tons

Country	Ammonia, all uses		Urea		Ammonium nitrate		Ammonium sulphate	
	Number of plants	Annual output	Number of plants	Annual output	Number of plants	Annual output	Number of plants	Annual output
Minimum transport costs—free exchange rates								
Mexico	2	599.0	0	0	0	0	4	711.0
Chile	2	551.7	2	258.8	2	413.7	0	0
Venezuela	2	349.8	3	528.2	1	6.3	0	0
Peru	2	471.4	0	0	1	126.3	8	1,598.0
Colombia	0	0	0	0	1[a]	32.8	0	0
Maximum transport costs—official exchange rates								
Mexico	3	947.5	2	439.0	1	190.0	4	711.0
Chile	2	408.9	1	165.0	2	223.0	0	0
Venezuela	1	165.2	1	184.5	1	6.3	1	87.7
Peru	2	450.3	0	0	1	126.5	7	1,514.0
Colombia	0	0	0	0	1[a]	32.8	0	0

Source: Table 3-8, Solutions 1 and 2.
a. Ammonia input for this plant is imported from Venezuela.

Table 3-8. Optimum Location of Production of Selected Nitrogenous Fertilizers in LAFTA, and Selected Alternatives, and their Costs, 1975

Product amounts in thousands of ammonia-equivalent tons

Product and producing country	Amount produced	Consuming countries
Solution 1: Ŝ239.2 million (minimum)[a]—optimum solution under minimum cost assumptions*		
Ammonia[b]		
Chile	551.7	Brazil, Chile
Mexico	599.0	Mexico
Peru	471.4	Peru[e]
Venezuela	349.8	Argentina, Colombia,[d] Venezuela
Urea		
Chile	155.1	Argentina, Brazil, Chile, Ecuador, Peru, Uruguay
Venezuela	319.9	Colombia, Mexico, Venezuela
Ammonium nitrate		
Chile	232.2	Argentina, Brazil, Chile, Ecuador, Mexico
Colombia	14.8	Colombia
Peru	56.9	Peru
Venezuela	3.3	Venezuela
Ammonium sulphate		
Mexico	184.8	Mexico
Peru	414.5	All others[e]
Solution 2: Ŝ279.4 million (maximum)[f]—optimum solution under maximum cost assumptions*		
Ammonia[b]		
Chile	408.9	Brazil, Chile
Mexico	947.5	Mexico
Peru	450.3	Peru[e]
Venezuela	165.2	Argentina, Colombia,[d] Venezuela
Urea		
Chile	99.0	Argentina, Chile, Uruguay
Mexico	262.7	Mexico
Venezuela	113.3	Brazil, Colombia, Ecuador, Peru, Venezuela
Ammonium nitrate		
Chile	145.5	Argentina, Brazil, Chile
Colombia	14.8	Colombia
Mexico	85.8	Mexico
Peru	57.8	Ecuador, Peru
Venezuela	3.3	Venezuela
Ammonium sulphate		
Mexico	184.8	Mexico
Peru	392.5	Argentina, Brazil, Colombia, Ecuador, Peru, Uruguay
Venezuela	22.0	Venezuela

*Footnotes to table appear on p. 96.

Table 3-8. (*continued*)

Product and producing country	Amount produced	Consuming countries

Solution 3: $\hat{S}$246.1 million (minimum)[a]

Ammonia[b]
| Venezuela | 1,971.9 | All[g,d,h] |

Urea
| Venezuela | 319.9 | Colombia, Mexico, Venezuela |
| Chile | 155.1 | All others |

Ammonium nitrate
| Colombia | 14.8 | Colombia |
| Venezuela | 292.4 | All others[i] |

Ammonium sulphate
| Venezuela | 599.3 | All[e] |

Solution 4: $\hat{S}$244.6 million (minimum)[a]

Ammonia[b]
Mexico	676.9	Mexico
Venezuela	727.5	Argentina, Colombia,[d] Venezuela
Chile	452.5	Brazil, Chile
Peru	115.4	Peru[e]

Urea
Chile	155.1	Argentina, Brazil, Chile, Ecuador, Peru, Uruguay
Mexico	262.7	Mexico
Venezuela	57.2	Colombia, Venezuela

Ammonium nitrate
Venezuela	102.5	Argentina, Ecuador, Mexico, Venezuela
Chile	133.0	Brazil, Chile
Colombia	14.8	Colombia
Peru	56.9	Peru

Ammonium sulphate
| Peru | 58.5 | Peru |
| Venezuela | 540.8 | All others[i] |

Solution 5: $\hat{S}$248.9 million (minimum)[a]

Ammonia[b]
Chile	452.5	Brazil, Chile
Mexico	414.2	Mexico
Venezuela	1,105.2	Argentina, Venezuela

Urea
| Chile | 155.1 | Argentina, Brazil, Chile, Ecuador, Peru, Uruguay |
| Venezuela | 319.9 | Colombia, Mexico, Venezuela |

Ammonium nitrate
| Chile | 133.0 | Brazil, Chile |

Table 3-8. (*continued*)

Product and producing country	Amount produced	Consuming countries
Venezuela	174.2	Argentina, Colombia, Ecuador, Mexico, Peru, Venezuela
Ammonium sulphate		
Venezuela	599.3	Argentina, Brazil, Colombia, Ecuador, Mexico, Peru, Uruguay, Venezuela

Solution 6: $280.0 million (maximum)[f]

Ammonia[b]		
Chile	459.3	Brazil, Chile
Mexico	947.5	Mexico
Venezuela	449.7	Argentina, Colombia,[d] Venezuela
Peru	115.4	Peru[h]
Urea		
Chile	149.4	Argentina, Brazil, Chile, Uruguay
Mexico	262.7	Mexico
Venezuela	62.9	Colombia, Ecuador, Peru, Venezuela
Ammonium nitrate		
Chile	145.5	Argentina, Brazil, Chile
Mexico	85.8	Mexico
Peru	56.9	Peru
Colombia	14.8	Colombia
Venezuela	4.2	Ecuador, Venezuela
Ammonium sulphate		
Mexico	184.8	Mexico
Peru	58.5	Peru
Venezuela	356.0	Argentina, Brazil, Colombia, Ecuador, Uruguay, Venezuela

Solution 7: $288.2 million (maximum)[e]

Ammonia[b]		
Chile	518.6	Argentina, Brazil, Chile
Mexico	947.5	Mexico
Venezuela	505.8	Venezuela
Urea		
Chile	149.4	Argentina, Brazil, Chile, Uruguay
Mexico	262.7	Mexico
Venezuela	62.9	Colombia, Ecuador, Peru, Venezuela
Ammonium nitrate		
Chile	202.2	Argentina, Brazil, Chile, Peru
Mexico	85.8	Mexico
Venezuela	19.2	Colombia, Ecuador, Venezuela

Table 3-8. (*continued*)

Product and producing country	Amount produced	Consuming countries
Ammonium sulphate		
Mexico	184.8	Mexico
Venezuela	414.5	Argentina, Brazil, Colombia, Ecuador, Peru, Venezuela, Uruguay

Solution 8: $\hat{S}245.2$ million (minimum);[a] $\hat{S}304.5$ million (maximum)[e]

Ammonia[b]		
Venezuela	1,971.9	All[g,d]
Urea		
Venezuela	475.0	All
Ammonium nitrate		
Venezuela	307.2	All
Ammonium sulphate		
Venezuela	599.3	All[i]

Solution 9: $\hat{S}246.7$ million (minimum)[a]

Ammonia[b]		
Chile	452.5	Brazil, Chile
Mexico	1,217.7	Mexico
Venezuela	186.3	Argentina, Colombia,[i] Venezuela
Peru	115.4	Peru
Urea		
Chile	155.1	Argentina, Brazil, Chile, Ecuador, Peru, Uruguay
Mexico	262.7	Mexico
Venezuela	57.2	Colombia, Venezuela
Ammonium nitrate		
Chile	133.0	Brazil, Chile
Colombia	14.8	Colombia[d]
Peru	56.9	Peru
Venezuela	102.5	Argentina, Ecuador, Mexico, Venezuela
Ammonium sulphate		
Mexico	540.8	Argentina, Brazil, Colombia, Ecuador, Mexico, Uruguay, Venezuela
Peru	58.5	Peru

Solution 10: $\hat{S}272.4$ million (minimum);[a] $\hat{S}310.7$ million (maximum)[f]

Ammonia[b]		
Mexico	1,971.9	All[g,d,h]
Urea		
Mexico	475.0	All

Table 3-8. *(continued)*

Product and producing country	Amount produced	Consuming countries
Ammonium nitrate		
Mexico	307.2	All[i]
Ammonium sulphate		
Mexico	599.3	All[e]

Solution 11: $\hat{S}$334.5 million (minimum);[a]
$\hat{S}$470.0 million (maximum)[l]—import solution

Ammonia[b]		
United States	1,971.9	All[g,d,h]
Urea		
United States	475.0	All
Ammonium nitrate		
United States	307.2	All[i]
Ammonium sulphate		
United States	599.3	All[e]

Solution 12: $\hat{S}$253.5 million (minimum);[a] $\hat{S}$333.8 million (maximum)[f]

Ammonia[b]		
Chile	1,971.9	All[g,d,h]
Urea		
Chile	475.0	All
Ammonium nitrate		
Chile	307.2	All[i]
Ammonium sulphate		
Mexico	184.8	Mexico
Peru	59.2	Ecuador, Peru
Venezuela	355.3	Argentina, Brazil, Colombia, Uruguay, Venezuela

Solution 13: $\hat{S}$266.5 million (minimum); $\hat{S}$273.7 million (maximum)—
national solution

Ammonia[b]		
Argentina	131.2	Argentina
Brazil	618.7	Brazil
Chile	15.7	Chile
Colombia	65.8	Colombia
Mexico	956.2	Mexico
Peru	143.6	Peru
Venezuela	40.7	Venezuela
Urea		
Argentina	93.5	Argentina

Table 3-8. *(continued)*

Product and producing country	Amount produced	Consuming countries
Brazil	50.4	Brazil
Chile	2.5	Chile
Colombia	51.0	Colombia
Mexico	271.4	Ecuador, Mexico, Peru, Uruguay
Venezuela	6.2	Venezuela
Ammonium nitrate		
Argentina	12.5	Argentina
Brazil	123.1	Brazil
Chile	9.9	Chile
Colombia	14.8	Colombia
Mexico	85.8	Mexico
Peru	57.8	Ecuador, Peru
Venezuela	3.3	Venezuela
Ammonium sulphate		
Argentina	22.6	Argentina
Brazil	284.1	Brazil
Mexico	184.8	Mexico
Peru	85.8	Colombia, Ecuador, Peru, Uruguay
Venezuela	22.0	Venezuela

Note: Paraguay did not present a demand study, and therefore is excluded from these solutions.

a. This is the cost under the minimum cost assumptions—minimum transport costs and free exchange rates.

b. Ammonia for direct use and as inputs into urea, ammonium nitrate, and ammonium sulphate.

c. The ammonia that Peru produces is the input for its own production of ammonium nitrate and ammonium sulphate.

d. The ammonia that Colombia imports is the input for its own production of ammonium nitrate.

e. Chile does not consume ammonium sulphate.

f. This is the cost under the maximum cost assumptions—1963 published transport rates and official exchange rates.

g. Ecuador and Uruguay do not consume ammonia in pure form nor do they import it for their own production of other nitrogenous fertilizers.

h. The ammonia that Peru imports is the input for its own production of ammonium nitrate and ammonium sulphate.

i. Uruguay does not consume ammonium nitrate.

concentrated in the optimum based on minimum costs (Solution 1 in Table 3-8) than in the optimum based on maximum costs (Solution 2).[20] All other solutions shown are deviations from this optimum, but in many cases the deviations are small. For example, in the minimum cost case, the change in absolute cost to the area of concentrating all production of fertilizers in Venezuela would be on the order of 4 percent of the total cost

20. The national solution shows the lowest total cost for the maximum cost case, but, as explained below, this result is based on a number of very rough cost estimates, so is not considered the optimum.

of production and transportation. In the maximum cost case, the deviations widen, but they are still comparatively small relative to possible errors in costs.

Imports from outside the area and autarkic production[21] present the limiting cases of alternatives to the optimum. Importing is costly, even in the minimum cost solution, for which U.S. f.o.b. prices of ammonia and the other products are assumed to be lower than present world prices.[22] It appears that high transport costs and the relatively low price of natural gas in Latin America make it possible for some production there to compete with imports from third countries.

The total cost of autarkic production is not so clear-cut. The costs of domestic production of all the products under consideration in Brazil and Argentina are based on approximations. Brazil is now (1970) producing ammonium using naphtha as the raw material, but Brazilian costs of ammonia and ammonium nitrate were estimated assuming that coke oven gas would be the raw material for ammonia and nitric acid.[23] The plant is presumed to be located in Santos and the prices shown in Table 3-9 for the two products in Brazil reflect both the 25 percent correction to production costs for distribution and sales costs (which are also included in all other costs discussed below) and the cost of transport from Santos to consumption points. This estimated price is made the maximum cost, since the plant described is a relatively small one.

The maximum cost for Argentina is estimated by taking this figure for Brazilian production costs and adding transportation costs from Buenos Aires to consumption points. Minimum prices for ammonia in both Argentina and Brazil are assumed to be the same as the import price c.i.f. consumption points. Minimum prices for urea and ammonium sulphate in these countries are approximated arbitrarily by assuming them to be in the same proportion to c.i.f. minimum import price in Brazil (from the opti-

21. Autarkic or national production in this study means that those countries that presented cost studies produce for themselves and the most efficient among them produce for the other LAFTA countries.

22. In the minimum transport cost solution, U.S. f.o.b. prices are taken as the following: ammonia, $45; ammonium nitrate, $50; urea, $70; ammonium sulphate, $35. In the maximum transport cost solution, the prices used are $75, $70, $101, and $44, respectively. By 1975, U.S. f.o.b. prices for ammonia may fall below $45. Therefore, even the minimum estimates of U.S. f.o.b. prices may be too high.

23. ECIEL, *Optimum Location of Specific Industries*, Vol. 2, App. A to production costs.

Table 3-9. Prices of Selected Nitrogenous Fertilizers from Selected Sources in LAFTA, 1975

Simones per ammonia-equivalent ton

Consuming country	Ammonia[a]		Urea[b]		Ammonium nitrate[c]		Ammonium sulphate[d]	
	Minimum costs	Maximum costs	Minimum costs	Maximum costs	Minimum costs	Maximum costs	Minimum costs	Maximum costs
Optimum location[e]								
Argentina	59.3	79.8	113.9	144.9	169.1	235.4	234.3	276.3
Brazil	66.3	87.7	117.6	151.5	161.8	217.7	242.0	288.6
Chile	39.4	59.7	84.6	117.2	130.3	185.2	...	...
Colombia	...	...	105.6	138.3	137.6	203.3	205.4	268.3
Ecuador	...	...	96.1	127.3	135.9	226.5	177.3	191.0
Mexico	42.9	42.0	92.4	106.2	127.4	134.4	147.7	148.8
Peru	...	...	102.9	133.8	128.1	128.5	151.1	151.5
Uruguay	...	...	86.2	117.2	...	...	170.8	213.5
Venezuela	36.3	37.0	86.9	91.8	169.3	155.2	156.5	185.3
Imports[f]								
Argentina	85.2	144.5	185.5	263.7	248.9	375.7	296.5	396.9
Brazil	100.4	159.7	187.9	266.0	252.0	378.9	301.1	400.4
Chile	88.8	162.3	157.0	234.4	216.0	338.0	...	...
Colombia	...	...	173.8	269.2	219.1	354.6	281.9	434.2

Ecuador	...	...	170.0	239.4	206.2	317.1	291.9	434.2
Mexico	57.8	87.8	132.9	184.2	132.3	176.4	171.8	205.6
Peru	...	...	176.0	255.7	218.7	329.5	299.6	427.7
Uruguay	...	...	157.8	236.0	...	...	232.6	331.1
Venezuela	73.6	130.0	149.5	224.0	182.1	285.1	238.2	353.8
National production[g]								
Argentina	85.2	106.5	125.8	125.8	173.2	173.2	258.9	258.9
Brazil	100.4	107.9	125.8	125.8	173.2	173.2	258.9	258.9
Chile	141.4	171.5	363.3	483.2	313.5	383.8	...	...
Colombia	...	...	126.8	183.1	161.4	227.3	211.9[h]	274.3[h]
Ecuador	...	...	137.9[i]	153.5[i]	163.7[h]	183.2[h]	183.8[h]	197.0[h]
Mexico	41.8	41.8	105.7	105.7	134.2	134.2	148.6	148.6
Peru	...	...	147.6[i]	175.2[i]	136.8	136.8	157.5	157.5
Uruguay	...	...	135.1[i]	159.9[i]	...	...	177.3[h]	218.5[h]
Venezuela	81.3	81.3	352.0	352.0	200.1	200.1	229.5	229.5

Source: Derived from Table 3-8.
a. For final use, not as input to fertilizer production.
b. To calculate price per ton of urea, multiply by 0.6.
c. To calculate price per ton of ammonium nitrate, multiply by 0.45.
d. To calculate price per ton of ammonium sulphate, multiply by 0.26.
e. Solutions 1 and 2 (see Table 3-8).
f. Solution 11.
g. Solution 13.
h. From Peru.
i. From Mexico.

99

mum locations) as ammonium nitrate cost is to its minimum import price (from optimum location). For all products except ammonia, maximum price is taken equal to minimum price.

While this estimating process may seem rather superficial, no direct information on cost of production was available at the time this study was made.[24] At the same time, Argentina and Brazil are both potential producers of nitrogenous fertilizers, and both intend to become nearly self-sufficient in these products by 1975. Their emergence as producers drastically reduces the market for Chilean and Venezuelan fertilizers and therefore raises prices to those countries still buying them.

The total cost to the area of having completely national production based on integrated plants filling domestic demand in Mexico, Colombia, Chile, Peru, Argentina, Brazil, and Venezuela is $266.5 million (minimum cost) and $273.7 million (maximum cost). Under the minimum cost assumptions, the absolute cost of national production is relatively high; but under the maximum cost assumptions, the cost of national production relative to the optimum distribution of plants could even be negative, owing to the large increase in transport costs and to the assumptions about Brazilian and Argentine domestic prices. Although the Argentine and Brazilian costs are approximate, the Brazilian figures indicate that it is the cost of production of ammonia, not of final products net of ammonia, that is high relative to those for Venezuela and Chile. It seems that even if ammonia costs are not competitive, Brazil and Argentina, by importing ammonia from Chile and Venezuela, could compete in the production of final fertilizers.[25] Clearly, however, there is only small probability that the

24. Since these estimates were made, the Brazilians began construction of an integrated fertilizer plant in Santos for the production of ammonia, ammonium nitrate, and diammonium phosphate. Production was to begin in 1969–70. The projected price of ammonia at this plant (Ultrafertil, S.A.) is $93.70 per metric ton. See U.S. Agency for International Development, Brazil, *Brazil—Ultrafertil S.A.*, Capital Assistance Paper, AID-DLC/P-465 (Aug. 18, 1966), Annex IV, Exhibit 10. This confirms that the ammonia cost estimates shown in Table 3-9 for Brazil under national production are underestimates. Brazilian solid fertilizer prices are also underestimated here, perhaps more than ammonia price. The ECLA study (*La Oferta de Fertilizantes*, p. 33) shows the price of natural gas in Argentina to be about twice the Chilean price and about the same as the Mexican price. Assuming that Argentine ammonia production would use 1,000 m³ of gas per ton of ammonia, this would add about $4.00 per ton to the Chilean price, taking all other costs equal. Since the Argentine market will only be 131,000 ammonia-equivalent tons in 1975, full advantage cannot be taken of large-scale production, and so the price of $85–100 per ton of ammonia seems reasonable.

25. For urea production, a cheap source of carbon dioxide other than ammonia production is necessary.

prices in Table 3-9 will prevail in each country under the national production solution (that is, that they will equal theoretical costs of production and distribution plus profit), since prices will reflect tariff protection, which can be expected to increase for final fertilizers in Argentina and Brazil with the initiation of production in the face of falling world prices. While, in view of this, the total cost of national production shown here is likely to be an underestimate, an opposite effect would arise if Venezuela, Chile, and Colombia, with small domestic markets, could export to non-LAFTA members. Exporting would tend to reduce domestic prices in those countries, and would thus reduce the total cost to the area of national production.

The Influence of Exchange Rates

The prices in Table 3-9 reflect not only production and transport costs, but also the rates of exchange used between the national currencies and the simón. Two rates of exchange are different for the minimum and the maximum cost cases: The escudo is altered from 5.0 to the simón in the former case to 3.5 to the simón in the latter, and the Colombian peso from 17.5 to 13.5 per simón. These changes are made because of the uncertainty that pervaded the choice of a "true" rate for the period in which costs were estimated. The change has little effect on the configuration of optimum locations of production and of supply flows, since transportation rates also are increased in the maximum alternative. Because there are a very large number of exchange rate combinations that could be tested in this problem, it is not possible to establish a range that would permit a given location to compete with other locations in the various markets, assuming various plant configurations. This type of comparison is made in the tractor and lathe studies, but these products involve only a few solutions.

In Table 3-10 the exchange rate problem is presented by comparing c.i.f. prices of the four products studied under the assumption that the total area demand for all of them is supplied by one location. The table shows the approximate implicit indifference exchange rates between Mexican pesos, Chilean escudos, Venezuelan bolivars, and simones, assuming that production is concentrated in Mexico, Chile, Venezuela, or the United States, and that minimum transport costs prevail.

In general, as might be expected, the farther the producer from the consumption point, the less competitive he is in supplying it. So Chile can compete with Venezuela and Mexico in the southern cone at rates of ex-

Table 3-10. Prices of Nitrogenous Fertilizers and Implicit Indifference Exchange Rates in LAFTA, 1975[a]

Producing country, product, price ratio, and currencies exchanged	Consuming country								
	Argentina	Brazil	Chile	Colombia	Ecuador	Mexico	Peru	Uruguay	Venezuela
Prices in simones per ton									
Chile[b]									
Ammonia	55.1	65.4	38.4	...	...	51.6	...	...	46.4
Urea	114.0	117.7	84.6	106.2	96.1	87.5	103.0	86.3	90.2
Ammonium nitrate	169.1	161.8	130.3	151.4	135.9	127.4	145.2	...	127.0
Mexico[e]									
Ammonia	71.0	84.1	55.9	...	...	41.4	...	...	53.2
Urea	163.9	164.1	133.3	147.0	138.8	106.6	148.5	136.0	122.8
Ammonium nitrate	222.8	221.4	185.5	195.0	183.5	133.8	195.5	...	161.6
Ammonium sulphate	254.1	257.2	...	220.9	198.6	147.8	220.2	189.8	170.6
Venezuela[d]									
Ammonia	54.2	67.1	40.5	...	...	44.5	...	...	31.2
Urea	125.9	216.0	95.0	102.2	99.1	89.0	108.8	98.2	83.4
Ammonium nitrate	167.8	166.3	133.4	135.4	132.3	113.9	140.5	...	94.3
Ammonium sulphate	235.8	238.8	...	213.8	191.9	158.8	204.6	171.9	167.2
United States									
Ammonia	85.2	100.4	88.8	...	...	57.8	...	...	73.6
Urea	185.5	187.9	157.0	173.8	170.0	132.9	176.0	157.8	149.5
Ammonium nitrate	248.9	252.0	216.0	219.1	206.2	132.3	218.7	...	182.1
Ammonium sulphate	296.5	301.1	...	281.9	291.9	171.8	299.6	232.6	238.2
Price ratios									
Mexican to Chilean									
Ammonia	1.29	1.28	1.46	...	...	0.80	...	...	1.25
Urea	1.44	1.39	1.58	1.38	1.44	1.22	1.44	1.59	1.36

102

Ammonium nitrate	1.32	1.37	1.42	1.22	1.35	1.04	1.35	...	1.26
Venezuelan to Chilean									
Ammonia	0.98	1.02	1.05	...	...	0.86	...	...	0.67
Urea	1.10	1.07	1.12	0.96	1.03	1.02	1.06	1.14	0.92
Ammonium nitrate	0.99	1.03	1.02	0.89	0.97	0.89	0.97	...	0.74
Venezuelan to U.S.									
Ammonia	0.64	0.67	0.46	...	...	0.77	...	...	0.42
Urea	0.68	0.67	0.60	0.59	0.58	0.67	0.62	0.62	0.56
Ammonium nitrate	0.67	0.66	0.62	0.62	0.64	0.86	0.64	...	0.52
Ammonium sulphate	0.80	0.79	...	0.76	0.66	0.92	0.68	0.74	0.70
Indifference exchange rates									
Pesos per escudo[e]									
Ammonia	3.22	3.20	3.65	...	...	2.00	...	...	3.12
Urea	3.60	3.48	3.95	3.45	3.60	3.05	3.60	3.98	3.40
Ammonium nitrate	3.30	3.42	3.55	3.05	3.38	2.60	3.38	...	3.15
Bolivars per escudo[f]									
Ammonia	0.88	0.92	0.94	...	...	0.78	...	...	0.60
Urea	0.99	0.96	1.01	0.86	0.93	0.92	0.95	1.03	0.83
Ammonium nitrate	0.89	0.93	0.92	0.80	0.87	0.80	0.87	...	0.67
Bolivars per dollar[g]									
Ammonia	2.88	3.02	2.07	...	...	3.46	...	...	1.89
Urea	3.06	3.02	2.70	2.66	2.61	3.02	2.79	2.79	2.52
Ammonium nitrate	3.02	2.98	2.79	2.79	2.88	3.87	2.88	...	2.34
Ammonium sulphate	3.60	3.56	...	3.42	2.97	4.14	3.06	3.33	3.15

a. Assuming minimum transport costs and free exchange rates.
b. Chile does not intend to produce ammonium sulphate. The exchange rate is 5 escudos per simón.
c. The exchange rate is 12.5 pesos per simón.
d. The exchange rate is 4.5 bolivars per simón.
e. Calculated by multiplying the ratio of Mexican to Chilean price by 2.5 (the number of pesos per escudo).
f. Calculated by multiplying the ratio of Venezuelan to Chilean price by 0.9 (the number of bolivars per escudo).
g. Calculated by multiplying the ratio of Venezuelan to U.S. price by 4.5 (the number of bolivars per dollar).

change between their currencies much less favorable to it than those it requires farther to the north. Similarly, to compete with Chilean production in the South, Mexico and Venezuela need more favorable exchange rates for their currencies than they do to compete in northern Latin America. Table 3-10 shows, for example, that if the exchange rate were 3.82 pesos per escudo (which implies an exchange rate of 3.26 escudos per simón, if the peso-simón rate is held at 12.5 pesos per simón), Chile would be competitive with Mexico in urea only in the Chilean and Uruguayan markets. At the other extreme, the rate would have to fall to 3.05 pesos per escudo (4.1 escudos per simón) for Chile to compete in ammonia in the Mexican market. This implies that at the official rates (3.5 escudos per simón) of 1965, the year costs were estimated, Chile would be hard pressed to compete with either Mexican or Venezuelan industrial ammonia and final fertilizers at minimum freight rates. The table makes clear that, to sell ammonia in Mexico, Venezuela would require an exchange rate lower than 2.6 pesos per bolivar; and that to compete in Venezuela, Mexico would require a rate of 5.04 pesos per bolivar, or 22.6 pesos per simón (at 4.5 bolivars to the simón). Therefore, at official rates, Venezuela is in a good position relative to Mexico, and the rates would have to shift considerably in Mexico's favor for it to become competitive in most markets.

As far as Argentina is concerned, an integrated plant (Petrosur, S.A.) located at Campana, in Buenos Aires province, has been in operation since May 1968. It required an investment of $25 million, 40 percent of which was financed by the Inter-American Development Bank. A complementary plant operates at Rosario. Existing capacity of the main plant (per day) is 200 tons of ammonia, 162 tons of urea, and 147 tons of ammonium sulphate. The raw material is natural gas, piped from Campo Duran (Salta province), and imported sulphur.[27]

Some Qualifications to the Results

There are several sources of error in the production costs used to estimate the optimum configuration of plants. The most obvious is the curve for Colombian ammonia production, since cost per unit rises between the 100,000 and 200,000 ton plants (Table 3-3). Assuming that only the small-

27. See *La Chacra*, Vol. 40 (March 1970), p. 12.

est plant—the 16,500 ton plant—and the 100,000 ton plant enter the estimate of the long-run cost curve, the estimate yields the following equations:

$$C_A = 1.00 + 0.0493\ X;$$
$$C'_A = 0.78 + 0.0380\ X,$$

where

C_A = total cost of ammonia in millions of simones at an exchange rate of 13.5 pesos per simon

C'_A = total cost of ammonia in millions of simones at an exchange rate of 17.5 pesos per simon

X = output in thousands of metric tons.

At 200,000 tons of output, the equations imply unit costs at the plant of $54.3 and $41.9 per metric ton under, respectively, the maximum and minimum assumptions about transport costs and exchange rates. At 68,000 tons of output (Colombia's domestic market in 1975), this range of costs rises to $64.0 to $49.5 per ton. This exercise shows that, even under the transport costs and exchange rates most favorable to it, Colombia, with costs of $49.5 per ton, cannot compete with Venezuelan ammonia imports, with costs of $48.1 per ton, if she produces only for the domestic market. However, if Colombia can export ammonia, then under the same assumptions she can compete with Venezuelan imports ($41.9 per ton versus $48.1 per ton). Assuming either minimum transport costs or an exchange rate of 13.5 pesos per simón eliminates any Columbian advantage even if Colombia can find export markets.

Another possible error is in the investment estimated for Venezuelan ammonia plants. Taking the largest plant in each country, investment per ton-year of ammonia output at capacity is as follows:

	Annual output (thousands of tons)	Investment (simones)		Exchange rate per simón
		Total (millions)	Per ton-year	
Chile	330.0	16.70	50.6	5 escudos
Colombia	100.0	8.45	84.5	13.5 pesos
Mexico	299.4	19.2	64.2	12.5 pesos
Peru	330.0	23.1	70.0	26.8 soles
Venezuela	330.0	13.8	41.8	4.5 bolivars

Raising Venezuelan investment to the more "reasonable" level of $17.1

million, or by $10.0 per ton-year, increases unit cost by $3.1 (adjusted for sales and distribution costs). Such a change would increase the total cost of production for the area and would push Solutions 3, 4, 5, and 8 further from the optimum, but would not alter their order.[27]

A third error is in sulphuric acid cost for Peruvian ammonium sulphate production. The Peruvian cost is one-third the Venezuelan and less than one-half the Mexican cost. Even a small correction upward of the Peruvian price would shift the optimum location of ammonium sulphate production from Peru to Mexico and Venezuela, and the lowest cost solution would be Solution 2 for the minimum cost case and Solution 6 for the maximum cost case.

One way to get at differences in technical coefficients, although not in the prices, of inputs is to assume that the coefficients relating inputs per ton of output are the same for all countries. Venezuela's coefficients are taken as the benchmark, and the optimum solutions and shadow prices solved for. The results appear in Table 3-11.

Besides the somewhat lower total cost of production and transportation, the primary difference between this set of optima and those shown in Table 3-8 is the shift of ammonium sulphate production away from Peru to Mexico and Venezuela. In the minimum cost case with equal coefficients, Chile produces much more ammonia and urea than in the minimum cost case optimum solution where coefficients are allowed to vary.

The shadow prices of each product at each market derived from the equal-technology optimum solutions are shown in Table 3-12. In general, these prices are somewhat lower than those in Table 3-9.

Capital Investment Requirements

The total investment necessary to meet 1975 demand can be determined from the investments specified for the plants of various sizes shown in Tables 3-3 to 3-6,[28] and by interpolating for other sizes. Since this invest-

27. A similar problem occurs in urea production, in which Chile and Venezuela show about $40 per ton-year investment in the largest plants, against approximately $60 per ton-year for Mexico and Colombia. For ammonium nitrate all investments per ton-year are the same except in Peru, where it is 25 percent lower. For ammonium sulphate, Mexican investment per ton-year is 25 percent lower than Venezuelan or Peruvian investment. No correction is made for any of these variations.

28. For investment figures, see Carnoy (ed.), *Optimum Location of Specific Industries*.

Table 3-11. Optimum Location of Production of Selected Nitrogenous Fertilizers in LAFTA, and Selected Alternatives, and their Costs, Assuming Equal Technology in All Producing Countries, 1975[a]

Thousands of ammonia-equivalent tons

Product and producing country	Amount produced	Consuming countries
Minimum cost assumptions:[b] $\hat{S}$*233 million*		
Ammonia		
Chile	602.7	Argentina, Brazil, Chile, Peru[c]
Mexico	971.6	Mexico
Venezuela	397.6	Venezuela
Urea		
Chile	155.1	Argentina, Brazil, Chile, Ecuador, Peru, Uruguay
Mexico	262.7	Mexico
Venezuela	57.2	Colombia, Venezuela
Ammonium nitrate		
Chile	164.5	Argentina, Brazil, Chile, Colombia, Ecuador, Venezuela
Mexico	85.8	Mexico
Peru[d]	56.9	Peru
Ammonium sulphate		
Mexico	208.9	Colombia, Mexico, Venezuela
Peru[d]	59.2	Ecuador, Peru
Venezuela	331.2	Argentina, Brazil, Uruguay
Maximum cost assumptions:[e] $\hat{S}$*265 million*		
Ammonia		
Chile	462.8	Argentina, Brazil, Chile
Mexico	947.5	Mexico
Peru	118.2	Peru[f]
Venezuela	443.4	Colombia,[g] Venezuela
Urea		
Chile	149.4	Argentina, Brazil, Chile, Uruguay
Mexico	262.7	Mexico
Venezuela	62.9	Colombia, Ecuador, Peru, Venezuela
Ammonium nitrate		
Chile	146.4	Argentina, Brazil, Chile, Ecuador
Colombia[h]	14.8	Colombia
Mexico	85.8	Mexico
Peru	56.9	Peru
Venezuela	3.3	Venezuela
Ammonium sulphate		
Mexico	184.8	Mexico
Peru	61.3	Colombia, Ecuador, Peru
Venezuela	353.2	Argentina, Brazil, Uruguay, Venezuela

a. The technology in all countries is assumed to be the same as in Venezuela.
b. Projected 1975 maritime transport rates and free exchange rates.
c. Peru imports ammonia from Chile to produce ammonium nitrate and ammonium sulphate.
d. Ammonia input imported from Chile.
e. Current published transport rates and official exchange rates.
f. Peru produces ammonia for its own production of ammonium nitrate and ammonium sulphate.
g. Colombia imports ammonia from Venezuela for ammonium nitrate production.
h. Ammonia input imported from Venezuela.

Table 3-12. Prices of Nitrogenous Fertilizers in LAFTA Countries Derived from Optimum Solution, Assuming Equal Technology in All Producing Countries, 1975

Simones per metric ton

Consuming country	Ammonia	Urea	Ammonium nitrate	Ammonium sulphate
	Minimum cost assumptions[a]			
Argentina	51.4	109.8	162.3	246.5
Brazil	61.6	113.5	155.0	249.5
Chile	34.7	80.5	123.5	...
Colombia	...	82.6	144.6	217.6
Ecuador	...	92.0	129.1	190.5
Mexico	39.8	74.5	112.3	144.4
Peru	...	98.8	132.8	164.3
Uruguay	...	82.1	...	182.6
Venezuela	34.6	63.9	120.2	167.2
	Maximum cost assumptions[b]			
Argentina	76.1	133.9	229.4	292.6
Brazil	81.3	140.6	211.8	291.1
Chile	53.3	106.2	179.2	...
Colombia	...	132.2	209.0	273.7
Ecuador	...	121.2	189.2	205.7
Mexico	40.0	74.7	112.5	144.7
Peru	...	127.7	128.7	160.2
Uruguay	...	106.2	...	228.7
Venezuela	33.9	85.6	173.3	177.1

Source: Derived from Table 3-11.

a. These are the prices derived from the optimum solutions based on projected 1975 maritime transport rates and free exchange rates.

b. These are the prices derived from the optimum solutions based on current published transport rates and official exchange rates.

ment should take account of existing (1963) plants, what is relevant is the *additional* investment in producing countries necessary to meet demand. To be complete, this calculation requires a set of optimum solutions beyond those presented above: It would be desirable to know what the optimum solution would be if 1963 production were assumed to continue (even if subsidization is needed). Under those circumstances, fixed demand in each LAFTA country, for purposes of the linear programming model, consists of the difference between 1975 demand and 1963 production, which is shown in Table 3-13.

After a comparison of Tables 3-2 and 3-13, it is not surprising to find that no change takes place in the optimum locations of *new* plants under the minimum and maximum cost assumptions. The only important differ-

Table 3-13. Demand for Ammonia and Nitrogenous Fertilizers in LAFTA, Net of 1963 Production, 1975

Thousands of metric tons of ammonia-equivalent units

Consuming country	Ammonia[a]	Urea[b]	Ammonium nitrate[c]	Ammonium sulphate[d]
Argentina	1.1	93.5	12.3	19.6
Brazil	158.8	50.4	109.5	282.0
Chile	3.1	2.5	9.9	0.2
Colombia	−9.9	44.6	9.0	1.3
Ecuador	...	3.2	0.9	0.7
Mexico	388.8	238.9	23.5	143.3
Peru	...	0.5	41.4	55.3
Uruguay	...	3.0	...	24.5
Venezuela	9.2	3.4	−4.7	16.1
Total	551.1	440.0	201.8	543.0

Source: ECIEL, *The Demand for Chemical Fertilizers.*
a. Includes ammonia to be used in the production of fertilizers other than those studied here.
b. One unit of urea equals 0.60 unit of ammonia.
c. One unit of ammonium nitrate equals 0.45 unit of ammonia.
d. One unit of ammonium sulphate equals 0.26 unit of ammonia.

ence in the number of plants required occurs in ammonium nitrate because of the high level already reached by Mexico in 1963. Table 3-14 shows the investment required under the various alternatives presented in the study. Alternative 1 assumes Solution 1, the minimum cost optimum in 1975 with no account taken of existing (1963) plants in the region; Alternative 2 also assumes Solution 1, but accounts for plants existing in those countries in 1963. Alternatives 3 and 4 both assume all plants in Venezuela, but the former counts on the production of plants existing in 1963, while the latter excludes it.

The arbitrary assumptions on the size of plants and their order in time make the total investment figures highly tenuous; in general, they constitute a minimum investment, since the largest possible plants are assumed. As the figures stand, the area will have to invest, under Alternatives 1 and 2, a minimum of $183 million in plant and equipment between 1963 and 1975. In Alternatives 3 and 4, investment in plant and equipment will be a minimum of $144 million.

Welfare Benefits and Costs

With the prices given in Table 3-9, and the methodology developed in Appendix C, estimates are made of the welfare benefits to each country of

Table 3-14. Total Investment Required in Nitrogenous Fertilizer Production in LAFTA, 1963–75

Simón amounts in millions; capacity in thousands of tons

Alternative and producing country	Ammonia — Number	Ammonia — Capacity per plant	Ammonia — Simones	Urea — Number	Urea — Capacity per plant	Urea — Simones	Ammonium nitrate — Number	Ammonium nitrate — Capacity per plant	Ammonium nitrate — Simones[b]	Ammonium sulphate — Number	Ammonium sulphate — Capacity per plant	Ammonium sulphate — Simones	Total investment for period
Alternative 1													
Mexico	2	330	$38.4	...	...	...	...	...	...	4	180	$3.2	$41.6
Chile	2	330	37.6	1, 1	{150, 100}	$11.6	2	220	$23.6	...	...	...	72.8
Peru	1	{330, 180}	39.1	...	...	...	1	160	5.0	7	220	6.3	50.4
Colombia	...	...	...	...	...	...	1	40	2.3	...	...	...	2.3
Venezuela	1	{330, 100}	23.1	3	200	19.8	1	50	2.7	...	...	...	45.6
Total	6	2,260	138.2	5	850	31.4	5	690	33.6	11	2,260	9.5	212.7
Alternative 2[c]													
Mexico	2	330	38.4	...	...	...	...	...	...	3	180	3.2	41.6
Chile	1	330	28.0	1, 1	{150, 100}	11.6	2	220	23.6	...	...	...	63.2
Peru	1, 1	{132, 330}	34.1	...	...	...	1	120	4.0	7	220	6.3	44.4
Venezuela	1, 1	{108, 330}	17.1	2, 1	{200, 100}	17.5	...	...	...	...	...	...	34.6
Total	7	1,890	117.6	5	750	29.1	3	560	27.6	10	2,080	9.5	183.8
Alternative 3													
Venezuela	6	330	102.6	4	200	26.4	3, 1	{200, 100}	29.0	10, 1	{220, 100}	9.7	167.7
Total	6	1,980	102.6	4	800	26.4	4	700	29.0	11	2,300	9.7	167.7
Alternative 4													
Venezuela	5, 1	{330, 100}	91.5	3, 1	{200, 150}	25.5	2	220	17.9	9, 1	{220, 100}	8.8	143.7
Total	6	1,750	91.5	4	750	25.5	2	440	17.9	10	2,080	8.8	143.7

Source: ECIEL, Martin Carnoy (ed.), *The Optimum Location of Specific Industries in the Latin American Free Trade Association (including Venezuela)* (Brookings Institution 1966; processed).

a. For definitions of alternatives to optimum, see text, p. 109.

b. Includes investment in nitric acid plants.

c. Colombia is omitted from this list, because it is assumed that the present capacity of the ammonium nitrate plant at Barrancabermeja can satisfy 1975 demand and that, [therefore no net investment] is required from 1963 to 1975.

buying from the optimum location versus (1) importing and (2) autarkic production. These estimates, calculated on an annual basis, divided into a production effect and a consumption effect,[29] and based on both the minimum and maximum prices of Table 3-9, are shown in Table 3-15. The total benefits of producing at the optimum location versus importing from the United States range between $80 million and $147 million in 1975, depending on whether minimum transport cost and projected U.S. prices or maximum transport cost and 1965 U.S. prices are used in the estimate. Gains attributable to the production effect represent about 27 to 38 percent of the costs of production and transportation of these products in 1975. The total welfare cost of national production in the minimum cost case is only $23 million, or about 10 percent of total annual production and transport cost in 1975. Considering the assumption made with regard to Brazilian and Argentine domestic production costs, this low figure is not surprising. In the maximum transport cost case, there is a net benefit to the region of $9 million of producing nationally, again due to the Argentine and Brazilian cost assumption.

Nominal and Effective Tariffs

In order to get an idea of the present structure of tariffs on fertilizers in Latin America, Table 3-16 presents both nominal and effective tariffs by country for 1966. The latter refer to protection of value added afforded by the nominal tariff on the finished products, in this case value added to the cost of ammonia. If autarkic production begins in earnest in Latin America, tariffs on final fertilizers may be raised considerably. It is noteworthy that currently many of the effective tariffs on final fertilizers are negative because of the relatively much higher tariff on ammonia.

Summary

Under the assumptions of minimum maritime transport rates and free exchange rates, ammonia and final nitrogenous fertilizers could be produced at minimum cost to the LAFTA region by a number of production

---

29. See Chap. 2 for an explanation of these terms.

Table 3-15. Welfare Benefits and Costs of Selected Alternatives to Optimum Location of Production of Nitrogenous Fertilizers in LAFTA Countries, Assuming Minimum and Maximum Transport Costs, 1975

Thousands of simones

Country	Ammonia		Urea		Ammonium nitrate		Ammonium sulphate		Total	
	Production effect	Total	Production effect	Total	Production effect	Total	Production effect	Total	Production effect	Total
Buying from optimum location[a] versus U.S. imports[b]—minimum transport costs and free exchange rates										
Argentina	−46	56	4,154	5,483	676	838	1,112	1,256	5,988	7,633
Brazil	3,632	4,576	2,252	2,928	7,170	9,178	13,750	15,400	26,804	32,082
Chile	73	119	98	139	516	691	...	...	687	949
Colombia	...	...	2,100	2,772	753	979	116	137	2,969	3,888
Ecuador	...	...	237	332	46	58	83	110	366	500
Mexico	4,265	5,033	7,282	8,884	437	446	3,821	4,127	15,805	18,490
Peru	...	...	21	28	2,988	4,004	4,420	6,630	7,429	10,662
Uruguay	...	...	116	164	...	...	1,967	2,832	2,083	2,996
Venezuela	170	259	117	159	39	40	1,171	1,475	1,497	1,933
Total	8,186	10,043	16,377	20,889	12,625	16,234	26,440	31,967	63,628	79,133
National production[c] versus buying from optimum location[a]—minimum transport costs and free exchange rates										
Argentina	−46	−56	−958	−1,006	−42	−42	−530	−562	−1,576	−1,666
Brazil	−3,632	−4,576	−408	−424	−1,317	−1,422	−4,743	−4,933	−10,100	−11,355
Chile	−95	−213	−163	−437	−742	−1,254	...	...	−1,000	−1,904
Colombia	...	...	−914	−1,005	−305	−332	−13	−13	−1,232	−1,350
Ecuador	...	...	−161	−196	−23	−25	−8	−8	−192	−229
Mexico	533	544	−3,156	−3,408	−542	−569	−273	−273	−3,438	−3,706
Peru	...	...	−15	−18	−377	−388	−310	−316	−702	−722
Uruguay	...	...	−93	−106	...	...	−167	−170	−260	−276
Venezuela	−184	−280	−208	−520	−84	−91	−1,102	−1,366	−1,578	−2,257
Total	−3,424	−4,581	−6,076	−7,120	−3,432	−4,123	−7,146	−7,641	−20,078	−23,465

112

Buying from optimum location[d] *versus U.S. imports*[b]—*maximum transport costs and official exchange rates*

Argentina	93	132	6,099	8,600	1,090	1,416	1,873	2,285	9,155	12,433
Brazil	6,358	8,964	3,283	4,531	11,521	15,784	22,957	27,548	44,119	56,828
Chile	124	231	148	148	832	1,182	...	...	1,104	1,561
Colombia	...	...	3,456	5,115	1,298	1,778	214	278	4,969	7,171
Ecuador	...	...	337	486	9	11	128	210	474	707
Mexico	9,046	14,021	11,717	16,052	2,768	3,211	7,699	9,162	31,230	42,446
Peru	...	...	31	45	4,460	7,939	5,761	11,119	10,252	19,103
Uruguay	...	...	176	265	...	...	1,883	2,410	2,059	2,676
Venezuela	231	558	335	576	238	338	1,653	2,413	2,457	3,884
Total	15,852	23,906	25,582	35,818	22,216	31,659	42,168	55,425	105,819	146,809

National production[c] *versus production at optimum location*[d]—*maximum transport costs and official exchange rates*

Argentina	−52	−61	1,762	1,903	740	873	375	386	2,825	3,101
Brazil	−2,684	−3,006	1,128	1,240	5,357	6,000	8,199	8,691	12,000	12,925
Chile	−120	−248	−224	−575	−962	−1,482	...	...	−1,306	−2,304
Colombia	...	...	−1,693	−1,964	−332	−352	−11	−11	−2,306	−2,327
Ecuador	...	...	−122	−135	6	7	−7	−7	−123	−135
Mexico	...	...	...	...	...	...	...	...	...	...
Peru	...	...	−15	−18	...	...	−310	−316	−325	−334
Uruguay	...	...	−95	−112	...	...	−104	−105	−199	−217
Venezuela	−184	−275	−194	−445	−113	−129	−654	−732	−1,145	−1,581
Total	−3,040	−3,590	547	−106	4,696	4,917	7,488	7,906	9,421	9,128

Sources: Tables 3-2 and 3-8.
a. Solution 1.
b. Solution 11.
c. Solution 13.
d. Solution 2.

Table 3-16. Nominal and Effective Tariffs on Nitrogenous Fertilizers in LAFTA, 1966

Percent

Country	Ammonia Nominal tariff	Urea Nominal tariff	Urea Effective tariff[a]	Ammonium nitrate Nominal tariff	Ammonium nitrate Effective tariff[a]	Ammonium sulphate Nominal tariff	Ammonium sulphate Effective tariff[a]
Argentina	212.0	0.3	[b]	0.3	[b]	0.3	[b]
Brazil	31.6	9.6	[b]	9.6	−8.6	9.6	[b]
Chile	620.0	3,400.0	4,920.0	[c]	[c]	17.0	[b]
Colombia	20.0	1.0	−19.1	1.0	−29.4	1.0	[b]
Ecuador	59.0	43.0	[b]	45.0	[b]	55.0	[b]
Mexico	36.0[d]	4.0	−28.1	3.0	−26.2	42.0	47.9
Peru	116.5	20.0	[b]	20.0	−73.5	20.0	−62.0
Uruguay	n.a.	148.0	[b]	178.0	[b]	178.0	[b]
Venezuela	2.2	0	−1.2	0	−1.4	0	−0.5

Source: U.S. Department of Commerce, Bureau of International Commerce.

n.a. Not available.

a. The effective tariff equals $\dfrac{t_f - (1 - v)t_a}{v}$,

where

t_f = nominal tariff on final fertilizer

t_a = nominal tariff on ammonia

v = value added to ammonia cost by fertilizer industry per simón of output of final fertilizer.

b. Value added was not available, so effective tariff could not be computed.

c. Prohibited.

d. On imports from LAFTA countries.

configurations, ranging from plants in five countries to production concentrated in Venezuela. If transport costs are based on published rates and official rates of exchange are assumed, the optimum shifts to a more dispersed production pattern; and even an autarkic solution—under which each country that submitted costs for this study produces for its own market and the more efficient among them supply those that did not—becomes acceptable.

Of the alternatives available under the assumption of minimum costs and free exchange rates, the more widely dispersed pattern is more viable if the possible distortions of Colombian and Venezuelan data are corrected. Somewhat lower delivered prices result when technology in all countries is assumed to be the same as that in Venezuela, but the location of production alters very little.

The autarkic solution, which political considerations make a very real possibility, would probably involve opposition to lower tariffs on these products in the region. In that sense, the total costs and prices estimated in this study would be much lower than the effective prices that would prevail with this alternative. It should also be clear that lower transport costs for fertilizers would be more likely with greater trade among LAFTA members. Hence, while autarkic production may be the optimum given current rates, it would prevent the movement to the lower total costs embodied in the minimum cost estimates. If this assumption is correct, the $273 million cost of the maximum cost national solution should be compared with the $239 million cost of the optimum solution under minimum cost assumptions. The results of the comparison imply that the additional cost to the area of autarkic production would be $34 million annually.

CHAPTER FOUR

Methanol and Formaldehyde

LIKE NITROGENOUS FERTILIZERS and other chemical products, the methanol-formaldehyde group can play an important role in industrial integration in Latin America. Since both production and consumption are currently a small fraction of the area's potential demand for these products, immediate benefits to the area of free trade in them might be small, but future gains could be large and at small cost in terms of displacing current production.

Methanol is used primarily as an input into formaldehyde, and formaldehyde, in turn, is used in manufacturing resins for molding powders, textile preparations, adhesives, laminates, and paints, as well as in disinfectants, soap, and explosives, and in metallurgy. With the expansion of industrial production, then, the consumption of formaldehyde is expected to increase rapidly. The other end uses of methanol—as a solvent, in airplane fuel, and in laboratories—are not as crucial to the early and middle stages of industrial growth, and are therefore not expected to stimulate production as much in coming years.

Production and Consumption—1963 and 1975

The relation between consumption and production in 1963 in the countries of the Latin American Free Trade Association (LAFTA) appears in

116

Table 4-1. Production and Apparent Consumption of Methanol and Formaldehyde, 1963, and Projected Demand, 1975, in LAFTA

Thousands of metric tons

Consuming country	*Methanol*[a]			*Formaldehyde*[b]		
	Production, 1963	Consumption		Production, 1963	Consumption	
		1963	1975[c]		1963	1975[c]
Argentina	3.4	8.6	15.5	9.8	9.8	26.5
Brazil	8.0	11.0	106.6	18.5	18.5	219.1
Chile	...	0.5	7.0	0.2	0.4	15.0
Colombia	...	2.3	7.3	5.0	5.1	13.0
Ecuador	...	...	...	...	...	0.1
Mexico	...	5.4	29.7	7.3	7.3	23.8
Peru	...	...	...	...	1.0	13.4
Uruguay	...	...	...	...	0.5	1.0
Venezuela	...	...	1.4	n.a.	0.5[d]	2.9
Total	11.4	27.8	167.5	40.8	43.2	314.8

Source: ECIEL, *The Demand for Chemical Fertilizers, Tractors, Paper and Pulp, Milk Concentrates, and Lathes in the Latin American Free Trade Association (including Venezuela)* (Brookings Institution, 1966; processed), Vol. 1.

n.a. Not available.

a. As methanol and in domestic production of formaldehyde. If the country imports all formaldehyde (Peru and Uruguay), methanol consumption is taken to be zero.

b. In 37 percent solution.

c. Midpoint of minimum and maximum projections.

d. 1960 consumption.

Table 4-1. Formaldehyde production (40,800 metric tons) almost matched consumption in that year (43,100), but the manufacture of methanol was confined to Argentina and Brazil and total production met only 40 percent of demand. Of the 27,800 metric tons consumed, 17,800 were for the production of formaldehyde, and 10,000 for other uses.

The consumption of formaldehyde is projected to grow at a rapid 18 percent average annual rate during the 1963–75 period, from 43,000 to 315,000 tons. Its distribution alters rather substantially for some countries: Argentina's share drops from 23 percent in 1963 to 8.5 percent in 1975, Brazil's increases from 43 percent to almost 70 percent, and both the Colombian and Mexican shares contract significantly. That part of methanol demand that serves formaldehyde production grows, of course, at the same rate as formaldehyde consumption (assuming that all formaldehyde is produced in the area). Methanol for other uses, however, is projected to increase at the much lower rate of 11 percent annually, from

Table 4-2. Projected Total Market Demand for Methanol in Direct Form and Formaldehyde, by LAFTA Country, 1975

Thousands of metric tons of methanol-equivalent units

	Product	
Consuming country	*Methanol*	*Formaldehyde*[a]
Argentina	4.0	11.5
Brazil	11.4	95.2
Chile	0.3	6.7
Colombia	0.5	5.6
Mexico	19.4	10.3
Peru	...	5.8
Uruguay	...	0.4
Venezuela	0.1	1.2
Total	35.7	136.7

a. One ton of formaldehyde equals 0.435 ton of methanol.

10,000 to 35,700 tons (see Table 4-2).[1] If all methanol and formaldehyde used in the area is manufactured there, a total of 172,400 methanol-equivalent tons would be required.[2]

The expected productive capacities for methanol and formaldehyde in Latin America in 1965, as projected by a 1962 ECLA study,[3] were 32,500 tons and 71,300 tons, respectively, approximately 19 and 22.5 percent of projected 1975 demand. While the total value of the products involved is small, the results here are representative of those for a whole range of petroleum- and natural gas-based chemicals whose large-scale production is just beginning in Latin America. In the case of methanol and formaldehyde, production to meet 80 percent of 1975 consumption could be located in an optimum manner without displacing existing capacity.

Structure of Costs and Economies of Scale

Table 4-3 shows the structure of costs, and unit costs, for various size plants at Punta Arenas, Chile; Puerto La Cruz or Puerto Miranda, Vene-

1. The total of methanol for other uses and for formaldehyde that appears in Table 4-1 is different from the sum of the demand for methanol-equivalent units of formaldehyde plus methanol "in direct form" (Table 4-2) because Peru and Uruguay are not considered here as potential producers of formaldehyde, and so consume a negligible amount of methanol.

2. One ton of formaldehyde requires 0.435 ton of methanol.

3. ECLA, *La Industria Química en America Latina*, Vol. I, E/CN.12/628/Add. 1 (1962), pp. 18–19.

zuela; San Martín, Mexico; and Cali or Medellín, Colombia. The breakdown of methanol costs is strikingly similar in the three countries. The largest deviations, which occur in the 23,000 ton Venezuelan plant, are probably due to the fact that it is a converted ammonia plant. Chilean formaldehyde has relatively heavier capital costs (depreciation plus the alternative cost of capital, which is 8 percent per annum) and lower proportional raw material costs than either Colombia or Venezuela. Otherwise the formaldehyde distributions are approximately the same.

Economies of Scale

The costs per ton for each country by capacity of plant shown in the last column of Table 4-3 indicate that the changes in average cost are similar for the different locations.[4] A comparison of the changes in average cost that occur with a small change in production in a plant of 20,000 metric tons annual output of methanol for various countries produces the following slopes of the average cost curve:

Chile 11.5×10^{-4} simones/ton (at 5 escudos per simón);
Mexico 16.5×10^{-4} simones/ton (at 12.5 pesos per simón);
Venezuela 17.8×10^{-4} simones/ton (at 4.5 bolivars per simón)

When 3.5 escudos per simón is used as the exchange rate, the Chilean figure rises to 12.8×10^{-4} simones per ton. The variation in average cost change associated with formaldehyde production is much greater at 20,000 methanol-equivalent tons (47,000 tons of formaldehyde):

Chile 47.5×10^{-5} simones/ton (5 escudos per simón);
Colombia 13.0×10^{-5} simones/ton (17.5 pesos per simón);
Venezuela 23.0×10^{-5} simoncs/ton (4.5 bolivars per simón).

The Chilean figure is 56.8 at 3.5 escudos per simón, and the Colombian, 16.5 at 13.5 pesos per simón. Changes in average cost for formaldehyde are for value added to the methanol input, and although technology should not be very different in the various plants, it is clear from Table 4-3 that Chile's production of formaldehyde is more capital intensive than Colombia's or Venezuela's even if the capital cost of methanol is excluded from

4. If a Cobb-Douglas production function and equal prices of inputs are assumed, equal changes in average cost over a given range of output implies equal economies or diseconomies of scale in production.

Table 4-3. Cost Structure of Methanol and Formaldehyde Production in LAFTA

Percent of total costs

Country and plant capacity in tons per year	Materials	Direct labor	Utilities	Maintenance	Depreciation	Supervision	Insurance	Opportunity cost of capital	Other	Total	Cost per ton in national currency
Methanol											
Chile											
16,500	9.4	6.6	10.9	3.3	27.7	a	2.6	20.0	19.5	100.0	334.00
25,000	10.1	5.7	11.8	3.3	29.0	a	2.6	20.1	17.3	100.0	305.50
33,000	11.2	5.2	13.1	3.4	29.8	a	2.7	20.6	14.0	100.0	278.00
Mexico											
15,000	8.7	4.3	16.3	8.8	29.4	1.4	2.9	23.5	4.9	100.0	1,362.22
25,000	10.0	2.8	18.7	8.6	28.8	0.9	2.9	23.0	4.2	100.0	1,190.48
33,000	10.6	2.6	19.8	8.5	28.2	0.9	2.8	22.6	4.0	100.0	1,119.59

Venezuela

23,000	8.5	2.7	18.6	11.3	28.3	0.8	3.4	22.7	3.7	100.0	383.48
33,000	8.2	3.4	15.1	12.0	29.9	0.5	3.6	23.9	3.5	100.0	292.34
55,000	8.8	3.2	16.2	11.7	29.3	0.3	3.5	23.4	3.5	100.0	271.66

Formaldehyde

Chile

10,000	54.6	8.0	1.0	1.4	13.8	a	1.6	12.5	7.1	100.0	295.50
20,000	63.7	4.7	1.2	1.4	12.3	a	1.4	11.3	4.1	100.0	253.12
40,000	67.6	4.1	1.2	1.2	10.7	a	1.2	10.0	3.8	100.0	237.70

Colombia

6,000	79.1	2.4	0.4	2.2	5.5	0.2	0.5	5.9	3.8	100.0	976.17
10,000	82.0	1.5	0.4	2.0	5.0	0.1	0.5	5.5	3.0	100.0	941.80
30,000	88.2	1.0	0.8	1.3	3.3	0.1	0.3	4.1	0.9	100.0	875.83

Venezuela

5,000	59.8	12.7	2.0	3.0	7.3	4.1	0.9	5.8	4.5	100.0	246.11
20,000	75.8	4.0	2.5	2.0	5.1	1.3	0.6	4.1	4.5	100.0	194.35

a. Included in other.

121

the calculation. The explanation of large economies of scale, then, are consistent with the more capital-intensive production process in Chile. Capital costs are, however, a higher percentage of value added in Colombia than in Venezuela, yet economies of scale are greater in the latter. These differences in the slope of the average cost curve are probably due to differences not only in economies of scale, but also in prices of inputs and in factors that cannot be identified from the available data.

The Optimum Location

This section explores the determination of the economic "best" location of production through minimizing the cost at which LAFTA members fill their needs for methanol and formaldehyde; it also discussed the implications of these solutions for the expansion of plant capacity. Cost minimization to the area entails supplying the fixed demand in 1975 (see Table 4-2) to the various consumption points in the area at the lowest possible cost of production plus transportation. Four possible production points—those that presented data—are considered for methanol: Punta Arenas, Chile; San Martín, Mexico; Puerto La Cruz or Puerto Miranda, Venezuela; and the United States (importation into the area at f.o.b. New York price); and four for formaldehyde: Punta Arenas; Cali or Medellín, Colombia; Puerto La Cruz or Puerto Miranda; and the United States. Three of the four locations have both methanol and formaldehyde production possibilities, and the linear programming model used allows separate or integrated plants at each of these. Plants are restricted to a maximum size of 60,000 tons for methanol and 47,000 tons for formaldehyde (20,000 methanol-equivalent tons). Only formaldehyde costs are presented for Colombia (no methanol capacity is planned), and only methanol costs for Mexico, despite the capacity it already has in formaldehyde. One of the solutions tried assumes that Mexico would satisfy its own formaldehyde needs.

With eight possible plant locations (four each for methanol and formaldehyde production), there are 2^8, or 256, possible solutions. A sampling of them is shown in Table 4-4. These various "local optima" are the result of systematically eliminating certain plants and including others. Thus, for example, if Venezuela is excluded from consideration, the lowest cost pattern clearly will be different from what it would be if all locations (that is, all for which data were available for study) were candidates for plant sites.

Table 4-4. Optimum Location of Production of Methanol and Formaldehyde in LAFTA, and Selected Alternatives, and their Costs, 1975

Product amounts in thousands of methanol-equivalent tons

Producing country	Methanol		Formaldehyde	
	Amount produced	Consuming countries	Amount produced	Consuming countries
Solution 1: Ŝ32.0 million (minimum);[a] Ŝ39.0 million (maximum)[b]—				
optimum solution under both sets of assumptions				
Colombia[c]	...	...	5.6	Colombia
Venezuela	172.4	All	131.1	All but Colombia
Solution 2: Ŝ32.1 million (minimum);[a] Ŝ39.1 million (maximum)[b]				
Venezuela	172.4	All	136.7	All
Solution 3: Ŝ32.4 million (minimum)[a]				
Chile	21.8	Argentina, Brazil, Chile, Colombia	...	...
Colombia[d]	...	...	5.6	Colombia
Venezuela	150.6	Mexico, Venezuela	131.1	All but Colombia
Solution 4: Ŝ32.6 million (minimum);[a] Ŝ39.3 million (maximum)[b]				
Colombia	...	...	5.6	Colombia
Mexico	19.4	Mexico	...	...
Venezuela	153.0	All but Mexico	131.1	All but Colombia
Solution 5: Ŝ33.3 million (minimum)[a]				
Chile	7.0	Chile	6.7	Chile
Colombia	...	...	5.6	Colombia
Mexico	19.4	Mexico	...	...
Venezuela	146.0	Argentina, Brazil, Colombia, Venezuela	124.4	Argentina, Brazil, Mexico, Peru, Uruguay, Venezuela
Solution 6: Ŝ33.7 million (minimum);[a] Ŝ43.4 million (maximum)[b]				
Chile	172.4	All	131.1	All but Colombia
Colombia[d]	...	...	5.6	Colombia
Solution 7: Ŝ34.1 million (minimum);[a] Ŝ44.1 million (maximum)[b]				
Chile	172.4	All	136.7	All
Solution 8: Ŝ34.0 million (minimum);[a] Ŝ42.9 million (maximum)[b]				
Chile	153.0	All but Mexico	131.1	All but Colombia
Colombia	...	...	5.6	Colombia
Mexico	19.4	Mexico	...	...
Solution 9: Ŝ34.2 million (minimum);[a] Ŝ43.2 million (maximum)[b]				
Chile	153.0	All but Mexico	136.7	All
Mexico	19.4	Mexico	...	...

Table 4-4. (*continued*)

Producing country	Methanol		Formaldehyde	
	Amount produced	Consuming countries	Amount produced	Consuming countries
Solution 10: Ŝ38.5 million (minimum);[a] *Ŝ49.2 million (maximum)*[b]— *national solution under both sets of assumptions*				
Argentina	15.5	Argentina	11.5	Argentina
Brazil	106.6	Brazil	95.2	Brazil
Chile	7.0	Chile	6.7	Chile
Colombia	...	...	5.6	Colombia[c]
Mexico	29.7	Mexico	10.3	Mexico
Venezuela	13.6	Colombia, Venezuela	7.4	Peru, Uruguay, Venezuela
Solution 11: Ŝ35.7 million (minimum)[a]				
Chile	172.4	All	...	...
Colombia[d]	...	...	136.7	All
Solution 12: Ŝ36.8 million (minimum);[a] *Ŝ48.6 million (maximum)*[b]— *import solution*				
United States	172.4	All	136.7	All
Solution 13: Ŝ38.4 million (minimum)[a]				
Chile	...	...	107.1	Argentina, Brazil, Uruguay
Colombia	...	...	29.6	Chile, Colombia, Mexico, Peru, Venezuela
United States	172.4	All	...	...
Solution 14: Ŝ50.4 million (maximum)[a]				
Chile	...	...	24.4	Argentina, Chile, Peru, Uruguay
Colombia	...	...	5.6	Colombia
United States	172.4	All	...	...
Venezuela	...	...	106.7	Brazil, Mexico, Venezuela

Note: Ecuador and Paraguay presented demand projections for neither product. Peru and Uruguay presented none for methanol.

 a. This is the cost under the minimum cost assumptions—minimum transport costs and free exchange rates.

 b. This is the cost under the maximum cost assumptions—1963 published transport rates and official exchange rates.

 c. Methanol input imported from Venezuela.

 d. Methanol input imported from Chile.

The results of the program, with the restriction in plant size, show that under both minimum and maximum cost assumptions, the lowest cost method for meeting 1975 demand is integrated methanol-formaldehyde plants in Venezuela (three methanol plants and seven formaldehyde plants) and a formaldehyde plant in Colombia, the methanol for which is imported from Venezuela (see Solution 1 in Table 4-4). A number of the alternative solutions are very close in cost to the optimum; they range from concentrating production in Venezuela to confining it to Chile.

A distribution of the entire range of solutions, by cost, is presented in Figure 4-1. The curves graph cumulative percent of local optima by their total cost. In the minimum cost alternative, about one-third of the local optima are within $1.5 million of the optimum, and in the maximum cost alternative, one-third are within $0.8 million. Taking into account the possibility of errors in the data—especially the $7 million spread between the minimum and maximum cost optima—one could argue that all but the 10 percent most expensive local optima could be considered the "best" distribution of plants. Even if the difference between the costs of the minimum and maximum cost solutions were halved, more than half of the minimum cost alternative solutions could be the optimum location. It is also evident that the distribution of solutions is quite skewed in both cases: The median of the local optima is far below the mean. This agrees with the findings of Vietorisz and Manne.[5]

Shadow Prices

The shadow prices associated with Solutions 1, 5, and 12 are shown in Table 4-5. They represent three important production alternatives: (a) to locate all production at the lowest cost sites (Solution 1); (b) to import all methanol and formaldehyde from the United States (Solution 12); or (c) to produce on a national basis (Solution 10)—that is, each country supplies its own demand, and no imports are allowed except from Venezuela into Colombia, which does not intend to produce methanol, and into Peru and Uruguay, which will not produce formaldehyde.

Because the price of methanol to Argentina and Brazil from Venezuela, the minimum cost location, is slightly higher than the import price, these two countries, from their own point of view, would be better off importing methanol from the United States. However, the price of the remaining 121,300 tons of methanol produced in Venezuela would be raised by $0.65 per ton, or a total of $79,000. The increase in cost to Argentina and Brazil of buying from Venezuela is $45,000, so the area taken as a whole

5. Thomas Vietorisz and Alan S. Manne, "Chemical Processes, Plant Location, and Economies of Scale," in Alan S. Manne and Harry M. Markowitz (eds.), *Studies in Process Analysis: Economy-Wide Production Capabilities* (John Wiley & Sons, 1963) pp. 152–53.

Figure 4-1. Cumulative Percentage of Alternative Patterns of Production of Methanol and Formaldehyde in LAFTA, by Annual Cost

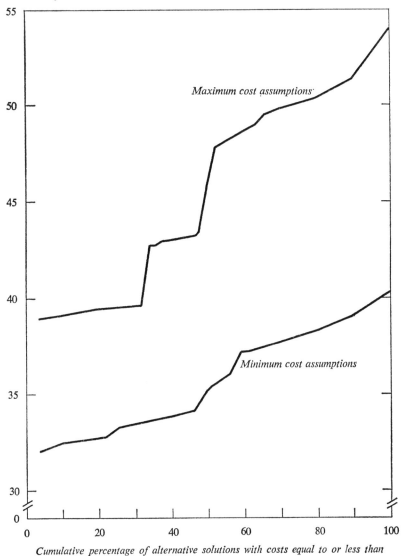

Total cost of solution to area (millions of simones per year)

Maximum cost assumptions

Minimum cost assumptions

Cumulative percentage of alternative solutions with costs equal to or less than amount shown

Table 4-5. Prices of Methanol and Formaldehyde from Selected Sources in LAFTA, 1975

Simones per methanol-equivalent metric ton

Consuming country	Optimum location[a]				Imports[b]				National production[c]			
	Methanol		Formaldehyde		Methanol		Formaldehyde		Methanol		Formaldehyde	
	Minimum costs	Maximum costs	Minimum costs	Maximum costs	Minimum costs	Maximum costs	Minimum costs	Maximum costs	Minimum costs	Maximum costs	Minimum costs	Maximum costs
Argentina	113.3	142.1	196.4	246.1	108.3	138.8	228.2	308.8	108.3	138.8	228.2	308.8
Brazil	121.7	147.6	216.6	263.8	119.4	139.6	253.7	334.4	119.4	139.6	253.7	334.4
Chile	98.5	122.4	172.6	212.0	109.6	151.6	192.1	261.1	147.6	251.2	287.1	328.1
Colombia	101.6	122.9	182.7	212.0	120.8	168.3	226.0	293.4	142.2	163.2	205.5	251.5
Ecuador	...	...	...	...	...	...	...	...	...	...	...	...
Mexico	107.3	127.6	184.8	223.5	108.7	137.3	219.3	286.3	125.9	125.9	219.3	286.3
Peru	...	...	170.0	223.1	...	...	200.0	272.1	...	...	218.1	270.4
Uruguay	...	...	180.7	234.1	...	...	211.9	290.4	...	...	228.8	281.7
Venezuela	84.9	85.2	137.5	138.1	108.0	147.0	211.9	296.9	125.5	125.5	175.7	175.7

a. Table 4-4, Solution 1.
b. Solution 12.
c. Solution 10.

127

is better off if Argentina and Brazil do not import from the United States. This case is exceptional, but certainly not inconsistent with the model. It highlights the possibility of resistance to integration by countries whose markets are sufficiently large to absorb the output of plants of optimum size, given favorable raw material costs, but that, when confronted with the choice between importing more cheaply from outside the region or more expensively from within it, see the possibility of getting the best of both worlds by a combination of autarky and reliance on imports from the developed countries. The linearized program minimizes *total* cost to the area, and it is possible that the cost to any single consuming country is higher when it buys from the optimum rather than from some other source. This situation could arise because the existence of economies of scale implies that average costs of production (and therefore long-run marginal costs) increase when output declines at any one location.

Influence of Exchange Rates

Table 4-6 shows the approximate indifference rates of exchange for minimum transport costs, assuming that all production for both products takes place at the specified location. The rates indicate, for example, that at minimum transport costs and an exchange rate of 5 escudos per simón, Chile is competitive with the United States in every market but that for methanol in Mexico; however, at minimum transport costs and an exchange rate of 3.5 escudos per simón, Chile could not compete with the United States in any market. By way of comparison with the data in Table 4-6, the following are the ratios of prices, and the indifference rates, at maximum transport costs and an exchange rate of 3.5 escudos per simón:

Country	Ratio of Chilean to U.S. price		Indifference exchange rate	
	Methanol	Formaldehyde	Methanol	Formaldehyde
Argentina	0.99	0.83	3.48	2.90
Brazil	1.06	0.86	3.70	3.01
Chile	0.82	0.89	2.87	3.12
Colombia	0.96	0.99	3.36	3.48
Mexico	1.18	1.02	4.12	3.56
Peru	...	0.89	...	3.12
Uruguay	...	0.83	...	2.90
Venezuela	0.96	0.90	3.36	3.15

Given the maximum costs, Chile is competitive with the United States at 3.5 escudos per simón everywhere except in Mexico in both products and in Brazil in methanol.

Capital Investment Requirements

The investment required between 1965 and 1975 to build the plants specified by the lowest cost pattern of production (Solution 1 in Table 4-4) and by the "modified national" alternative to it (Solution 5) is calculated from the cost and investment data presented by each country for the various plant sizes at their respective eligible production points.[6] Table 4-7 lists the results of these calculations for three alternatives.

Alternatives 1 and 3 both assume the optimum pattern; the difference is that Alternative 1 takes account of plants in existence in 1965 only in Venezuela and Colombia, while Alternative 3 assumes existing capacity everywhere, including that in Argentina, Brazil, and Mexico. Alternative 2, which corresponds to modified national production, also assumes existing capacity. The total investment required by 1975 to meet regional demand with regional production runs between $37 million (with, in addition, subsidies to existing plants so that they can compete with the new installations) and about $48 million. Most of the investment is for methanol production, which is relatively low in the region at present; this explains the small difference between capital requirements for Alternatives 1 and 3—that is, the small effect that inclusion of existing capacity has on total required investment in the 1965–75 period.

Welfare Benefits and Costs

As is noted in Appendix C, the welfare costs to other countries of a decision by any one country to produce for its own consumption (when it is not the optimum location) are not likely to be large, since such a small curtailment of their markets would not force the more efficient plants to

6. The limitation on size of plant should be noted. No data on fixed investment for methanol and formaldehyde plants are available for Brazil and Argentina, nor for the latter in Mexico. Therefore, required investment could be estimated only for the "modified national" solution, in which the possible locations of production are confined to countries that presented costs.

Table 4-6. Prices of Methanol and Formaldehyde and Indifference Exchange Rates in LAFTA, 1975[a]

Producing country,[a] product, price ratio, and currencies exchanged	Consuming country[b]							
	Argentina	Brazil	Chile	Colombia	Mexico	Peru	Uruguay	Venezuela
	Prices in simones per methanol-equivalent metric ton							
Venezuela[c]								
Methanol	113.3	121.7	98.5	101.6	107.3	...	...	84.9
Formaldehyde	196.2	216.4	172.4	182.5	184.6	169.8	180.5	137.3
Chile[d]								
Methanol	101.9	113.1	90.2	112.1	120.2	...	...	99.6
Formaldehyde	199.4	227.8	175.6	210.4	220.2	181.2	181.4	195.1
United States								
Methanol	108.3	119.4	109.6	120.8	108.7	...	...	108.0
Formaldehyde	228.2	253.7	192.1	226.0	219.3	200.0	211.9	211.9

Price ratios

Chilean to Venezuelan								
Methanol	0.90	0.93	0.92	1.10	1.12	. . .	. . .	1.17
Formaldehyde	1.02	1.05	1.02	1.15	1.19	1.07	1.00	1.42
Chilean to U.S.								
Methanol	0.94	0.95	0.82	0.93	1.10	. . .	. . .	0.92
Formaldehyde	0.87	0.90	0.91	0.93	1.00	0.91	0.86	0.92
Indifference exchange rates								
Escudos per bolívar[e]								
Methanol	0.99	1.03	1.02	1.22	1.24	. . .	. . .	1.29
Formaldehyde	1.13	1.16	1.13	1.28	1.32	1.19	1.11	1.58
Escudos per dollar[f]								
Methanol	4.70	4.75	4.10	4.65	5.50	. . .	. . .	4.60
Formaldehyde	4.35	4.50	4.55	4.65	5.00	4.55	4.30	4.60

a. Assuming minimum transport costs and free exchange rates; also assuming that, in each case, the given plant location produces all the methanol and formaldehyde for the area, except for Colombia, which produces its own when Venezuela and Chile are the producers for the area.
b. Ecuador presented no demand study.
c. The exchange rate is 4.5 bolivars per simón.
d. The exchange rate is 5.0 escudos per simón.
e. Calculated by multiplying the ratio of Chilean to Venezuelan price by 1.11 (the number of escudos per bolívar).
f. Calculated by multiplying the ratio of Chilean to U.S. price by 5 (the number of escudos per dollar).

Table 4-7. Total Investment Required in Production of Methanol and Formaldehyde in LAFTA, 1965–75

Simón amounts in millions; capacity in thousands of tons

Alternative[a] and producing country	Methanol Plants Number	Methanol Plants Capacity per plant[b]	Methanol Simones	Formaldehyde Plants Number	Formaldehyde Plants Capacity per plant[b]	Formaldehyde Simones	Total investment for period
Alternative 1							
Venezuela	3	60	Ŝ31.8	7	47	Ŝ7.3	Ŝ39.1
Colombia	...	...	...	1	10	3.5	3.5
Total	3	180	31.8	8	339	10.8	42.6
Alternative 2							
Chile	1	8	1.5	1	15	1.3	2.8
Colombia	...	...	...	1	10	3.5	3.5
Mexico	1	33	8.3	...	...	...	8.3
Venezuela	2 / 1	60 / 20	26.8	6	47	6.4	33.2
Total	5	181	36.6	8	307	11.2	47.8
Alternative 3							
Venezuela	2	60	26.8	6	47	6.4	33.2
Colombia	...	...	...	1	10	3.5	3.5
Total	2	120	26.8	7	292	9.9	36.7

Source: ECIEL, Martin Carnoy (ed.), *The Optimum Location of Specific Industries in the Latin American Free Trade Association* (*including Venezuela*) (Brookings Institution, 1966; processed).
 a. For definitions of alternatives, see p. 129.
 b. Except for total.

reduce output to levels at which unit costs would be greatly increased. If, however, all the producing countries studied here, plus Argentina and Brazil, should decide to serve themselves, even the most efficient plants, cut off from a large segment of their markets, would be forced to reduce their output to levels where unit costs would increase appreciably.

The data in Table 4-8 show the total increase in cost resulting from a national production policy, including the increase in cost to these four countries owing to the reduced scale of production at their sources of supply. The potential welfare benefits of buying from the optimum location within the area rather than importing from the United States total between

Table 4-8. Welfare Benefits and Costs of Selected Alternatives to Optimum Location of Production of Methanol and Formaldehyde in LAFTA Countries, 1975

Thousands of simones

Consuming country	Methanol		Formaldehyde		Total, both products	
	Production effect	Total	Production effect	Total	Production effect	Total
Buying from optimum location[a] versus U.S. imports[b]—minimum costs						
Argentina	−23	−23	316	342	293	319
Brazil	−28	−28	3,093	3,371	3,065	3,343
Chile	3	3	116	122	119	125
Colombia	8	9	194	218	202	227
Mexico	21	21	304	335	325	356
Peru	...	...	148	161	148	161
Uruguay	...	...	11	12	11	12
Venezuela	2	2	41	52	43	54
Total	−17	−16	4,222	4,613	4,206	4,597
Buying from optimum location[a] versus U.S. imports[b]—maximum costs						
Argentina	−11	−11	594	672	583	660
Brazil	−101	−98	5,273	6,012	5,173	5,914
Chile	7	8	270	302	277	310
Colombia	16	20	332	396	349	415
Mexico	173	180	506	577	680	758
Peru	...	...	245	273	245	273
Uruguay	...	...	18	20	18	20
Venezuela	4	5	88	95	92	100
Total	88	104	7,326	8,347	7,417	8,450
National production[c] versus buying from optimum location[a]—minimum costs						
Argentina	23	22	−316	−342	−293	−319
Brazil	28	27	−3,093	−3,371	−3,065	−3,343
Chile	−10	−12	−460	−615	−470	−627
Colombia	−15	−18	−112	−119	−127	−137
Mexico	−312	−340	−305	−335	−617	−675
Peru	...	...	−217	−247	−217	−247
Uruguay	...	...	−17	−20	−17	−20
Venezuela	−3	−3	−36	−41	−39	−45
Total	−289	−324	−4,557	−5,090	−4,845	−5,413
National production[c] versus buying from optimum location[a]—maximum costs						
Argentina	11	11	−594	−672	−583	−660
Brazil	101	98	−5,273	−6,012	−5,173	−5,914
Chile	−18	−29	−497	−636	−516	−665
Colombia	−15	−18	−190	−209	−205	−227
Mexico	...	...	−506	−577	−506	−577
Peru	...	...	−220	−244	−220	−244
Uruguay	...	...	−16	−18	−16	−18
Venezuela	−3	−3	−35	−40	−38	−43
Total	76	59	−7,331	−8,408	−7,256	−8,348

Sources: Tables 4-2 and 4-5.
a. Solution 1, Table 4-4.
b. Solution 12.
c. Solution 10.

$4.6 million and $8.5 million annually for the two products. The welfare cost of nationalistic production totals $5.4 million to $8.3 million. The size of this last figure is due largely to the welfare cost to Brazil of producing its own formaldehyde. Table 4-9 shows the nominal and effective tariff on methanol and formaldehyde in 1966.

Table 4-9. Nominal and Effective Tariffs on Methanol and Formaldehyde, by LAFTA Country, 1966

Percent[a]

| | Methanol | Formaldehyde | |
Country	nominal tariff	Nominal tariff	Effective tariff[b]
Argentina	86.5	206.5	n.a.
Brazil	31.6	86.6	n.a.
Chile	200.0	77.0	−30.8[c]
Colombia	20.0	30.0	53.7
Ecuador	71.0	41.0	n.a.
Mexico	12.2	18.4	n.a.
Peru	104.0	40.6	n.a.
Uruguay	160.0	38.0	n.a.
Venezuela	550.0	296.0	−17.9

Source: U.S. Department of Commerce, Bureau of International Commerce.
n.a. Not available.
a. Specific duties are translated into percent of Venezuelan c.i.f. price.
b. The effective tariff equals $\dfrac{t_f - (1 - v)t_m}{v}$,

where
t_f = nominal tariff on formaldehyde,
t_m = nominal tariff on methanol, and
v = value added to methanol cost by formaldehyde production per simón of formaldehyde output.
c. Minimum negative effective tariff.

CHAPTER FIVE

Tractors

THE MANUFACTURE OF TRACTORS is a complex process, which reaches into the highest levels of industrialization. Like automobiles, tractors require a ready supply of various types of steel, iron castings, electrical equipment, and machine tools. In Latin America, especially in the larger economies where some production of these goods takes place, these products are highly protected and their manufacture is characterized by a small number of producers.

The control over the importation of parts and raw materials for tractors is tightened by the requirements imposed by Latin American countries regarding the domestically produced elements of manufactures. Such content requirements are complex and their application ranges from total weight to value added.[1] Since content requirements, as well as import duties, differ from country to country, the structure of tractor firms in Argentina, Brazil, and Mexico (the three countries where tractors are now manufactured) varies considerably.[2]

1. The general development law in Mexico, for example, requires that the minimum level of value added in the plant itself be 10 percent of total *direct* cost. Direct cost includes raw materials, semifinished and finished parts, electrical energy, fuel, direct labor, and depreciation of equipment. The 10 percent minimum can be applied only to direct labor, fuel, and energy. Import content is limited to 40 percent of direct cost. For the evolution of Argentine content requirements, see José Maria Dagnino Pastore, *La Industria del Tractor en la Argentina* (Buenos Aires: Centro de Investigaciones Economicas, Instituto Torcuato di Tella, 1966), Chap. 1.

2. Bernard Munk, "Content Protection and the Theory of the Firm" (University of Chicago, March 1966; processed).

To present a reasonable estimate of the best location of tractor production in the Latin American Free Trade Association (LAFTA), this chapter begins with an analysis of demand projections, and proceeds to compare costs in LAFTA's producing countries with prices in third countries. Only the institutes in Argentina and Brazil estimated tractor production costs, so Mexico cannot be included in the study as a possible production point.

Nevertheless, Mexico clearly must figure in regional plans for tractor production. At the time the data were being collected, however, Mexican tractor production was essentially an assembly operation and its costs are thus not comparable with those for Argentina and Brazil. A future study would have to take Mexican production into account.

Standardization of Tractor Size

Demand projections, cost projections, and transport rates are all estimated in terms of a tractor of 50 horsepower at the pulley (belt). This does not imply that the study is relevant only if all tractors produced in Latin America are 50-horsepower units. It does imply a direct relation between the best locations for the production of a standard size tractor and for a range of sizes—that is, that the country with an advantage in the production of a 50-horsepower tractor also has an advantage in 35-horsepower and 80-horsepower tractors. While standardization on the demand side overestimates considerably the size of the largest feasible plant in Latin America in terms of one size of tractor, it is also reasonable to assume that in certain size ranges, there is enough interchangeability in production that, given 1975 projected demand, very large plants could still operate near capacity.

Only the Instituto di Tella (Argentina) and Nacional Financiera (Mexico) reported tractor purchases in 1963 and the projected demand in 1975 corrected for horsepower differences. Since "quality" varies widely among tractors of different sizes, any meaningful projection of the demand for tractors requires standardization on the basis of market valuation of these quality differentials. Assuming that average prices of various size tractors in an economy accurately reflect their value to that economy, the projected number of the different size tractors could be converted into a standard size through a horsepower-price relationship in each country. Given such a relationship, any size tractor could be made equivalent to any other size, not necessarily linearly. The details of the procedure for standardizing tractor sizes are given in Appendix D.

Projected Demand for Tractors

Table 5-1 summarizes the projected growth of demand by LAFTA countries (except Venezuela, for which no estimates were made) between 1963 and 1975. The largest current and potential consumers of tractors are Argentina, Brazil, and Mexico. Although Mexico had no plants in 1963, two have gone into production since that time. For the most part, projections of the number of tractors were made by adding changes in the stock of tractors (estimated on the basis of cultivated area and tractors per 1,000 hectares of cultivated area) to the demand for replacement of depreciated stock. It should be clear that projections of cultivated area alone may either overestimate increases in tractor stock, as in Brazil, or seriously underestimate them, as in Argentina. If Argentina's agricultural price policy is changed, for example, tractor demand could be double the projection for 1975 shown in Table 5-1. As the figures now appear, Argentine consump-

Table 5-1. Purchases of Tractors in 1963 and Projected Demand for Tractors in 1975, in LAFTA Countries

50-horsepower-equivalent units

Country	1963	1975[a]
Argentina[b]	12,435	16,337
Brazil	7,648	25,542
Chile	1,652	2,674
Colombia	1,342	3,670
Ecuador	83	145
Mexico[b,c]	6,175	10,182
Paraguay[d]	124	457
Peru[e]	570	814
Uruguay[d]	1,453[f]	2,623
Total	31,482	62,444

Source: Table D-2 data multiplied by demand projections presented in ECIEL, *The Demand for Chemical Fertilizers, Tractors, Paper and Pulp, Milk Concentrates, and Lathes in the Latin American Free Trade Association (including Venezuela)* (Brookings Institution, 1966; processed).

a. Midpoint of minimum and maximum projections. Range for total in 1975: 55,496–69,630.

b. No conversion made, since original results are in terms of 50-horsepower tractors.

c. Includes used tractors (imports) in 1963.

d. Argentine consumption structure used.

e. Colombian consumption structure used.

f. 1961.

tion increases only slightly between 1963 and 1975. In addition, the demand projections for Mexico may be distorted by the inclusion of used tractor imports in the 1975 estimates. In 1963, used units accounted for 23 percent of total wheel tractor consumption. The projections assume perfect substitution between new and used tractors coming into Mexico. While this is an extreme assumption, it would be just as extreme to assume that, if imports of used tractors ceased, new tractor purchases would not increase. Reality lies somewhere between the two assumptions, and the projection shown in Table 5-1 could be considered an overestimate.

Between 1963 and 1975, the total demand for tractors in LAFTA (not including Venezuela) is projected almost to double from 31,000 to 62,000 50-horsepower-equivalent units.[3] Unlike chemicals and paper, in which existing capacity is a small fraction of 1975 demand, present capacity for tractor production in Argentina and Brazil alone is approximately 52,000 units. If Mexican capacity and the possibility of additional shifts are included, total available capacity at present is probably larger than maximum projected demand in 1975 (69,630 compared with 62,444 units). If economies of scale in tractor manufacture are to be realized as a result of an optimum pattern of production, certain portions of existing capacity must be consolidated.

How the consolidation takes place depends in part on the relative costs of tractor production in the producing countries. Tables 5-2 and 5-3 summarize the cost structures for Argentina and Brazil. Although the proportions of total cost are not corrected to the standard unit, the unit costs shown in Table 5-3 are for 50-horsepower-equivalent tractors in each plant. Because the Argentine data are confidential, it is not possible to connect the cost breakdown (percentage) figures and the unit cost by plant.

The percentages for various types of cost for the Argentine and Brazilian plants are quite similar. Materials, which are the most important single element of costs, seem to be a slightly higher proportion of total cost in Brazil, especially considering that total costs in Argentina are shown net of opportunity costs of capital. If opportunity cost were included, the percentage for materials would fall by a few points. Two things may explain this difference: (1) In the absence of data, the cost of marketing and sales is taken as a constant 20 percent of total cost in Brazil. While this ratio

---

3. For simplicity's sake, any reference hereafter to tractors or units is to be understood to mean tractors or units of 50-horsepower equivalent.

Table 5-2. Structure of Costs of Production of Tractors, Uncorrected for Horsepower, by Firm, Argentina, 1963

Percent of total cost

Category of cost	Argentine firms[a]				
	A	B	C	D	E
Materials	50.32	44.34	60.85	48.10	75.42
Raw materials					
Domestic	3.39	0.06	0.54	2.87	2.42
Imported	7.92	1.19	...	7.81	1.82
Semifinished products					
Domestic	...	...	4.78	2.87	3.09
Imported	0.74	...	...	7.81	4.55
Parts and components					
Domestic	25.14	22.41	42.26	10.39	47.08
Imported	13.13	20.68	13.27	16.35	16.46
Direct labor	2.98	1.04	3.50	1.48	1.86
Production	2.04	0.53	2.76	1.11	1.50
Assembly	0.94	0.51	0.74	0.37	0.36
General costs of fabrication					
Services	2.47	3.10	0.76	1.88	1.43
Supplies	2.40	1.23	0.05	...	0.26
Depreciation charged to fabrication	3.60	4.24	4.86	5.89	1.12
Other general costs of fabrication	7.06	6.16	5.97	4.82	4.13
General expenditures	0.07	...	0.06	1.19	0.90
Taxes	3.11	0.50	0.53	0.20	0.39
General costs of commercialization	9.23	22.79	1.29	17.15	1.23
Taxes	1.85	1.29	0.53	0.51	0.52
Sales commission	16.91	15.31	21.60	18.78	12.80
Total cost of production (not including opportunity costs)[b]	100.00	100.00	100.00	100.00	100.00
Total import content[c]	21.79	21.87	18.05	31.97	22.83

Source: José Maria Dagnino Pastore, *La Industria del Tractor en Argentina* (Buenos Aires: Centro de Investigaciones Económicas, Instituto Torcuato di Tella, 1966), p. 9.27.

a. Breakdown is for 1963 production levels, not capacity.

b. Opportunity cost of capital is included in the total price of Table 5-4, but is not available as a percent of total cost.

c. Includes only current material inputs.

is approximately the average for the Argentine plants, Brazilian commercialization costs could be different. If they are higher, materials would form a lower percentage of the total and the wholesale price (equal here to total cost) would be higher. (2) In both countries, the plants with higher percentages in materials are apparently those with a larger element of assembly

Table 5-3. Structure of Costs of Production of Tractors, Uncorrected for Horsepower, by Firm, Brazil, 1965

Percent of total cost

	Plant 1		Plant 2	
Category	Actual production, 1,407 units	Capacity, 5,000 units	Actual production, 3,600 units	Capacity, 8,500 units
Materials	52.3	58.5	64.5	67.6
Raw materials	2.6	3.0	0.0	0.0
Component parts				
Imported	4.2	4.7	5.4	5.7
Domestic	45.4	50.8	58.8	61.6
Auxiliary parts	0.0	0.0	0.3	0.3
Services	0.5	0.6	0.1	0.1
Energy	0.4	0.4	0.0	0.0
Fuel	0.1	0.2	0.0	0.0
Direct labor	0.8	0.9	0.3	0.3
Salaries	0.5	0.5	0.2	0.2
Social charges	0.3	0.4	0.1	0.1
General costs of production	12.0	10.8	6.6	6.9
Maintenance	0.3	0.3	0.2	0.3
Depreciation	8.4	9.4	1.1	1.1
Indirect labor	0.7	0.2	0.2	0.1
Social charges	0.7	0.2	0.0	0.0
Production engineering	1.8	0.6	0.7	0.7
Taxes	0.0	0.0	4.4	4.7
Administration expenses	3.2	1.0	5.2	2.3
Payroll	1.3	0.4	1.4	0.6
Social charges	0.6	0.2	0.6	0.3
Others	1.3	0.4	3.2	1.4
Opportunity cost of capital[a]	11.2	8.2	3.2	2.7
Total costs	80.0	80.0	80.0	80.0
Commercialization costs (0.25 costs)	20.0	20.0	20.0	20.0
Total costs plus commercialization costs	100.0	100.0	100.0	100.0
Unit cost				
Cruzeiros (thousands)	10,524	9,410	9,427	8,990
Simones[b]	5,689	5,086	5,096	4,859
Adjusted[c]	5,888	5,264	5,733	5,466

Source: Universidade de São Paulo, Faculdade de Ciencias Economicas e Administraçao, *Trator Agricola* (São Paulo: Universidade de São Paulo, 1966).

a. On the basis of 8 percent.

b. 1 simón equals 1,850 cruzeiros (official rate, July 1965).

c. Plant 1 costs are for a 47-horsepower tractor and Plant 2 costs for a 40.5-horsepower tractor (at the pulley). Using equation (3) to adjust total cost to 50 horsepower yields an adjustment factor of 1.035 for Plant 1 and 1.125 for Plant 2.

relative to production. The most obvious example is the Brazilian plant with an 8,500 unit capacity, which apparently is entirely an assembly operation (that is, all materials are finished components).

The level of domestic content is considerably higher in Brazil than in Argentina. Imported materials represent only about 5 percent of total cost in the two Brazilian plants, but the Argentine proportion varies between 13 and 30 percent. The effect of such a difference is to raise Brazilian costs relative to Argentine costs; for, if content requirements forced Argentina, with its higher costs, to substitute domestic materials to the extent that its proportion of imported materials matched Brazil's, its production costs would be much higher relative to Brazil's. In fact, increases in domestic content requirements in Argentina since 1963 have undoubtedly contributed to rises in real costs. With the 1963 year-end simón cost at the official exchange rate at 100, the cost of material to the tractor industry rose to 123 in June 1965 and tractor list price (in simones) to 121. However, deflating by official rates may be very misleading: While the official rate of pesos to the simón rose 27 percent from December 1963 to July 1965, the black market rate almost doubled, and the cost of living and wholesale prices each rose about 40 percent. Deflating by the average price rise, real tractor list prices increased only 6.5 percent, and real material costs, 14 percent.[4] If black market rates are used to deflate tractor costs or prices, real costs and prices fell by about 25 percent. In a comparison of costs in Brazil (July 1965) and in Argentina (December 1963), the importance of real increases in Argentine costs becomes apparent.

Table 5-4 shows costs of production of a tractor in the plants of various size in Argentina and Brazil for output at capacity and at the level of the time the data were taken. List prices are also shown for Argentina, Italy, Great Britain, and the United States. Costs at actual production levels are essentially equal in Brazil and Argentina at official rates of exchange. List prices in these two countries are also very similar and are considerably higher than prices in Europe and the United States. The primary difference between production in Argentina and Brazil on the one hand and in the more developed countries on the other is the scale of the plant. John Deere, the largest U.S. tractor manufacturer, produces about 25,000 units

---

4. Tractor list price and material cost data are provided by an anonymous U.S. tractor manufacturer. Exchange rate and average price level data are from W. R. Grace and Co., "Latin American Exchange Rates: Monthly Report" (memorandum to Mr. J. P. Grace, Jr., January 1964 and August 1965; processed).

Table 5-4. Costs of Production and Price per Tractor in Selected Countries

| | Total cost of production[a] | | | | |
| | At actual production level | | At plant capacity | | |
Country	Simones	Number of units	Simones	Number of units	Price
Argentina[b]					
Plant 1	11,629	918	5,694	3,300	
Plant 2	7,152	1,061	6,904	1,730	
Plant 3	6,802	1,798	5,610	3,520	$6,150[c]
Plant 4	6,113	2,720	5,334	4,520	
Plant 5	5,599	4,617	4,718	12,300	
Brazil[d]					
Plant 1	5,888	1,407	5,264	5,000	
Plant 2	5,733	3,600	5,466	8,400	
Italy	n.a.	...	n.a.	...	3,038[e]
Great Britain	n.a.	...	n.a.	...	2,460[f]
United States	n.a.	...	n.a.	...	4,647[g]

Sources: Actual production costs—Argentina, Dagnino Pastore, *La Industria del Tractor*, pp. 4.35, 4.37, 7.11, 7.12, 7.17; Brazil, Table 5-3. Prices—Dagnino Pastore, *La Industria del Tractor*, p. 4.67.
n.a. Not available.
a. Includes commercialization costs.
b. Data are for 1963; exchange rate is 135 pesos per simón.
c. Price is five-plant average, derived from equation (3); see App. D, p. 252.
d. Data are for 1965; exchange rate is 1,850 cruzeiros per simón.
e. Price as of September 1964 for OM 513 tractor.
f. Price as of first quarter 1964, for Massey-Ferguson 65 tractor.
g. Average price of 50-horsepower diesel standard tractor, derived from equation (1); see App. D, p. 252.

annually in each of its two Iowa plants; Massey-Ferguson, the largest British firm, produces about 80,000 tractors annually in one plant.[5]

Prices

In the linearized programming model, prices in Brazil and Argentina are compared with the average price of a tractor imported from the United States. It is clear from Table 5-4 that imports from Europe are less expensive; the European tractor probably has fewer extras and is more com-

5. U.S. tractor prices are so much higher than British prices because (1) U.S. manufacturers produce more varieties of tractors to meet specific needs of U.S. farmers (who have the higher incomes with which to satisfy their demands); and (2) U.S. firms retool more often than the British, so depreciation and amortization of equipment are more rapid. Steel prices are almost the same in the two countries; and wage differences are probably not a contributing factor because labor plays only a small part in tractor cost.

parable with Argentine and Brazilian models. Despite the lower price of British tractors, however, Argentina and Brazil, in the years before they began manufacturing tractors, imported largely from the United States and European countries other than Britain. In the 1951–57 period, West Germany, the United States, Italy, and France were the leading tractor exporters to Argentina, and in 1953–60, the United States was by far the largest exporter of tractors to Brazil, followed by West Germany, Great Britain, Italy, Sweden, and Czechoslovakia.[6] It is not necessary, then, to compare LAFTA production with the lowest cost foreign source (Great Britain) in order to estimate the welfare gains or losses over importing. The United States is chosen as the country for comparison simply because U.S. prices are used for this purpose in the other product studies. Because of the use of U.S. tractor prices described above, the welfare gains to regional production relative to importing may be considered maximum gains to LAFTA for this particular product.

Optimum Location of Production

From the production costs (Tables 5-2 and 5-3), the fixed demands (Table 5-1), and transportation costs between production points (United States, Argentina, and Brazil) and consumption points in LAFTA,[7] the minimum cost locations of production for LAFTA consumption can be determined. The difficulty encountered in using Brazilian production cost curves is that unit costs in the larger plant (2) are higher than those in the smaller plant (1). Total costs in the two plants at capacity yield a long-run curve with diseconomies of scale. This result is considered unrepresentative, so the short-run costs for Plant 2 are taken as a proxy for a Brazilian long-run cost curve. Plant 2 also covers a range of output more relevant for the comparison. The marginal cost for Plant 1 is $268 less than that for Plant 2, so that taking the latter's curve as representative may distort

6. República de Argentina, Secretaria de Estada de Hacienda, Dirección Nacional dc Estadística y Censo, *Comercio Exterior* (annual issues for the years 1951–57); Estados Unidos do Brazil, Ministerio da Fazenda, Servicio de Estatística Económica e Financiera, *Comercio Exterior do Brazil* (annual issues for the years 1953–60).

7. ECIEL, Martin Carnoy (ed.), *The Optimum Location of Specific Industries in the Latin American Free Trade Association (including Venezuela)*, Vol. 1: *Tractors* (Brookings Institution, 1966; processed), Table 14.

Brazilian costs upward. The curves for the two plants show both much smaller changes in average cost with changes in output and higher marginal costs than the Argentine long-run curve.

The significance of such differences becomes clear in the estimate of the optimum location of production and the shadow prices associated with alternative production points. The linear programming model is solved here for both sets of demand projections in 1975, for two rates of exchange of Argentine pesos relative to Brazilian cruzeiros and U.S. dollars, and for two plant sizes—unlimited (62,000 units) and 20,000 units. Only one set of transport rates is used because of the similarity between published rates and formula-determined rates.[8] Table 5-5 gives the resulting optimum solutions, and some alternatives to it.

The solutions indicate that the ability of Latin America to compete with the United States in tractors and the optimum location of production within the area are sensitive to exchange rates, but that the maximum plant size allowed is not crucial for establishing the optimum pattern. The best location for production in 1970 and 1975 is Argentina, although, as Table 5-6 demonstrates, Argentina's advantage over the United States is rather narrow at the official rate of exchange, at which Argentina would, in fact, lose the Mexican market. Because U.S. tractor prices are much higher than those of European manufacturers, Argentina's advantage over the United States does not imply an advantage over all foreign imports. Quite to the contrary: Even under the most favorable circumstances—production at the optimum location and the higher peso-to-simón ratio—an Argentine tractor would cost about $1,000 more than a similar imported British model.

Even under the circumstances most advantageous to it (an exchange rate of 135 pesos per simón and a limitation of 20,000 units on plant size), confining tractor production to Brazil would still cost the area over 17 percent more than the optimum pattern. The possible error in choosing the Plant 2 over the Plant 1 curve is approximately 5 percent, but even if it were corrected, a 10 percent difference in c.i.f. wholesale prices from the two sources would still remain at official rates of exchange (see Table 5-7). The cost of national production, in which Brazil produces only for its own market, is much smaller. In the case most favorable to Brazil, the annual cost to the area would be Ŝ19 million, borne almost entirely by Brazil

8. See App. B.

Table 5-5. Optimum Location of Production of Tractors in LAFTA, and Selected Alternatives, and their Costs, 1975

Thousands of tractors; millions of simones

Solution and producing country	Number of tractors produced	Consuming countries	Cost, by plant size limit Unlimited (62,000)	20,000
155 pesos and 1,850 cruzeiros per simón				
Solution 1—optimum solution			Ŝ251.1	Ŝ262.7
Argentina	62.4	All		
Solution 2			342.1	347.1
Brazil	62.4	All		
Solution 3—import solution			321.9	321.9
United States	62.4	All		
Solution 4—national solution			288.0	293.5
Brazil	25.5	Brazil		
Argentina	36.9	All other		
135 pesos and 1,850 cruzeiros per simón				
Solution 1—optimum solution			287.2	296.1
United States	10.2	Mexico		
Argentina	52.2	All others		
Solution 2			286.7	299.9
Argentina	62.4	All		
Solution 3			342.1	347.1
Brazil	62.4	All		
Solution 4—import solution			321.9	321.9
United States	62.4	All		
Solution 5—national solution			309.3	315.4
Brazil	25.5	Brazil		
Argentina	36.9	All others		

Note: Venezuela did not present a demand study for tractors, and is therefore not included in these solutions.

itself. The secondary effect of reducing total Argentine production, when plants are limited to 20,000 units, is negligible.

The prices given in Tables 5-6 and 5-7 show that the increased production called forth by expanded markets can exert significant downward pressure on the price of tractors manufactured in Latin America. Existing plants in Argentina and Brazil (1964) produce annually between 1,000 and 4,000 tractors of all sizes.

Table 5-6. Tractor Prices Associated with Various Patterns of Production, for LAFTA Countries, and Selected Exchange Rates, 1975[a]

Simones

Consuming country	Optimum location[b]		Imports from the United States	National production[c]	
	155 pesos/simón	135 pesos/simón		155 pesos/simón	135 pesos/simón
Argentina	4,074	4,671	5,117	4,037	4,634
Brazil	4,177	4,773	5,297	5,440	5,440
Chile	4,138	4,734	5,299	4,101	4,697
Colombia	4,444	5,040	5,196	4,407	5,003
Ecuador	4,431	5,027	5,248	4,394	4,990
Mexico	4,428	5,024	4,802	4,391	4,987
Paraguay	4,090	4,687	5,131	4,053	4,650
Peru	4,439	5,036	5,362	4,402	4,999
Uruguay	4,129	4,725	5,118	4,092	4,688

Source: Table 5-5.
a. Plant size is limited to 20,000 units.
b. Argentina.
c. Brazil produces for domestic market; Argentina for all others. Because of the plant size limitation, Argentine prices under national production are $37 lower than prices from the optimum location. There is less excess capacity in the national production case than in the optimum solution.

The Influence of Exchange Rates

Table 5-7 estimates, by the use of indifference exchange rates, the degree of advantage of Argentine over Brazilian and U.S. tractor production. The rates reflect c.i.f. wholesale price differentials. The table shows that the ratio of Argentine pesos to Brazilian cruzeiros is well below the ratio of official exchange rates implied in the simón prices. The price ratios can be applied to relative exchange rates at any point in time, assuming that costs fluctuate to the same degree as the rates. A small experiment can reveal whether, at prices of July 1965 (the date of the Brazilian study) and at the official exchange rate between pesos and cruzeiros, Argentine tractors could be competitive in Brazil. When $4,773 (the Brazilian price of Argentine tractors) is multiplied by 1.21 (the increase in tractor list price, deflated by the increase in the official exchange rate between January 1, 1964 and June 30, 1965), the result is $5,775; this indicates that at official rates of exchange, Argentina could not compete in Brazil. In fact, at official rates, Argentina could not compete with either Brazil or the United States in any LAFTA country. If, however, Argentina had altered official rates in response to changes in the average price level, the relationship of Argentine to Brazilian and U.S. tractor prices would have changed by only 6.5 per-

Table 5-7. Comparative Prices of Tractors Produced in Argentina, Brazil, and the United States, by Consuming Country, 1975, and Indifference Exchange Rates[a]

Simones

Consuming country	Production point			Ratio of Argentine to Brazilian price	Ratio of Argentine to U.S. price	Indifference exchange rates	
	Argentina[b]	Brazil[c]	United States			Pesos per cruzeiro[d]	Pesos per dollar[e]
Argentina	4,671	5,520	5,117	0.85	0.91	0.062	123
Brazl	4,773	5,418	5,297	0.88	0.90	0.064	122
Chile	4,734	5,596	5,299	0.85	0.90	0.062	122
Colombia	5,040	5,861	5,196	0.86	0.97	0.063	131
Ecuador	5,027	5,873	5,248	0.86	0.96	0.063	130
Mexico	5,024	5,853	4,802	0.86	1.04	0.063	140
Paraguay	4,687	5,514	5,131	0.85	0.91	0.062	123
Peru	5,036	5,881	5,362	0.86	0.94	0.063	127
Uruguay	4,725	5,489	5,118	0.86	0.92	0.063	124

a. Assumes 20.000 unit limit on plant capacity, and that all tractor production takes place at each production point.
b. 135 pesos per simón.
c. 1,850 cruzei·os per simón.
d. The ratio of Argentine to Brazilian prices times 0.073 (the number of pesos per cruzeiro).
e. The ratio of Argentine to U.S. prices times 135 (the number of pesos per U.S. dollar).

147

cent. Because of Argentina's weakening exchange reserve position in the first six months of 1965, there is reason to believe that the official rate overvalued the currency, and that subsequent changes in it have put Argentine tractor producers in a more favorable position relative to their Brazilian and U.S. counterparts.

Welfare Benefits and Costs

Table 5-8 shows the welfare benefits and costs of various production policies in the area. The benefit of buying from the optimum location in the region, rather than importing from the United States, is approximately 18 percent of total costs of tractor production and transport in the free exchange rate case, and 8 percent when the official exchange rates are assumed. The "production" cost of national production rather than buying from the optimum location is between $15 million and $25 million annually, or between 5 and 9 percent of total cost. Table 5-9 shows tariff rates on 50-horsepower tractors by country in 1966.

Summary

Tractor production in Latin America is currently characterized by many small plants producing for local markets at prices approximately 40 percent higher than the United States c.i.f. price (net of tariffs), and more than 100 percent higher than the British price. Current capacity in Argentina, Brazil, and Mexico is sufficient to fill 1975 projected demand; and at present levels of production and exchange rates the cost of a 50-horsepower tractor is slightly lower in Brazil than in Argentina, given the size of the plant. With expanded production, however, Argentine economies of scale would appear to be greater and, at higher levels of output, they would lead to lower costs than in Brazil. This may be due, it should be noted, to the nature of the sampled plants in Brazil, which apparently operate much more as assembly operations than those in Argentina. Economies of scale would be expected to be greater in the more integrated production process.

Although the results of the linear program (which seeks cost minimization for the area) indicate that Argentina is the "best" location of produc-

Table 5-8. Welfare Benefits and Costs of Selected Alternatives to Optimum Location of Production of Tractors in LAFTA Countries, under Selected Assumptions about Exchange Rates, 1975

Thousands of simones[a]

Consuming country	Buying from optimum location versus importing		National production versus buying from optimum	
	Production effect	Total	Production effect	Total
	155 pesos and 1,850 cruzeiros per simón[b]			
Argentina	13,281	15,008	...	...
Brazil	22,368	25,499	−24,498	−28,173
Chile	2,458	2,802	...	...
Colombia	2,302	2,509	...	...
Ecuador	71	77	...	...
Mexico	3,618	3,758	...	...
Paraguay	327	370	...	...
Peru	604	670	...	...
Uruguay	2,040	2,284	...	...
Total	47,069	52,977	−24,498	−28,173
	135 pesos and 1,850 cruzeiros per simón[b]			
Argentina	6,852	7,195	...	...
Brazil	12,171	12,901	−14,605	−15,628
Chile	1,406	1,490	...	...
Colombia	559	571	...	...
Ecuador	20	20	...	...
Mexico	...	...	...	...
Paraguay	169	177	...	...
Peru	242	249	...	...
Uruguay	983	1,022	...	...
Total	22,402	23,625	−14,605	−15,628

a. Plant size is limited to 20,000 50-horsepower units.
b. Transport costs are the same for the two alternatives.

tion to supply 1975 demand for tractors in LAFTA, several factors could affect this solution.

First, the Argentine cost estimate is made for December 1964 and the Brazilian estimate for June 1965. An adjustment of Argentine costs to the latter date makes Argentina a higher cost producer than either Brazil or the United States at the official rate of exchange of pesos for simones. However, the change in the official rate in Argentina between these dates does not reflect changes in price level in the same period. This points up

Table 5-9. Import Duties on Wheeled, 50-Horsepower Agricultural Tractors in LAFTA Countries, 1966

Percent of c.i.f. value

Country	For LAFTA members	For other countries
Argentina	301.0	301.0
Brazil	39.4	39.4
Chile	57.9	57.9
Colombia	2.0	2.0
Ecuador	0.0	34.0
Mexico	4.4	4.4
Paraguay	40.0	40.0
Peru	10.0	20.4
Uruguay	6.0	45.6

Source: U.S. Department of Commerce, Bureau of International Commerce.

the importance of the exchange rate in determining competitive advantage in a given product and in all products combined.

Second, the limitation of plant size to 20,000 units annually does not affect the optimum solution, and the solution is not very sensitive to plant size. But at the very small sizes of plant now in operation, the optimum would shift to importation.

Third, although at high levels of output Argentine tractors could be competitive with U.S. imports, the optimum location of production would be in Great Britain if it were included as a potential supplier to the area. Even at much larger average plant size, Latin American producers could not compete with the British.

Finally, Mexican production possibilities are not considered in the solution to the model.

No matter who has the competitive advantage within Latin America, the price of tractors domestically produced cannot fall without a much larger scale of production. Achievement of such a scale will follow from the growth of the market, but average plant size must also increase. Since the industry is one in which present capacity is large relative to future demand, competition among producers in different countries in the area will probably lead to concentration of production in fewer firms.

CHAPTER SIX

Lathes

MACHINE TOOLS ARE A GROUP of products that is particularly difficult to define, but that, at the same time, typify the goods in which Latin American economies can hope to expand their trade. This is a new industry in the region, still confined to its large, industrial countries. Its newness is illustrated by a description of the industry in 1946.[1] Hughlett points out that World War II provided unprecedented stimulus to metalworking industries and to the demand for machine tools. However, the small size of domestic markets and the complex techniques involved presented obstacles to any appreciable local production of basic industrial equipment. In Argentina, indeed, the new industry was not expected to survive the war; and, in any case, its products, "although reputed to be of fair quality, [did] not equal American or European machine tools."[2] In a milder form, this judgment applied to Brazil, which had the most developed machine tool industry in Latin America in 1946, producing about $5 million of equipment in that year.

In recent years, however, Argentina, Brazil, and, to a much lesser extent, Mexico have become major producers of machine tools. Argentina manufactured 9,414 machine tools in 1960, of which 3,720 were lathes, including 2,520 universal parallel lathes. In the same year, Brazil produced 8,943

1. Lloyd Hughlett, *Industrialization in Latin America* (McGraw-Hill, 1946), Chap. 7.
2. *Ibid.*, p. 197. Universal parallel lathes are comparable to toolroom or engine lathes in the United States.

machine tools in 1960, of which 3,766 were lathes including 2,238 universal parallel lathes; in addition, about 1,300 lathes were imported.[3] Mexico, on the other hand, produced a total of 2,360 machine tools from 1955 to 1964, of which 128 were lathes. In the same period, 12,964 lathes were imported.[4]

The demand projections to 1975 for countries of the Latin American Free Trade Association (LAFTA) are based on a study made by the Economic Commission for Latin America (ECLA) on machine tools in Brazil.[5] This very complete work yields data that permit the following steps in estimating demand:

1. The stock of machine tools is projected, using either projections of the planning agency of the country concerned, or a stable relationship of employees to machine tools used in metal transforming industries, or both.

2. In order to estimate the future demand for labor in the metal transforming sector, a relationship is found between value of production and the estimated number of employees, taking account of changes in productivity.

3. The stock of lathes is taken as a fixed proportion of the projection of the stock of machine tools, and the stock of universal parallel lathes is taken as a fixed percentage of the stock of lathes.

4. Changes in the stock of parallel lathes between 1965 and 1975 are assumed to represent the annual expansion demand.

5. Replacement demand is estimated from the average life of lathes and the average age of the stock in the base year.[6]

Projections of Demand and Cost Estimates

The Instituto de Economía de la Universidad Nacional de Chile made the most detailed projections for this study, estimating the future demand

3. ECLA, *La Fabricación de Maquinarias y Equipos Industriales en América Latina*, *II. Máquinas-Herramientas en el Brasil*, E/CN.12/633 (1962), Tables 20 and 34, and *IV. Las Máquinas-Herramientas en la Argentina*, E/CN.12/747 (1967), Table 26.

4. See ECIEL, *The Demand for Chemical Fertilizers, Tractors, Paper and Pulp, Milk Concentrates, and Lathes in the Latin American Free Trade Association (including Venezuela)* (Brookings Institution, 1966; processed). The Mexican section is produced by Gerencia de Programación Industrial, Nacional Financiera, S.A.

5. ECLA, *La Fabricación de Maquinarias: Brasil*, E/CN.12/633.

6. For a detailed derivation of projected demand in LAFTA countries, see ECIEL, *Demand for Chemical Fertilizers*.

Table 6-1. Projected Demand for Universal Parallel Lathes in LAFTA, 1975[a]

Number of lathes

Country	Minimum	Maximum
Argentina[b]	2,278	2,386
Brazil	2,264	2,721
Chile[c]	177	240
Colombia	429	987
Mexico	2,125	2,835
Paraguay	15	20
Total	7,288	9,189

Source: ECIEL, *The Demand for Chemical Fertilizers, Tractors, Paper and Pulp, Milk Concentrates, and Lathes in the Latin American Free Trade Association (including Venezuela)* (Brookings Institution, 1966; processed).

a. All universal parallel lathes are assumed to be 1,500 millimeters between points.

b. Taken as 48 percent of the projected demand for lathes as shown in Tables 3 and 6 of the Argentine study in ECIEL, *The Demand for Chemical Fertilizers.*

c. Two-thirds of the projected demand for type A (1,000 millimeter) and four-thirds of demand for type C added to demand for type B (1,500 millimeter).

for parallel lathes by size. For other projections the demand for parallel lathes of all sizes is considered to be represented by the demand for lathes 1,500 millimeters between points, a medium size that should not be very different from the average size used. The projections are shown in Table 6-1.

The total demand for the area is projected to be 8,239 universal parallel lathes in 1975 (midpoint of minimum and maximum projections). This estimate is understated because four countries, lacking data, did not present projections and because the estimate for Colombia is very approximate. Despite these possible distortions and the potential error from the arbitrary assumption that all lathes are standard 1,500 millimeter units, these fixed demands are used in the linearized programming model to determine the pattern of production that minimizes the cost of lathes to the area.

Costs of production are estimated for three countries: Argentina, Brazil, and Chile; their structure is shown in Table 6-2. Costs are not available for Mexico, even though Mexican lathe production should be accounted for in regional planning.

The table indicates that the Chilean plant is somewhat more capital intensive than those in Argentina and Brazil. Cost studies for both the latter countries cover actual operating plants, while the Chilean estimates are

Table 6-2. Cost Structure of Universal Parallel Lathe Production in LAFTA, 1975

Category	Argentina[a] Operating level, 231	Argentina[a] Capacity, 420	Brazil[b] capacity, 300	Chile[c] capacity, 181
Materials[d]	38.0%	42.2%	33.9%	37.6%
Direct labor	32.8	26.3	44.0	18.1[e]
Utilities	1.3	0.7	f	4.3
Maintenance	f	f	f	b
Depreciation	4.1	2.4	f	9.1
Supervision	g	g	f	1.4
Insurance	f	f	f	b
Opportunity cost of capital	7.6	4.5	13.8	15.4
Other	16.4	13.9	8.1	14.2
Total	100.0%	100.0%	100.0%	100.0%
Cost per unit in national currency	404,260	264,368	7,564,000	13,224

Source: ECIEL, Martin Carnoy (ed.), *The Optimum Location of Specific Industries in the Latin American Free Trade Association (including Venezuela)* (Brookings Institution, 1966; processed), Vol. 1.
  a. Percentages are based on costs in 1964 pesos.
  b. Percentages are based on costs in 1965 cruzeiros.
  c. Percentages are based on costs in March 1965 escudos. This plant produces lathes that are slightly smaller than 1,500 millimeters. Nevertheless, their costs are representative of those of the standard unit.
  d. Materials include semifinished and finished parts.
  e. Does not include indirect labor or technical personnel.
  f. Included in other.
  g. Included in direct labor.

based on a feasibility study by the Chilean Institute of Steel.[7] The fact that the Chilean plant is based on engineering estimates may explain why it is more capital intensive. It also suggests the possibility that the Chilean cost estimates would be lower than the Argentine and Brazilian estimates even if they were all for the same type plant. Furthermore, the Chilean lathe, of a different metal content, is only about half as heavy as the Argentine and Brazilian product.

Because data for each of the three countries are based on single plants, cost estimates are limited to short-run curves. Fixed costs (costs incurred at zero output) are taken equal to depreciation, opportunity costs of investment in fixed assets, taxes, interest paid on fixed assets, and administration expenses. These short-run cost curves are taken as proxies for long-run

7. Chilean Institute of Steel, "Feasibility of the National Production of Machine Tools" (March 1965; processed).

curves with a 500 unit limitation on annual output in order to find the optimum location of production in the area. The price of a 1,500 milli-meter parallel lathe f.o.b. the United States is taken as $4,000.

Transportation costs are added to variable production costs to obtain the total variable component. In the case of lathes (and tractors as well) transport costs among countries in the southern cone appear to be much lower overland than by sea. This is in marked contrast to bulk products, such as solid fertilizers, which apparently are much cheaper to ship around Cape Horn. Overland rates are taken from the United States to Mexico; São Paulo to Paraguay, Argentina, and Chile; and between Santiago and Buenos Aires. The international maritime transport rates calculated in the two ways described in Chapter 2 are so similar that only one set of trans-port rates is presented. Thus only the exchange rate implicit in production costs varies between the minimum and maximum cost alternatives.

The Optimum Location of Production

The results of the linear program, which yield the optimum location of lathe production in the region in 1975, are presented in Table 6-3 for two rates of exchange for both Argentina and Chile relative to Brazil and the United States. There are therefore four possible sets of solutions to the model, based on the following sets of exchange rates per simón:

Country and currency	Solution			
	A	*B*	*C*	*D*
Chile, escudo	5.0	3.5	5.0	3.5
Argentina, peso	155.0	155.0	140.0	140.0
Brazil, cruzeiro	2,200.0	2,200.0	2,200.0	2,200.0

The solutions shown in Table 6-3 hold, however, only when one plant in each location is assumed to be producing all the lathes demanded. Since costs described in the previous section relate to plants producing up to 500 lathes a year, this upper limit is imposed on the model to generate an alternative set of solutions. Using this limit, fixed costs are multiplied by the number of plants necessary in each producing country to supply the required number of lathes. If one country produces all lathes demanded in 1975 (8,400), seventeen plants are needed. Table 6-4 shows the solutions under this criterion.

Table 6-3. Optimum Location of Production of Lathes in LAFTA, and Selected Alternatives, and their Costs, 1975, under Selected Exchange Rate Assumptions, Assuming Unlimited Plant Capacity

Thousands of lathes; millions of simones

Solution and producing country	Number of units produced	Consuming countries	Cost of solution to the area
A. 5 escudos, 155 Argentine pesos, 2,200 cruzeiros[a]			
Solution 1—optimum solution			$21.9
Chile	8.2	All	
Solution 2			24.6
Argentina	8.2	All	
Solution 3—national solution			28.1
Argentina	3.0	Argentina, Colombia, Paraguay	
Brazil	2.5	Brazil	
Chile	0.2	Chile	
Mexico[b]	2.5	Mexico	
Solution 4			29.7
Argentina	2.2	Argentina	
Brazil	2.5	Brazil	
Chile	1.0	Chile, Colombia, Paraguay	
Mexico[b]	2.5	Mexico	
Solution 5			30.0
Brazil	8.2	All	
Solution 6—import solution			36.3
United States	8.2	All	
B. 3.5 escudos, 155 Argentine pesos, 2,200 cruzeiros[a]			
Solution 1—optimum solution			24.6
Argentina	8.2	All	
Solution 2—national solution[c]			28.6
Argentina	3.0	Argentina, Colombia, Paraguay	
Brazil	2.5	Brazil	
Chile	0.2	Chile	
Mexico[b]	2.5	Mexico	
Solution 3			30.0
Brazil	8.2	All	
Solution 4			30.2
Brazil	8.0	Argentina, Brazil, Colombia, Mexico, Paraguay	
Chile	0.2	Chile	
Solution 5			30.9
Chile	8.2	All	
Solution 6—import solution			36.3
United States	8.2	All	

Table 6-3. (*continued*)

Solution and producing country	Number of units produced	Consuming countries	Cost of solution to the area
C. 5 escudos, 140 Argentine pesos, 2,200 cruzeiros[a]			
Solution 1—optimum solution			21.9
Chile	8.2	All	
Solution 2			27.3
Argentina	8.2	All	
Solution 3—national solution[d]			28.5
Argentina	2.2	Argentina	
Brazil	2.5	Brazil	
Chile	1.0	Chile, Colombia, Paraguay	
Mexico[b]	2.5	Mexico	
Solution 4[e]			29.0
Argentina	3.0	Argentina, Colombia, Paraguay	
Brazil	2.5	Brazil	
Chile	0.2	Chile	
Mexico[b]	2.5	Mexico	
Solution 5			30.0
Brazil	8.2	All	
Solution 6—import solution			36.3
United States	8.2	All	
D. 3.5 escudos, 140 Argentine pesos, 2,200 cruzeiros[a]			
Solution 1—optimum solution			27.3
Argentina	8.2	All	
Solution 2—national solution[c]			29.6
Argentina	3.0	Argentina, Colombia, Paraguay	
Brazil	2.5	Brazil	
Chile	0.2	Chile	
Mexico[b]	2.5	Mexico	
Solution 3			30.0
Brazil	8.2	All	
Solution 4[e]			30.2
Brazil	8.0	Argentina, Brazil, Colombia, Mexico, Paraguay	
Chile	0.2	Chile	
Solution 5			30.9
Chile	8.2	All	
Solution 6—import solution			36.3
United States	8.2	All	

Note: Ecuador, Peru, Uruguay, and Venezuela did not present demand studies for lathes, and are therefore not included in these solutions.

a. Per simón; transport costs are assumed to be the same for all solutions. See explanation, p. 155.
b. At Brazilian costs.
c. Same as Solution A-3.
d. Same as Solution A-4.
e. Same as Solution B-4.

Table 6-4. Optimum Location of Production of Lathes in LAFTA, and Selected Alternatives, and their Costs, 1975, under Selected Exchange Rate Assumptions, Assuming Plants of 500 Unit Capacity

Thousands of units; millions of simones

Solution and producing country	Number of units produced	Consuming countries	Cost of solution to the area
A. 5 escudos, 155 Argentine pesos, 2,200 cruzeiros[a]			
Solution 1—optimum solution			§24.5
Chile	8.2	All	
Solution 2			26.3
Argentina	8.2	All	
Solution 3—national solution			31.2
Argentina	2.2	Argentina	
Brazil	2.5	Brazil	
Chile	1.0	Chile, Colombia, Paraguay	
Mexico[b]	2.5	Mexico	
Solution 4			31.3
Argentina	3.0	Argentina, Colombia, Paraguay	
Brazil	2.5	Brazil	
Chile	0.2	Chile	
Mexico[b]	2.5	Mexico	
Solution 5			34.5
Brazil	8.2	All	
Solution 6—import solution			36.3
United States	8.2	All	
B. 3.5 escudos, 155 Argentine pesos, 2,200 cruzeiros[a]			
Solution 1—optimum solution			26.3
Argentina	8.2	All	
Solution 2—national solution[c]			31.4
Argentina	3.0	Argentina, Colombia, Paraguay	
Brazil	2.5	Brazil	
Chile	0.2	Chile	
Mexico[b]	2.5	Mexico	
Solution 3			34.6
Brazil	8.2	All	
Solution 4			34.6
Chile	8.2	All	
Solution 5			34.7
Brazil	8.0	Argentina, Brazil, Colombia, Mexico, Paraguay	
Chile	0.2	Chile	
Solution 6—import solution			36.3
United States	8.2	All	

Table 6-4. (*continued*)

Solution and producing country	Number of units produced	Consuming countries	Cost of solution to the area
C. 5 escudos, 140 Argentine pesos, 2,200 cruzeiros[a]			
Solution 1—optimum solution			24.5
Chile	8.2	All	
Solution 2			29.0
Argentina	8.2	All	
Solution 3—national production[d]			32.1
Argentina	2.2	Argentina	
Brazil	2.5	Brazil	
Chile	1.0	Chile, Colombia, Paraguay	
Mexico[b]	2.5	Mexico	
Solution 4[c]			32.2
Argentina	3.0	Argentina, Colombia, Paraguay	
Brazil	2.5	Brazil	
Chile	0.2	Chile	
Mexico[b]	2.5	Mexico	
Solution 5			34.5
Brazil	8.2	All	
Solution 6—import solution			36.3
United States	8.2	All	
D. 3.5 escudos, 140 Argentine pesos, 2,200 cruzeiros[a]			
Solution 1—optimum solution			29.0
Argentina	8.2	All	
Solution 2—national solution			32.7
Argentina	3.0	Argentina, Colombia, Paraguay	
Brazil	2.5	Brazil	
Chile	0.2	Chile	
Mexico[b]	2.5	Mexico	
Solution 3			34.5
Brazil	8.2	All	
Solution 4			34.6
Chile	8.2	All	
Solution 5[d]			35.1
Argentina	2.2	Argentina	
Brazil	2.5	Brazil	
Chile	1.0	Chile, Colombia, Paraguay	
Mexico[b]	2.5	Mexico	
Solution 6—import solution			36.3
United States	8.2	All	

Note: Ecuador, Peru, Uruguay, and Venezuela did not present demand studies for lathes, and are therefore not included in these solutions.

a. Per simón; transport costs are assumed to be the same for all solutions. See explanation, p. 155.
b. At Brazilian costs.
c. Same as Solution A-4.
d. Same as Solution A-3.

Shadow Prices and Indifference Rates

The solutions put the optimum location for lathe production in either Chile or Argentina, depending on the exchange rate between the two. Table 6-5 presents the shadow prices implicit in the set of solutions that assumes limited plant size (those shown in Table 6-4). Table 6-6 gives the approximate ratio of currencies that would render each purchasing country indifferent about whether it bought from Chile or Argentina. A difficulty arises because the data years are different for the two countries— 1964 for Argentina and 1965 for Chile. If it can be assumed, however, that a "new" peso rate in March 1965 can be calculated by multiplying whole-sale price increases between June 1964 and March 1965 by the June 1964 exchange rate, the new rate would be 174 pesos per simón and costs in simones would be the same as in 1964.

The ratios shown in Table 6-6 can be applied to the "new" rate, and suggest an indifference rate of exchange between Chile and Argentina of 37.2–38.0 pesos per escudo. The official rate (trade rate for Chile) in March 1965 was 51 pesos per escudo. At that rate, Chile cannot compete with Argentina in lathes. If similar calculations are made for the cruzeiro and the peso, the indifference rates involving the new peso would be 16.7 cruzeiros per new peso, compared with the official rate (free rate for Brazil) of 12.3 cruzeiros per peso. Even at the new rate, Brazil cannot compete with Argentina. At the March 1965 official rate of 630 cruzeiros per escudo, Brazil can compete with Chile in every country but Chile and Argentina.

Table 6-5. Shadow Prices for Lathes in LAFTA, 1975
Simones

Consuming country	Optimum location[a]			National production[a]		
	A-1 and C-1	B-1 and D-1	Importing from U.S.	A-3 and C-3	B-2	D-2
Argentina	2,775	2,962	4,334	2,976	2,991	3,304
Brazil	2,860	3,042	4,502	3,928	3,928	3,928
Chile	2,726	3,014	4,420	2,822	4,007	4,007
Colombia	3,006	3,270	4,348	3,103	3,298	3,612
Mexico	3,050	3,315	4,028	4,296	4,296	4,296
Paraguay	2,806	2,987	4,346	2,903	3,016	3,329

a. Keyed to Table 6-4 solution sets.

Table 6-6. Prices of Lathes and Indifference Exchange Rates in LAFTA, 1975

Producing country, price ratios, and currencies exchanged	Consuming country					
	Argentina	Brazil	Chile	Colombia	Mexico	Paraguay
	Lathe prices in simones					
Argentina[a]	2,962	3,042	3,014	3,270	3,315	2,987
Chile[b]	2,775	2,860	2,726	3,006	3,050	2,806
Brazil[c]	3,986	3,929	4,042	4,264	4,297	3,997
	Price ratios					
Argentine to Chilean	1.07	1.06	1.09	1.09	1.09	1.06
Brazilian to Chilean	1.44	1.37	1.48	1.42	1.41	1.42
Brazilian to Argentine	1.34	1.29	1.34	1.30	1.30	1.34
	Indifference exchange rates					
Pesos per escudo[d]	33.2	32.8	33.8	33.8	33.8	32.8
Cruzeiros per escudo[e]	632	602	650	625	620	625
Cruzeiros per peso[f]	19.0	18.3	19.0	18.5	18.5	19.0

a. The exchange rate is 155 pesos per simón.
b. The exchange rate is 5 escudos per simón.
c. The exchange rate is 2,200 cruzeiros per simón.
d. Calculated as the ratio of the Argentine to the Chilean price times 31 (the number of pesos per escudo).
e. Calculated as the ratio of the Brazilian to the Chilean price times 440 (the number of cruzeiros per escudo).
f. Calculated as the ratio of the Brazilian to the Argentine price times 14.2 (the number of cruzeiros per peso).

At a free exchange rate of 440 cruzeiros per escudo, Brazil cannot compete with Chile anywhere.

The absolute cost to the region of a national production policy decreases with the rate of exchange of escudos and pesos per simón. This is due, of course, to the large demand for lathes in Brazil, and to the decreasing relative costs of supplying Brazil on the basis of a domestically oriented (national) production policy. The relative cost to the area of such a policy also decreases when a limit of 500 lathes per firm is imposed. It should be noted that the cost to the area of Mexican autarkic production is probably overestimated, because it is based on Brazilian costs. Since Mexico has eliminated tariffs on LAFTA-manufactured lathes, it is likely that Mexico's production costs are lower than Brazilian costs (see Table 6-7). In a Solution D situation, then, it is possible that the cost to the area of a nationalistic policy is negligible.

Table 6-7. Tariffs on 1,500 Millimeter Lathes in LAFTA, 1966
Percent[a]

Levying country	LAFTA	Third countries
Argentina	28.8	175.0
Brazil	22.0	76.0
Chile	10.0	38.5
Colombia	16.0	16.0
Ecuador	15.5	31.8
Mexico	0	17.4
Paraguay	10.5	50.0
Peru	7.0	31.0

Source: U.S. Department of Commerce, Bureau of International Commerce.
a. Specific duties are translated into percent of U.S. f.o.b. price.

A Note on Tariffs

Current (1966) tariff rates within LAFTA for lathes are shown in Table 6-7. Interestingly enough, in all but the Argentine case, intra-LAFTA tariffs are lower than the price difference between national and optimum production. That Mexico imposes no duty on intra-LAFTA imports suggests that Mexican costs are overstated as a result of the assumption that they are the same as those in Brazil.

Capital Investment Requirements

The investment required to finance the production of lathes to meet demand in 1975 is presented in Table 6-8 for two cases. In the first, Argen-

Table 6-8. Investment Required for Lathe Production in LAFTA, 1963–75[a]

Investment and conditions	Producing and consuming countries	
	Argentina for all but Brazil	Chile for all but Brazil
Investment (thousands of simones)	1,144	1,544
Number of plants	12	12
Units of annual output per plant	500	500
Exchange rate per simón	155 pesos	5 escudos

a. In both cases, no plants are assumed to exist in 1963.

Table 6-9. Welfare Benefits and Costs of Selected Alternatives to Optimum Production of Lathes in LAFTA, 1975

Thousands of simones

Consuming country	Minimum cost assumptions				Maximum cost assumptions			
	Buying from optimum location[a] versus importing from U.S.[b]		National production[e] versus buying from optimum location[a]		Buying from optimum location[d] versus importing from U.S.[b]		National production[e] versus buying from optimum location[d]	
	Production effect	Total	Production effect	Total	Production effect	Total	Production effect	Total
Argentina	2,398	3,069	−466	−485	2,275	2,798	−711	−754
Brazil	2,780	3,586	−2,162	−2,573	2,628	3,259	−1,889	−2,172
Chile	207	271	−16	−17	193	237	−151	−176
Colombia	932	1,146	−90	−92	818	956	−294	−309
Mexico	2,050	2,377	−2,477	−2,987	1,671	1,854	−2,135	−2,455
Total	8,367	10,449	−5,211	−6,154	7,585	9,104	−5,180	−5,866

a. Solutions A-1 and C-1 (see Table 6-4).
b. Solution A-6.
c. Solutions A-3 and C-3.
d. Solutions B-1 and D-1.
e. Solution D-2.

tina, and, in the second, Chile, supplies the whole area but Brazil. Brazil currently has the capacity to cover projected demand to 1975; it would therefore be unrealistic to disregard it in calculating the required capital outlays. Furthermore, it seems probable that Brazil, because of the biases mentioned above, is not in the disadvantaged position indicated by the shadow prices in Table 6-5.

Welfare Benefits and Costs

Beyond the optimum locations and the cost to the area of second-best solutions, it would be useful to know the effects on individual members of policies that do not conform to the optimum pattern and to the free trade of lathes both within LAFTA and between LAFTA members and the rest of the world. As Table 6-5 makes clear, whether the optimum location is Chile or Argentina, the price of lathes imported from the United States is higher for every country in the area. Thus, all gain by not importing.

The welfare gain from regional production is over $9 million in the official exchange rate case and over $10 million when free rates are assumed (see Table 6-9). Considering the dubious nature of the Chilean cost figures, the former case yields a more reasonable estimate of regional prices, and therefore a better estimate of gains. However, the difference between the gains in the two cases is small. When official exchange rates are assumed, the gain from not importing attributable to the production effect represents 26 percent of the total maximum value of output in 1975. As in the tractor case, the comparison with U.S. lathes, instead of, say, European lathes, may overestimate the gain from not importing; nevertheless, the use of short-run cost curves as proxies for long-run curves, and the limitation of output of plant, would tend to bias upward possible future Latin American costs of production, and thus to bias welfare gains downward.

The cost of national rather than regional production is about $6 million annually in both the minimum and maximum cost estimates. Almost the entire cost would be borne by Mexico and Brazil. Yet it may be that the prices of neither country are as high as projected, so that the cost of national production could be substantially overestimated. On the other hand, if long-run cost curve estimates were available, they might show that no matter which country was the primary producer of lathes in the region, regional production on a large scale would provide significant gains over national production.

CHAPTER SEVEN

Powdered Milk and Cheese

ALTHOUGH THE MILK PRODUCT INDUSTRY has not generally been considered one in which benefits can be realized from increased market size and economies of scale, trade among members of the Latin American Free Trade Association (LAFTA) in products like powdered milk and cheese could, nevertheless, benefit consumers in many countries. The emphasis in this study thus far has been on industries in which costs decrease with increasing size, but specialization of production in industries characterized by constant or increasing costs can also result in benefits to the area if trade is created among the countries rather than simply diverted from one to the other. If one LAFTA country currently produces cheese behind a protective tariff, and another can produce it at a lower c.i.f. price, trade in cheese would benefit consumers in the first. If cheese production demonstrated economies of scale in the relevant output range, both countries would benefit from the lower prices made possible by the wider market facing producers in the lower cost country. In addition, a decreasing cost industry permits lower prices to countries currently importing from outside the region.

Almost all countries in LAFTA produce both cheese and powdered milk, but many have only a limited and expensive supply of fluid milk. Even to meet the nutritional requirements of their populations, many

LAFTA members need to import milk concentrates from countries with larger and cheaper supplies of the fresh product. The story for cheese is similar: Demand increases with population and income per capita; under these circumstances, the welfare cost of protecting limited domestic cheese industries in countries poor in fluid milk would increase every year unless tastes changed considerably. Cheese and powdered milk, then, are good examples of products that could become important items of trade among LAFTA countires.[1] They also typify the food processing industry in general, in that the supplies of materials, especially perishable raw materials, limit the size of plant.

Current and Projected Demand

As in other food processing industries, domestic production of powdered milk and cheese in recent years has nearly equaled domestic demand. In part this is a price effect: In all LAFTA countries (omitting Mexico, for which no study was made), tariffs on powdered milk and cheese are high (see Table 7-1), and this is reflected in domestic prices. Two countries, Peru and Venezuela, have only a 30 percent duty on powdered milk; both import a large proportion of their total supply. Argentina, which exports cheese, has one of the lower tariffs on the product, but even it is about 50 percent of value.

Tables 7-2 and 7-3 show the current and projected demand for the two products and the 1963 consumption. Of the two, current production of powdered milk is a much lower percentage of present and future consumption. Consumption is projected to increase at a rapid 7 percent a year, of which about 2.5 percent is attributable to population growth and about 4.5 percent to consumers' sensitivity to the lower price of powdered milk.[2]

1. Argentina already exports cheese to LAFTA, especially to Peru and Venezuela. See Juan Carlos de Pablo and Fernando Arturo Ibarra, *La Industria del Queso en la Argentina* (Buenos Aires: Fundación de Investigaciones Económicas Latinoamericanas, 1966).

2. The substitution effect may be even larger if it is assumed that the income effect is negative. In income groups where most direct powdered milk consumption takes place, however, the 4.5 percent may be due in part to a positive income effect. The coefficients of per capita income in the consumption regression equations vary from country to country for powdered milk. For Argentina, income elasticity, if measured for all milk concentrates, comes to 4.1; for Brazil, the income elasticity is gross of price changes and is 1.47; for Chile, the income elasticity with relative price held constant is 0.87; Ecuador, without prices held constant, 0.30; Paraguay, also gross of price changes, 0.22; Peru, net

Table 7-1. Nominal Tariffs on Powdered Milk and Cheese in LAFTA, 1966[a]

Percent

Levying country	Powdered milk	Hard cheese	Semihard cheese	Bland cheese
Argentina				
LAFTA	45.0	53.0	53.0	51.8[b]
Third countries	221.5	326.5	326.5	326.5
Brazil				
LAFTA and GATT	45.9	66.0	66.0	66.0[c]
Third (non-GATT) countries	62.9	100.0	100.0	100.0
Chile	200.0	174.0	174.0	195.0
Colombia	d	d	d	d
Ecuador	d	d	d	d
Mexico				
LAFTA	22.0	0	0	0
Third countries	22.0	824.0	824.0	824.0[e]
Paraguay	183.0	85.6	85.6	56.1
Peru				
Ecuador[f]	0	8.0	. . .	. . .
Other countries	31.1	94.0	94.0	94.0
Uruguay	114.5	177.1	177.1	180.1
Venezuela	30.5	44.5	44.5	44.5

Source: U.S. Department of Commerce, Bureau of International Commerce.

a. Specific duties are translated into percent of U.S. c.i.f. import price, except in the case of soft cheese, where optimum location price from Table 7.9 is used.

b. Rate to LAFTA on colonia cheese is 1.8 percent.

c. Rate to LAFTA and GATT on colonia cheese is 16.5 percent.

d. Importation prohibited.

e. Rate to third countries on colonia cheese is 531 percent.

f. Concessions to Ecuador under LAFTA agreement.

Cheese production, on the other hand, is not expected to increase as rapidly: Excluding Brazil, for which no study was made in 1963, demand is projected to grow at an annual rate of 2.8 percent, only slightly higher than average population growth in the area. The growth rate is dominated by developments in Argentine cheese consumption, which is felt to have reached such a high per capita level, given the price of substitutes (such as meat), that it has little probability of expanding much beyond the increase

of price changes, −0.04; Uruguay and Venezuela, gross of price changes, 4.1 and 0.86, respectively. The unusually high figures for Argentina and Uruguay are probably the result of the primarily industrial use of powdered milk in these two countries (in the manufacture of chocolate). It is also significant that in higher income countries, the income elasticity is higher; this means also that where the most powdered milk is being consumed, approximately 2.5 percent of the 4.5 percent of per capita increase in powdered milk demand can be ascribed to an assumed increase in per capita income in Latin America (income elasticity of 0.9 times 3.0 percent per capita income growth).

Table 7-2. Consumption and Production of Powdered Milk in LAFTA, 1963, and Projected Demand, 1975

Tons

Country	1963 Consumption	Production	1975 Demand[a]
Argentina	14,805	15,028	48,980
Brazil	53,413[b]	53,413	152,533
Chile	26,200	17,000	48,318
Colombia	6,512	7,012	12,425
Ecuador	1,154	709	4,195
Paraguay[c]	2,584	n.a.	2,064
Peru	604	n.a.	1,529
Uruguay	154	154	257
Venezuela	50,623	20,858	106,900
Total	156,049	114,174	377,200

Source: ECIEL, *The Demand for Chemical Fertilizers, Tractors, Paper and Pulp, Milk Concentrates, and Lathes in the Latin American Free Trade Association* (*including Venezuela*) (Brookings Institution, 1966; processed).

n.a. Not available.

a. Midpoint of minimum and maximum projections; range for total: 350,000–404,000 tons.

b. 1962.

c. The drop in the figures for Paraguay between 1963 and 1975 is due to the fact that the 1963 figure includes donations by CARE, while the 1975 demand does not.

in population. At such a low rate of growth in demand and at present production levels, domestic supply would be expected to continue to fill domestic demand if tariff barriers in the region were maintained. There are several unknowns here, however. The first is projected consumption in Brazil, which even conservatively approximated is the second largest in the area; the second is the effect on cheese consumption of lower prices in countries other than Argentina and Uruguay. If, for example, domestic prices of raw milk or cheese import prices fell in those countries, cheese consumption could increase greatly and domestic production would be insufficient to satisfy it. Inadequate data and the division of domestically produced varieties have prevented the calculation of price elasticities. For purposes of projecting the size of the regional market, however, two adjustments are made: (1) Cheese produced on farms is separated from total demand in Colombia and Ecuador; and (2) consumption is allocated among three types of cheese—hard paste, semihard paste, and bland (or soft) paste.[3] The adjusted consumption for 1975 shown in Table 7-4 can be considered the quantity that would figure in area trade.

3. See note 8, p. 217 for the types of cheese included in each category.

Table 7-3. Consumption of Cheese, 1963, and Projected Demand, 1975, LAFTA

Tons

Country	1963 Consumption	1963 Production	1975[a] Demand
Argentina	137,632	144,333	186,270
Brazil	[b]	[b]	143,800[c]
Chile	7,560	[d]	25,300
Colombia	13,000	13,000	21,548
Ecuador[e]	255	250	938
Paraguay	278	...	340
Peru	10,275[f]	10,275[g]	9,465
Uruguay	9,200[h]	9,200	12,200
Total	178,200	166,783[i]	256,060[j]

Source: ECIEL, *The Demand for Chemical Fertilizers.*
a. Midpoint of minimum and maximum projections; range for total: 246,000–266,000 tons.
b. No study was made for Brazil.
c. Based on per capita consumption of 1.5 kilograms in 1975.
d. No study of production was made for Chile.
e. Industrial cheese only; does not include cheese produced in agricultural establishments.
f. 1962.
g. No direct estimate, but it is known that consumption is met almost entirely by domestic production.
h. 1964.
i. Does not include Peru.
j. Does not include Brazil; including Brazil, 1975 total is 399,860.

Table 7-4. Demand for Cheese in LAFTA, 1975

Tons

Country	Type of cheese Hard	Type of cheese Semihard	Type of cheese Bland	Total
Argentina	47,898	45,237	93,135	186,270
Brazil[a]	37,300	34,600	71,900	143,800
Chile[a]	6,570	6,080	12,650	25,300
Colombia[b,c]	330	1,320	1,650	3,300
Ecuador[b,c]	95	380	475	950
Paraguay[a]	88	82	170	340
Peru[b]	2,470	2,280	4,750	9,500
Uruguay[a]	3,170	2,930	6,100	12,200

Source: ECIEL, *The Demand for Chemical Fertilizers.*
a. Apportioned on the basis of Argentine percentages.
b. Apportioned in the following way: Hard, 10 percent; semihard, 40 percent; and bland, 50 percent of total. These are the percentages estimated for Colombia. They are assumed to apply to Ecuador and Peru.
c. Industrially produced and imported cheese only.

Costs of Production

While all countries produce these products, it appears that the eastern area of the southern cone (southern Brazil, Uruguay, and Argentina), with its possibilities for expansion of milk production, would be the most likely area for the production of milk concentrates in LAFTA. But to determine the probable direction of trade in both cheese and powdered milk, if tariffs were reduced, requires comparative production costs and transportation charges between production and consumption points. Only two countries, Brazil and Uruguay, presented costs for powdered milk production; detailed data for Argentina are not available. Four production locations are included in the cheese estimates, but not all four apply to any single category of cheese. Argentina, Brazil, and Peru are considered for the production of bland paste cheese, and Argentina and Uruguay for the production of hard and semihard paste cheeses. The United States is considered a source of imports of all these products; however, in the case of semihard cheese only the U.S. wholesale prices of American and cheddar cheeses (semihard paste) are used. Prices of Italian parmesan cheese and Dutch full cream cheese are used for the prices of the hard and soft varieties, respectively. Freight rates are taken from the United States.

The projected structure of costs of production is presented in Table 7-5 for powdered milk and Table 7-6 for cheese. Total per unit cost is also

Table 7-5. Cost Structure of Powdered Whole Milk Production in LAFTA, 1975

	Producing country and plant output per year in tons		
Type of cost	*Brazil* *(3,400)*	*Uruguay* *(900)*	*United States*[a] *(3,620)*
Raw materials	79.0%	61.4%	79.0%
Direct labor[b]	2.6	7.7	14.8
Utilities	3.7	5.8	⎫
Maintenance	0.9	1.7	⎪
Depreciation	0.8	5.7	⎬ 6.2
Insurance	c	0.6	⎪
Opportunity cost	2.1	10.9	⎪
Other	10.9	6.2	⎭
Total	100.0%	100.0%	100.0%
Cost per kilogram in national currency	1,225[d]	9.46[e]	0.322[f]

Sources: ECIEL, Martin Carnoy (ed.), *The Optimum Location of Specific Industries in the Latin American Free Trade Association (including Venezuela)* (Brookings Institution, 1966; processed), Vol. 3. Scott H. Walker, Homer J. Preston, and Glen T. Nelson, *An Economic Analysis of Butter-Nonfat Dry Milk Plants*, University of Idaho Agricultural Experiment Station, Research Bulletin No. 20 (June 1953), Table 35.

a. Costs are based on average wholesale price of nonfat dry milk in 1964 and cost of capital and labor in nonfat dry milk plants in 1948–49 adjusted by the wholesale price index and wage changes in the food industry to 1964. This method biases the percentage in raw materials upward.

b. Includes indirect labor.

c. Included in other.

d. Mid-1964 cruzeiros (1,200 cruzeiros per simón).

e. 1963 pesos (21 pesos per simón).

f. Price of powdered whole milk (f.o.b. New York, 1964) equals $759 per metric ton.

shown for each plant size in each country. In Table 7-5 the present structure of costs for the United States is compared to those for Brazil and Uruguay for powdered milk; it should be noted, however, that U.S. cost is for nonfat powdered milk while the other two plants produce whole powdered milk.

The important difference in the cost structures for the three powdered milk plants appears in the percentage of raw material cost: This percentage rises with increased plant size, which is consistent with the theoretical cost structure; for the same plant size the U.S. and Brazilian percentages are the same. The inconsistency in the figure lies in the much lower price of fluid milk attributed to the production of powdered milk in the United States than in Brazil. Only part of the lower cost of the primary input is offset by the greater quantity of input required to produce dry nonfat milk (12.1 liters per kilogram) rather than dry whole milk (8.6 liters). Uruguayan input of fluid milk per kilogram of output is between these two figures (10.5 liters).

Joint Costs

One of the difficulties of estimating the costs of powdered milk is that it is a joint product with butter. If joint capital and utility costs are largely attributed to butter production, the percentage of raw materials in the total cost of powdered milk increases correspondingly. It should also be clear that the production of whole powdered milk would leave less fat for the production of butter; therefore, the implied price for the fluid milk used in dry milk production would be higher. The butter production of the Brazilian plant listed in Table 7-5, for example, is less than 6 percent of its powdered milk production (by weight); in the United States this percentage is considerably higher.[4] Under joint cost conditions, then, the implied price of fluid milk in the production of powdered milk depends on the amount of fat in the final product. While the prices shown in Table 7-7 are comparable for the South American countries, the U.S. implied price is very approximate. It is estimated that the price of fluid milk attributable

4. Scott H. Walker, Homer J. Preston, and Glen T. Nelson, *An Economic Analysis of Butter-Nonfat Dry Milk Plants*, University of Idaho Agricultural Experiment Station, Research Bulletin No. 20 (June 1953), Tables 34 and 35. It is not possible in comparing these tables to estimate the ratio of powdered milk to butter in each plant. With the smallest output of butter and the largest output of dry milk, however, the ratio is approximately the same as in the Brazilian plant. It is highly likely that the ratio in the U.S. plants is higher.

Table 7-6. Structure of Costs of Cheese Production in LAFTA, 1975

Type of cheese, producing country, and plant output per year in tons

	Hard paste			Semihard paste			Soft paste		
	Argentina (184)	Uruguay (450)	(900)	Argentina (304)	Uruguay (130)	(261)	Argentina (414)	Brazil (348)	Peru (132)
Raw materials	61.2%	62.3%	68.5%	56.2%	62.6%	69.0%	55.4%	72.6%	49.0%
Direct labor[a]	10.1	9.5	7.4	8.9	8.7	6.8	8.0	7.9	12.5
Utilities	0.8	2.0	1.7	5.2	1.9	1.7	7.9	6.5	b
Maintenance	b	1.9	1.5	b	2.0	1.5	b	b	b
Depreciation	1.1	6.4	3.5	1.0	6.5	3.6	1.4	2.9	12.3
Insurance	b	0.6	0.4	b	0.6	0.4	b	b	b
Opportunity cost	5.8	9.5	10.7	5.0	9.8	10.8	5.5	3.7	9.8
Other	21.1[c]	7.8	6.2	23.8[c]	8.0	6.1	21.7[c]	6.4	16.4
Total	100.0%	100.0%	100.0%	100.0%	100.0%	100.0%	100.0%	100.0%	100.0%
Cost per kilogram in national currency	111.1[d]	24.3[e]	22.3[e]	94.8[d]	21.2[e]	19.4[e]	72.5[d]	1,080[f]	22.2[g]

Source: Carnoy (ed.), *The Optimum Location of Specific Industries*, Vol. 3.
a. Includes indirect labor.
b. Included in "other."
c. Includes approximately 12 percent commercialization and sales cost.
d. 1964 pesos (140 pesos per simón).
e. 1965 pesos (35 pesos per simón).
f. 1965 cruzeiros (1,850 cruzeiros per simón).
g. 1965 soles (26.82 soles per simón).

Table 7-7. Wholesale Prices of Milk for Powdered Whole Milk Production in LAFTA, 1964–65

Simones per liter at the plant

Country	Implied price
United States	0.070
Argentina	0.038
Brazil	0.094
Peru	0.051
Uruguay	0.033

Source: Carnoy (ed.), *The Optimum Location of Specific Industries*, Vol. 3. Exchange rates per simón are: Argentina—140 pesos; Brazil—1,200 cruzeiros; Peru—26.82 soles; and Uruguay—21 pesos.

to the production of powdered whole milk in the United States, given the same labor and capital costs as for nonfat dry milk and assuming that 8.6 liters of fluid milk is required per kilogram of final product, is equal to 79 percent of the New York wholesale price for powdered whole milk divided by 8.6.

Price of Fluid Milk

The price of fluid milk in the various countries also affects cheese costs. If the Argentine cost structures shown in Table 7-6 are corrected for the inclusion of about 12 percent marketing costs, the percentage in raw materials in Argentina and Uruguay is similar, and so is the price of their milk. In a comparison of the cost structures in Argentine and Brazilian soft paste cheese plants (which are of similar size), the percentage in raw materials in the latter is significantly higher even when marketing costs are discounted. Total costs of production in Brazil and Peru are also much higher (adjusted for commercialization), but in Peru's case this can be assigned partly to a scale effect.

Differences in the wholesale price of dairy products between countries, or between areas in the same country, can be only partially explained by differences in the price of fluid milk. It is also, in turn, a function of cost of production of fresh milk and the nonlinear cost of transporting it. A model that expresses these relationships is set out in detail in Appendix F.

Despite the rather sophisticated methodology used to estimate costs of production of powdered milk, lack of data on transport costs and yields per acre of fresh milk preclude accurate estimates of cost functions. The yield of milk per hectare is assumed to be one-fourth that in the United

States and the transport cost for Brazil derived from that assumption is assumed to hold for Uruguay as well. In addition, it is assumed that the price of milk is fixed at the farm and is constant throughout the area from which the powdered milk plant draws its fresh milk. This is based on the assumption that farmers in the region where the plant is located have an alternative market for their milk and that the plant uses only a small fraction of total supply.

Since, as the calculations with the model indicate, the cost to the factory increases with the heavier raw milk transportation charges it incurs as it seeks to expand production, significant difficulties are encountered in attempts to determine an optimum location for this type of industry. Production would tend to be much more dispersed than it is for industries that are characterized by constant costs or by economies of scale in a much larger range of output. In Latin America price controls on milk have acted as price ceilings, in contrast with the United States, where the dairy farmer rather than the consumer is the intended beneficiary of price control and where the fixed price therefore acts as a floor. Expansion of output of processed dairy products in Latin America has been limited by these controls, but for the purposes of the present study, it is assumed that they would be removed (or altered) and the production of powdered milk and cheese allowed to expand in accordance with its optimum distribution.

Optimum Location of Production

The material and transportation costs, and the plant sizes, developed in Appendix E are used to determine the optimum location of powdered milk plants in Latin America. (The same calculations can be applied with respect to cheese production in each country.) In all of the estimates, it is assumed that the shadow transport rate calculated for Brazil, which accounts for the time required to bring fluid milk to a collection point or directly to the plant, applies to every country in the area. One of the tests of the appropriateness of the Brazilian estimate is to check the relation between the minimum average cost point estimated with the shadow rate and the actual output of the plants shown in Tables 7-5 and 7-6. In some cases (semihard cheese in Uruguay and bland cheese in Peru), the output at minimum average cost (in the optimum size plant) is larger than the output of the plant for which costs are shown. In those cases, economies of scale in production are assumed prevalent up to the turning-point output. The other three cases (Argentina—semihard and bland paste cheese, and Uruguay—hard paste cheese) are characterized by turning-point output less than actual output. It is assumed in those cases that diseconomies of scale prevail in the range between the turning-point and the actual output.

If turning-point outputs are underestimated in the Uruguayan and Argentine cases, it means that the shadow transport rate as estimated for Brazil (state of São Paulo) is an overestimate of the shadow rate in Argentina and Uruguay, and that the marginal cost of production of powdered milk and cheese is also overestimated for those countries. If the turning-point output is overestimated for Peru (the estimate is five times as high as the actual output of the plant), then the estimated marginal cost of production for Peru is biased downward. Since (1) the linearly approximated marginal cost of production derived for powdered milk in Uruguay is considerably lower than that in Brazil, (2) the marginal cost of bland paste cheese is higher in Peru than Brazil, and (3) the cost is lower in Argentina than in Brazil, the elimination of biases in costs would tend to make the comparative advantages of the optimum location even stronger in these cases. However, in hard and semihard paste cheeses, there is no way of determining which of the derived marginal costs is more biased, if indeed, a difference exists at all.

The solutions to the linearized programming model are found under the assumption of equal plant sizes in the producing countries. For powdered milk, annual output of each plant is assumed to be 3,400 metric tons; for hard paste cheese, 900 tons; for semihard cheese, 332 tons, and for bland cheese, 414 tons. These plant sizes represent the largest of the plants for which costs were estimated in all the countries observed in each product. Since costs rise with output in many cases, the average plant size assumed for this study acted to increase costs in those countries with lower average plant size. Where this assumption affects the optimum location of production within Latin America, it is discussed below. For imported hard cheese the f.o.b. price assumed is $1,357 per metric ton (for one-year-old parmesan of first quality, at the factory in Reggio Emilia, Italy); for semihard cheese the f.o.b. price assumed is $905 per metric ton (for full cream, factory, average factory price paid by wholesalers, Leeuwarden, Netherlands).[5] As explained above, all imports are assumed to originate in the United States.

5. Food and Agriculture Organization, *Production Yearbook*, Vol. 18 (1964), p. 386. The prices shown represent average prices for 1960–63. In the cases of hard and soft cheeses, the producer prices are adjusted for commercialization by multiplying that price by 1.25. This operation makes them compatible with the Latin American cost curves used. The resulting prices are $1,695 for hard cheese and $665 for soft cheese.

Table 7-8. Optimum Location of Production of Powdered Milk and Cheese in LAFTA, and Selected Alternatives, and their Costs, 1975

Thousands of metric tons; millions of simones

Solution and producing country	Amount produced	Consuming countries	Notes	Cost of solution to the area
		Powdered milk		
Solution 1			Optimum solution	Š310.8
United States	377.2	All		
Solution 2			Optimum in LAFTA	373.3
Uruguay	377.2	All	111 plants	
Solution 3				673.5
Brazil	377.2	All	111 plants	
Solution 4			National solution	492.9
Argentina	49.0	Argentina	At Uruguayan import price	
Brazil	152.5	Brazil	47 plants	
Uruguay	175.7	All others	52 plants	
Solution 5			Another form of national production	344.0
Argentina	49.0	Argentina	At Uruguayan import price	
Brazil	152.5	Brazil	47 plants	
Uruguay	0.2	Uruguay	1 plant	
United States	175.5	All others		
		Hard paste cheese		
Solution 1			Optimum solution	105.1
Uruguay	97.9	All	109 plants	
Solution 2				111.0
Argentina	97.9	All	109 plants	
Solution 3			National solution	108.8
Argentina	47.9	Argentina	54 plants	
Uruguay	50.0	All others	56 plants	
Solution 4			Import solution	180.9
United States	97.9	All		
		Semihard paste cheese		
Solution 1			Optimum solution	76.0
Uruguay	92.9	All	280 plants	
Solution 2				93.4
Argentina	92.9	All	280 plants	

Table 7-8. (*continued*)

Solution and producing country	Amount produced	Consuming countries	Notes	Cost of solution to the area
Solution 3			National solution	84.3
Argentina	45.2	Argentina	136 plants	
Uruguay	47.7	All others	144 plants	
Solution 4				97.7
United States	92.9	All	Import solution	
		Bland paste cheese		
Solution 1			Optimum solution[a]	150.9
United States	19.5	Chile, Colombia, Ecuador, Peru		
Argentina	171.3	All others		
Solution 2				151.6
Argentina	190.8	All	462 plants	
Solution 3				152.2
Argentina	186.0	All others		
Peru	4.8	Peru		
Solution 4			National solution	154.6
Argentina	114.1	Argentina, Chile, Colombia, Ecuador, Paraguay, Uruguay		
Brazil	71.9	Brazil		
Peru	4.8	Peru		
Solution 5			Import solution	155.0
United States	190.8	All		
Solution 6				165.2
Brazil	183.9	Argentina, Brazil, Chile, Paraguay, Uruguay	445 plants	
Peru	6.9	Colombia, Ecuador, Peru		
Solution 7				164.9
Brazil	190.8	All	462 plants	
Solution 8				200.2
Peru	190.8	All	462 plants	

Note: Mexico did not present demand studies for any of the products, and therefore is not included in these solutions. Venezuela is included only in the powdered milk solution.

a. The optimum solution for bland paste cheese, along with that under maximum cost assumptions for paper and pulp, is the only optimum solution that includes the United States. This is because the optimum location in LAFTA, Argentina, would require the construction of more than 400 plants in that country by 1975.

The results of the linear program show that Argentine and Uruguayan cheeses are competitive with imports at the official rates of exchange, but that powdered milk imports are cheaper than domestically produced dry milk. In the case of bland cheese, the prices of imports and of Argentine cheese are so close at the official rate that for all practical purposes the two sources are interchangeable. The optimum location for powdered milk production is the United States. The optimum location in LAFTA is Uruguay. The cost to the region (noting the omission of Mexico) of this "second best" solution would be $62 million annually. If powdered milk is produced in Argentina, Uruguay, and Brazil—assuming that Argentina can compete with Uruguay—it would cost the area an additional $182 million annually, or almost 60 percent of the cost of importing. For cheeses, Uruguay and Argentina are the optimum locations for production in the area. The additional costs to the area of national production in the countries for which costs have been estimated are very small. The national solution for bland paste cheese, in which Argentina produces for all countries but Brazil and Peru, costs the area only an additional $4 million annually, or less than 3 percent of the cost associated with the optimum location.

In all forms of the products, the number of plants in any country that is to provide the entire area with a type of cheese or powdered milk is quite large. It is assumed in estimating costs of dairy products that transporting milk is a constraint on the size of plants. If the plants are located in the same place, costs of production have been underestimated in this study; on the other hand, if it is possible to distribute smaller plants throughout the country (in cases where diseconomies of scale occur), costs have been overestimated. The problem of distributing plants over a region that is sufficiently large that the milk sources for the plants do not overlap is not solved by the model developed in Appendix E. A model that would deal with that problem would have to treat the varying distance from markets within the country as well as the transportation of raw material sources.

Indifference Exchange Rates

Tables 7-9 and 7-10 show the prices and indifference exchange rates associated with the various production locations. Since Uruguayan pesos were considered overvalued at 21 pesos per simón in 1964, it is possible

Table 7-9. Prices of Powdered Milk and Cheese in LAFTA, 1975

Simones per metric ton

Consuming country	Powdered milk	Hard paste cheese	Semihard paste cheese	Bland paste cheese
Optimum location[a]				
Argentina	966	1,062	808	778
Brazil	982	1,076	822	809
Chile	1,002	1,112	858	778
Colombia	1,000	1,135	881	783
Ecuador	1,012	1,126	872	776
Paraguay	965	1,059	805	782
Peru	1,008	1,130	876	785
Uruguay	952	1,046	792	793
Venezuela	1,022	n.a.	n.a.	n.a.
Imports from the United States				
Argentina	823	1,829	1,038	798
Brazil	840	1,872	1,081	841
Chile	827	1,809	1,018	778
Colombia	814	1,814	1,023	783
Ecuador	825	1,807	1,016	776
Paraguay	832	1,838	1,047	807
Peru	826	1,816	1,025	785
Uruguay	824	1,829	1,038	798
Venezuela	801	n.a.	n.a.	n.a.
National production[b]				
Argentina	963	1,118	989	778
Brazil	1,764	1,076	822	842
Chile	999	1,112	858	796
Colombia	997	1,135	881	865
Ecuador	1,009	1,126	872	856
Paraguay	962	1,059	805	782
Peru	1,005	1,130	876	971
Uruguay	949	1,046	792	793
Venezuela	999	n.a.	n.a.	n.a.

n.a. Not available.

a. The optimum locations in LAFTA are Uruguay for powdered milk and for hard and semihard paste cheese; and Argentina (and U.S. imports) for bland paste cheese.

b. Brazil and Argentina produce powdered milk for themselves (the latter at the Uruguayan import price) and Uruguay produces it for all others; Argentina produces hard and semihard paste cheeses for itself and Uruguay produces them for all others; and Brazil and Peru produce bland paste cheese for themselves, with Argentina supplying all others.

that changes since that time in the costs of production of powdered milk and in the rate of exchange have left Uruguay with a comparative advantage over imports. The relative change in Uruguay's favor would not have to exceed 25 percent in order for it to be competitive with imports in every country shown (Table 7-10). The correction of any overvaluation of the

Table 7-10. Prices and Implicit Indifference Exchange Rates for Selected Locations of Production of Powdered Milk and Cheese in LAFTA

Producing country, product, price ratio, and currencies exchanged[k]	Consuming country								
	Argentina	Brazil	Chile	Colombia	Ecuador	Paraguay	Peru	Uruguay	Venezuela
	Prices per metric ton in simones								
United States									
Powdered milk	823	840	827	814	825	832	826	823	801
Hard cheese	1,829	1,872	1,809	1,814	1,807	1,838	1,816	1,929	n.a.
Semihard cheese	1,038	1,081	1,018	1,023	1,016	1,047	1,025	1,038	n.a.
Bland cheese	789	841	778	783	776	807	785	789	n.a.
Argentina[b]									
Hard cheese	1,118	1,148	1,135	1,204	1,195	1,122	1,199	1,130	n.a.
Semihard cheese	989	1,020	1,006	1,075	1,066	993	1,070	1,004	n.a.
Bland cheese	778	809	796	865	856	782	860	793	n.a.
Brazil									
Powdered milk[c]	1,786	1,757	1,811	1,812	1,826	1,795	1,819	1,775	1,809
Bland cheese[d]	871	842	896	960	943	880	943	860	n.a.
Peru									
Bland cheese[e]	1,035	1,079	1,024	1,031	1,008	1,044	966	1,036	n.a.
Uruguay									
Powdered milk[f]	966	982	1,002	1,000	1,012	965	1,008	952	1,022
Hard cheese[g]	1,062	1,076	1,112	1,135	1,126	1,059	1,130	1,046	n.a.
Semihard cheese[g]	808	822	858	881	872	805	876	792	n.a.

Price ratios

Uruguayan to U.S.									
Powdered milk	1.17	1.17	1.21	1.23	1.23	1.16	1.22	1.16	1.25
Semihard cheese	0.78	0.76	0.84	0.86	0.86	0.77	0.85	0.76	n.a.
Uruguayan to Argentine									
Hard cheese	0.95	0.94	0.98	0.94	0.94	0.94	0.94	0.92	n.a.
Semihard cheese	0.82	0.81	0.85	0.82	0.82	0.81	0.82	0.79	n.a.
Brazilian to Argentine									
Bland cheese	1.12	1.04	1.13	1.10	1.10	1.13	1.10	1.08	n.a.
Indifference exchange rates									
Uruguayan pesos per dollar									
Powdered milk[b]	24.6	24.6	25.4	25.8	25.8	24.4	25.6	24.4	26.2
Semihard cheese[i]	16.4	16.0	17.6	18.1	18.1	16.2	17.8	16.0	n.a.
Uruguayan pesos per Argentine peso									
Hard cheese[j]	0.24	0.24	0.25	0.24	0.24	0.24	0.24	0.23	n.a.
Semihard cheese[j]	0.21	0.20	0.21	0.21	0.21	0.20	0.21	0.20	n.a.
Cruzeiros per Argentine peso									
Bland cheese[k]	147.84	137.28	149.16	145.20	145.20	149.16	145.20	142.56	n.a.

n.a. Not available.

a. In each case the producing country is assumed to supply all powdered milk or cheese to the area; minimum costs are assumed.
b. The exchange rate is 140 Argentine pesos per simón.
c. The exchange rate is 1,200 cruzeiros per simón.
d. The exchange rate is 1,850 cruzeiros per simón.
e. The exchange rate is 26.82 soles per simón.
f. The exchange rate is 21 Uruguayan pesos per simón.
g. The exchange rate is 35 Uruguayan pesos per simón.
h. Calculated as the ratio of Uruguayan prices to U.S. prices multiplied by 21 (the number of pesos per simón).
i. Calculated as the ratio of Uruguayan prices to U.S. prices multiplied by 35 (the number of pesos per simón). The Uruguayan exchange rate differs for the two products because the studies were made at different times.
j. Calculated as the ratio of Uruguayan prices to Argentine prices multiplied by 0.25 (the number of Uruguayan pesos per Argentine peso).
k. Calculated as the ratio of Brazilian to Argentine prices multiplied by 132 (the number of cruzeiros per Argentine peso).

Table 7-11. Welfare Benefits and Costs of Selected Alternatives to Optimum Location of Production of Powdered Milk and Cheese in LAFTA, 1975[a]

Thousands of simones

Country	Powdered milk		Hard cheese		Semihard cheese		Bland cheese		Total	
	Production effect	Total	Production effect	Total	Production effect	Total	Production effect	Total	Production effect	Total
	Optimum location in LAFTA[b] versus U.S. imports[c]									
Argentina	−7,005	−7,635	21,365	29,057	8,035	9,160	2,173	2,216	24,568	32,798
Brazil	−21,869	−23,618	17,258	23,643	6,826	7,918	2,327	2,373	4,541	10,316
Chile	−8,469	−9,400	2,862	3,750	837	921	...	...	−4,769	−4,729
Colombia	−2,306	−2,560	126	164	160	173	...	...	−2,020	−2,222
Ecuador	−786	−872	43	56	49	53	...	...	−694	−763
Paraguay	−280	−302	44	61	18	21	5	5	−212	−215
Peru	−274	−304	1,074	1,396	302	329	...	...	1,102	1,421
Uruguay	−26	−28	1,439	1,986	551	639	48	48	2,013	2,646
Venezuela	−23,708	−27,027	...	...	...	...	...	...	−23,709	−27,027
Total	−64,723	−71,746	44,211	60,113	16,778	19,214	4,553	4,642	821	12,225
	National production[d] versus optimum location in LAFTA[b]									
Argentina	−66,356	−92,898	−2,543	−2,620	−6,574	−7,297	...	...	−9,117	−9,917
Brazil	...	...	...	...	...	...	−2,327	−2,373	−68,683	−95,271
Chile	...	...	...	...	...	...	−196	−198	−196	−198
Colombia	...	...	...	...	...	...	−113	−118	−113	−118
Ecuador	...	...	...	...	...	...	−35	−37	−35	−37
Paraguay	...	...	...	...	...	...	...	...	...	...
Peru	...	...	...	...	...	...	−716	−802	−716	−802
Uruguay	...	...	...	...	...	...	...	...	...	...
Venezuela	...	...	...	...	...	...	...	...	...	...
Total	−66,356	−92,898	−2,543	−2,260	−6,574	−7,297	−3,387	−3,528	−78,860	−106,343

a. Minimum costs are assumed.
b. See Table 7-8, Solution 1 for hard and semihard paste cheese; Solution 2 for powdered milk and bland paste cheese.

Argentine peso in 1964 would also make that country more competitive in cheese production, relative to both third country imports and, possibly, Uruguayan production. Similar statements can be made in regard to Brazilian and Peruvian versus Argentine bland cheese production.

Welfare Benefits and Costs

Welfare costs associated with the alternative locations of production and with the present tariff structure are shown in Table 7-11. The gains to LAFTA from buying from the optimum location in LAFTA, rather than importing from outside the area, are negative for powdered milk and positive for cheese. The welfare costs of national production rather than buying from the optimum in LAFTA are relatively high, totaling $106 million, most of which results from the high cost of production of powdered milk in Brazil.

CHAPTER EIGHT

Paper and Pulp

PAPER AND THE WOOD PULP, or cellulose, from which it is made are produced in a highly developed industry in Latin America. In 1964, all countries in the Latin American Free Trade Association (LAFTA) produced paper, and every one but Ecuador and Paraguay supplied more than 50 percent of its own domestic demand.

The tables make plain that the major consumers of paper and pulp are also the major producers, and that production in those countries has increased more rapidly than consumption. In the fifteen years before 1964, paper and paperboard consumption in the area more than doubled, but production more than tripled, with the result that the region met nearly four-fifths of its own needs in 1964, compared with slightly under three-fifths in the earlier period (see Table 8-1).[1] Similarly, most LAFTA countries that year produced the greater part of their own wood pulp needs,

1. Care should be taken in making production-consumption comparisons for paper and paperboard. Many paper products are heavily protected in the countries under study, so that consumption may be a function of production. If a country prohibited imports of paper, production would immediately become 100 percent of consumption. As it now stands, production may be catching up to consumption because tariffs have been raised on an increased number of paper products. Newsprint presents an interesting example: While tariffs are high in Chile and Mexico, Argentina and Brazil offer low protection. Argentine production has fallen both in absolute terms and relative to consumption; Brazilian production has clearly risen, measured both ways, despite the low tariff (however, import licensing and prior deposit provisions, which are not included in the tariff, may have acted to stimulate domestic production).

Table 8-1. Paper and Paperboard Apparent Consumption and Production in LAFTA, Selected Years, 1949–64

Thousands of metric tons

Producing and consuming country	Total, paper and paperboard			Newsprint		
		Production			Production	
	Apparent consumption	Amount	Percent of domestic consumption	Apparent consumption	Amount	Percent of domestic consumption
1949–50						
Argentina	403.0	195.0	48.0%	109.0	0	...
Brazil	294.0	233.0	79.0	84.0	30.0	36.0%
Chile	65.0	45.0	70.0	26.0	10.0	38.0
Colombia	59.0	8.0	14.0	15.0	0	...
Ecuador	n.a.	0.3	3.0	n.a.	0	...
Mexico	184.0	125.0	68.0	49.0	2.0	4.0
Paraguay	n.a.	0	...	n.a.	0	...
Peru	31.0	18.0	58.0	9.0	0	...
Uruguay	48.0	25.0	52.0	17.0	0	...
Venezuela	45.0	5.0	11.0	9.0	0	...
Total	1,129.0	654.3	58.0	318.0	42.0	13.2
1955						
Argentina	410.0	283.6	69.2	111.0	21.6	10.7
Brazil	479.6	333.2	69.5	167.6	37.2	22.2
Chile	83.1	67.3	81.0	25.4	11.5	45.3
Colombia	96.1	29.2	30.4	21.6	0	...
Ecuador	13.4	0.6	4.5	7.4	0	...
Mexico	297.8	228.6	76.8	47.3	0	...
Paraguay	1.8	0.4	22.2	0.5	0	...
Peru	51.2	26.7	52.1	15.4	0	...
Uruguay	58.2	30.0	51.5	24.5	0	...
Venezuela	89.8	12.3	13.7	16.1	0	...
Total	1,581.1	1,011.9	64.0	436.8	70.3	16.1
1960						
Argentina	461.2	290.5	63.0	171.0	9.3	5.4
Brazil	664.8	474.4	71.4	230.2	65.8	28.6
Chile	86.1	105.8	ª	27.0	51.5	ª
Colombia	127.4	51.3	40.3	33.1	0	...
Ecuador	17.6	1.0	5.7	8.0	0	...
Mexico	553.4	412.4	77.0	103.9	14.0	13.5
Paraguay	3.0	0.4	14.3	1.2	0	...
Peru	75.8	46.9	62.1	18.1	0	...
Uruguay	60.5	39.0	64.5	20.0	0	...
Venezuela	138.2	48.8	35.3	23.5	0	...
Total	2,188.0	1,470.5	67.2	636.0	140.6	22.1

Table 8-1. *(continued)*

Producing and consuming country	Total, paper and paperboard			Newsprint		
		Production			Production	
	Apparent consump- tion	Amount	Percent of domestic consump- tion	Apparent consump- tion	Amount	Percent of domestic consump- tion
			1964			
Argentina	589.5	407.6	69.1	173.3	8.2	4.7
Brazil	725.7	650.3	89.6	184.3	118.5	64.3
Chile	129.6	160.3	a	42.7	77.1	a
Colombia	171.4	114.9	67.2	41.7	0	...
Ecuador	21.7	0.3	1.4	9.7	0	...
Mexico	682.0	557.7	81.8	114.6	15.6	13.6
Paraguay	4.5	0.9	20.0	1.4	0	...
Peru	110.2	59.8	54.3	37.1	0	...
Uruguay	61.6	36.5	59.2	23.6	0	...
Venezuela	216.1	132.6	61.4	38.1	0	...
Total	2,712.3	2,120.9	78.2	666.5	219.4	32.9

Sources: Juan B. Rodriguez Quintanilla, *La Industria del Papel y la Celulosa en el Peru* (Lima: Universidad Nacional Mayer de San Marcos, Instituto de Investigaciones Económicas, 1966; processed), App. 1; ECLA, *Pulp and Paper in Latin America* (1963), App. 1.
a. Net exports.

and Brazil and Chile were net exporters. As Table 8-2 demonstrates, regional output of wood and other fiber pulps in 1964 was almost five times its level in 1949–50, while net imports dropped off sharply.[2]

Given the circumstances, it is not surprising that the paper and pulp industry has been the object of a number of attempts to analyze prospects for production on a country-by-country basis.[3] Because the industry developed behind a high tariff wall (see Table 8-4), it is reasonable to assume that integration of paper and pulp production, except for newsprint, faces considerable opposition from vested interests, some of which may involve quite inefficient operations.

2. Because of its sharply different characteristics of supply and demand, newsprint is reported separately in these tables, and discussed separately below. See pp. 207–08.

3. Juan B. Rodriguez Quintanilla, *La Industria del Papel y la Celulosa en el Peru* (Lima: Universidad Nacional Mayor de San Marcos, Instituto de Investigaciones Económicas, 1966; processed).

United Nations, ECLA/FAO/DOAT, *El Papel y La Celulosa en America Latina: Situación Actual y Tendencias Futuras de la Demanda, Producción e Intercambio*, E/CN.12/570/Rev. 3 (1966) provides, on pp. 3–4, a list of United Nations documents pertaining to paper and pulp in Latin America.

Table 8-2. Paper Pulp Production in LAFTA, Selected Years, 1949–64[a]

Thousands of metric tons

Producing country	1949–50			1955			1960			1964		
	Wood pulp	Other fiber pulp	Total	Wood[b] pulp	Other fiber pulp[c]	Total	Wood[b] pulp	Other fiber pulp[c]	Total	Wood[b] pulp	Other fiber pulp[c]	Total
Argentina	11.0	23.0	34.0	22.1	33.8	55.9	46.4	26.9	73.3	67.4	40.0	107.4
Brazil	130.0	16.0	146.0	173.6	13.9	187.5	289.7	40.0	329.7	477.0[d]	93.0	570.0
Chile	14.0	5.0	19.0	17.8	2.2	20.0	102.2	2.7	104.9	174.1	0	174.1
Colombia	0.0	0.4	0.4	0.0	1.3	1.3	6.2	2.7	8.9	19.5	25.5	45.0
Ecuador	0.0	0.0	0.0	0.0	0.0	0.0	0.0	0.0	0.0	0.0	0.0	0.0
Mexico	58.0	3.0	61.0	82.4	11.5	93.9	174.5	60.5	235.0	238.7	79.9	318.6
Paraguay	0.0	0.0	0.0	0.0	0.0	0.0	0.0	0.0	0.0	0.0	0.0	0.0
Peru	0.0	5.0	5.0	0.0	13.0	13.0	0.0	28.0	28.0	0.0	42.7	42.7
Uruguay	0.0	3.0	3.0	2.0	3.3	5.3	2.0	3.0	5.0	3.7	2.5	6.3
Venezuela	0.0	0.0	0.0	6.1	0.0	6.1	0.0	0.0	0.0	0.0	14.2	14.2
Total	213.0	55.4	268.4	304.0	79.0	383.5	621.0	163.8	784.8	980.4	297.8	1,278.3

Source: Same as for Table 8-1.
a. Does not include newsprint.
b. Includes mechanical pulp and chemical wood pulp.
c. Includes other chemical pulp.
d. Estimates.

187

Table 8-3. Net Imports of Wood Pulp in LAFTA, Selected Years, 1950–64

Thousands of metric tons

	1949–50	1955	1960	1964
Argentina	70.0	202.4	86.2	149.0
Brazil	132.0	102.6	81.3	−267.0ª
Chile	25.0	38.7	7.3	−9.4ª
Colombia	1.0	23.8	31.1	37.1
Ecuador	0.0	0.0	0.0	0.0
Mexico	53.0	59.2	34.5	44.1
Paraguay	0.0	0.0	0.0	0.0
Peru	8.0	8.6	11.1	18.4
Uruguay	12.0	14.9	25.7	16.5
Venezuela	7.0	6.1	31.0	71.2
Total	308.0	456.3	308.2	59.9

Sources: ECLA, *El Papel y la Celulosa en America Latina*, App. 4; *Pulp and Paper in Latin America* (1963), App. 4.
a. Net exports.

Table 8-4. Nominal and Effective Tariffs on Pulp and Paper in LAFTA, 1965

Percent

	Pulp		Newsprint		Kraft paper		
Levying country	*Nominal: third countries*	*Nominal: LAFTA countries*	*Nominal: third countries*	*Nominal: LAFTA countries*	*Nominal: third countries*	*Nominal: LAFTA countries*	*Effective*ª
Argentina	38.0	1.8ᵇ	1.8	1.8	142.5	142.5	…
Brazil	26.0	1.0	1.0	1.0	316.0	316.0	924.0
Chile	39.1	39.1	90.0	90.0	ᶜ	ᶜ	…
Colombia	22.7	1.0ᵈ	1.0	0.0	46.3	46.3	62.5
Ecuador	40.1	0.0	24.8	4.4	44.0	44.0	…
Mexico	44.0ᵉ	30.0ᵉ	34.6	11.0	82.1	82.1	321.0
Paraguay	30.0	30.0	20.0	15.5	97.4	97.4	…
Peru	12.0	0.0	12.0	0.0	60.7	60.7	112.3
Uruguay	35.5	0.0	3.4	0.0	173.3	173.3	…
Venezuela	13.5	13.5	0.0	0.0	100.5	100.5	…

Sources: ECLA, *El Papel y la Celulosa en America Latina*, p. 136; see also U.S. Department of Commerce, Bureau of International Commerce.
  a. The effective tariff equals $t_f - (1 - v)t_a$,
where
   t_f = nominal tariff on kraft paper
   t_a = nominal tariff on chemical pulp
   v = value added to cellulose by kraft paper production per simon of kraft paper output.
  b. For pulp of 9 percent latifoliodas (broad-leafed trees).
  c. Imports prohibited.
  d. For pulp of 5 percent latifoliodas.
  e. Applies only to pulp of types not produced domestically.

The prospects of a substantial increase in the trade of paper and cartons among the countries of LAFTA, excluding newsprint, are not very promising, due principally to the fact that the majority of the countries are important producers of paper and cartons, satisfying a large part of domestic demand. This makes it very difficult to grant preferential tariffs in these products. One exception, perhaps, is computer cards, for which the capacity that already exists in . . . Argentina and Chile could satisfy regional demand.[4]

This study concerns the optimum location in LAFTA of production of one of the more important types of paper, kraft paper, including semi-kraft paper. These products are generally used in wrapping papers and container board, respectively. In addition, demand projections are made for newsprint and for the kraft pulp used in its production as well as in the production of kraft paper. The costs of Chilean newsprint are also compared with the United States-Canadian newsprint price.[5]

Four possible locations are considered for the production of pulp: the Bio-Bio region of South Central Chile, the state of Nuevo Leon in northern Mexico, the state of Santa Caterina in Southern Brazil, and Peru. The first three produce pulp from softwoods or soft-hardwood (eucalyptus), while the Peruvian costs are based on a bagasse pulp. In addition to these four locations, kraft paper costs are estimated for Colombia and Ecuador. The Colombian plants import softwood pulp and add domestic hardwood pulp to produce the paper. The Ecuadorian plant uses bagasse and waste paper

---

4. ECLA, *El Papel y La Celulosa*, p. 137. Author's translation.

5. One of the technical problems in this study is to homogenize pulp and paper output to make costs comparable. Newsprint has a lower kraft pulp equivalent than kraft paper, and hardwood pulp produces a paper of lower quality than softwood pulp does. In order to convert all these grades of pulp and paper into 100 percent kraft equivalents, the U.S. ratio of the price of each product to the price of unbleached kraft paper is used. Although these prices reflect supply and demand conditions rather than supply conditions alone, available data do not permit more sophisticated adjustments.

Adjustments were made by applying the following factors to the tonnage:

Product	Conversion factor	Basis for factor
Cellulose for newsprint	0.770	U.S. ratio of prices of newsprint to prices of 100% kraft paper
Container and semikraft paper	0.662	U.S. ratio of prices of liner board to prices of 100% kraft paper

Final demand is then shown in kraft cellulose-equivalent tons. More exactly, one ton of paper should equal 1.05 tons of cellulose, because of waste. For purposes of this study, however, it is assumed that one ton of 100 percent kraft cellulose is equivalent to one ton of kraft paper.

Table 8-5. Production and Consumption of Kraft Paper in LAFTA, 1963

Thousands of metric tons

Producing and consuming country	Production	Consumption
Argentina	42[a]	42
Brazil	85	85
Chile	40	40
Colombia	48	48
Ecuador	n.a.	8
Mexico	211	218
Paraguay	0	n.a.
Peru	22	22
Uruguay	3	3
Total	451	466

Source: ECIEL, *The Demand for Chemical Fertilizers, Tractors, Paper and Pulp, Milk Concentrates, and Lathes in the Latin American Free Trade Association (including Venezuela)* (Brookings Institution, 1966; processed).

n.a. Not available.

a. 1962 data.

to produce pulp, but a breakdown of production costs between pulp and paper was not possible.

Projections of Demand

Kraft paper consumption is expected to increase from 466,000 tons in 1963 to 1,356,000 tons in 1975 (see Tables 8-5 and 8-6).[6] Mexico accounts for almost half the 1963 consumption and almost 40 percent of 1975 production. Argentine consumption is assumed equal to production for the purposes of projection. Even though consumption of kraft paper was met almost entirely from domestic production, the 1963 output represented only one-third of the midpoint of the 1975 projections.

Demand for cellulose (shown in Table 8-7) is estimated on the basis of its use in kraft paper and newsprint, according to the known conversion factor.[7] In turn, for the purposes of Table 8-7, all kraft paper used in the region is assumed to be produced there. Newsprint production in the region

6. The 1975 figure is the midpoint of the minimum and maximum projections reported in Table 8-6.

7. The cellulose considered here is kraft unbleached cellulose used in the production of kraft and semikraft papers. It has other uses, but the data given here do not include them.

Table 8-6. Projected Demand for Kraft Paper in LAFTA, 1975

Metric tons

Country	Minimum	Maximum
Argentina	n.a.	n.a.
Brazil	227,947	306,362
Chile	57,700	73,700
Colombia	122,900	132,000
Ecuador[a]	260,000	326,000
Mexico[b]	454,600	610,000
Paraguay	544	646
Peru	53,000	70,000
Uruguay	5,148	12,537
Venezuela	n.a.	n.a.
Total	1,181,839	1,531,245

Source: ECIEL, *The Demand for Chemical Fertilizers.*

n.a. Not available.

a. These figures include banana boxes. A more recent projection (July 1967) made in Ecuador shows that the figures here may be slightly high.

b. Includes in the minimum projection, 273,600 tons, and in the maximum, 366,000 tons, of semikraft papers.

Table 8-7. Demand for Cellulose for Use in Kraft Paper and in Newsprint in LAFTA, 1975

Thousands of metric tons of kraft cellulose

Consuming country	Cellulose for kraft paper	Cellulose for newsprint[a]
Argentina	45.7[b]	11.7
Brazil	267.2	133.4
Chile	54.8[c]	41.0
Colombia	127.6	0
Ecuador	293.0	0
Mexico	424.2[d]	30.6
Paraguay	0.6	0
Peru	61.5	0
Uruguay	8.8	0
Venezuela	n.a.	0
Total	1,283.4	216.7

Sources: Tables 8-6 and 8-14.

n.a. Not available.

a. Derived from domestic production of newsprint. One ton of cellulose for newsprint is taken as 0.770 of a ton of kraft cellulose. See note 5, p.189.

b. Kraft paper demand refers to domestic production figures only, and does not represent total demand. This figure was calculated by projecting current demand using the projected percentage increase for "other" papers.

c. Equals demand for wrapping paper plus 0.662 times demand for container paper. See note 5, p. 189.

d. Equals demand for kraft paper plus 0.662 times demand for semikraft paper. See note 5, p. 189.

is based on the percentage of consumption supplied by domestic producers in recent years.

The projected demand for cellulose (Table 8-8, pages 194–95) is estimated on the hypothesis that part of it will be consumed by kraft paper producers and part by newsprint producers in Latin America; projections of newsprint production, in turn, are based on the percentage of consumption supplied by domestic producers in recent years. Cellulose is expressed in terms of kraft unbleached cellulose, because the costs shown below are estimated for this product. Kraft cellulose refers to the production of sulphate chemical pulp for all uses. This study is concerned, however, only with the consumption of pulp in two types of paper production.

Cost Structure

Table 8-8 shows the percentage breakdown and total cost of production for kraft cellulose and kraft paper.[8] The most pronounced deviation appears for the Mexican kraft paper plant, where raw materials constitute 83.8 percent of total cost and value added is very low. It should be noted that this plant, unlike the other kraft paper plants shown, is not integrated; that is, unbleached kraft cellulose enters the plant in dried form and is processed into paper. Nevertheless, the value added may be considerably underestimated for this plant. According to the cost curve, kraft paper net of pulp input costs $36.7 per metric ton at 60,000 tons of output in Mexico compared with $66.4 in Chile (at 5 escudos per simón) and $134.4 in Peru.

In Mexico and Chile, the two countries for which softwood costs are available, the cost of production of bleached cellulose presented here

---

8. Costs for each country had to be adjusted to a standardized basis for purposes of intercountry comparisons. Like the demand data, costs were adjusted with U.S. price ratios, although these correspond closely to the same data gleaned from Latin American cost figures. Bleaching pulp provides an example of the close correspondence between U.S. and Latin American adjustment factors. The ratio of U.S. prices for bleached and unbleached chemical sulphate pulp is 1.203; the average for Chile and Mexico is 1.190 (1.254 and 1.125, respectively).

For all adjustments, see ECIEL, Martin Carnoy (ed.), *The Optimum Location of Specific Industries in the Latin American Free Trade Association (including Venezuela)*, Vol. 4: *Pulp and Paper* (Brookings Institution, 1966; processed).

Except where noted, the cost breakdowns are shown for plants producing unbleached, dried cellulose. However, costs of production for all plants are adjusted to those for unbleached, dried pulp for estimating the minimum cost location. In the case of the 105,000 ton Chilean plant, for example, the cost of 533 escudos per ton is lowered by eliminating the bleaching process and raised by including the drying process.

differ by so much in the free exchange rate case that if Mexican production costs are to equal Chilean, the cost of softwood in Mexico would have to be less than $1 per cubic meter. The price in Chile of softwood is estimated to be $4.05 and $5.79 per cubic meter for exchange rates of 5 escudos and 3.5 escudos per simón, respectively. The cost to the Mexican plant is $12.00. At the official rate of exchange, however, Mexican costs would have to fall only to $10.30, almost twice the Chilean price, for Mexican costs of production to equal Chilean costs. One difference is that Chilean plants use 5.8 cubic meters per ton of bleached cellulose and the Mexican plant uses 4.8 cubic meters per ton for unbleached. Estimates made by the United Nations use 5.3 and 4.8 cubic meters per ton for bleached and unbleached cellulose, respectively.[9]

The cost curves derived from the data shown in Table 8-8 are considered long-run when there are two or more observations of plant capacity, and short-run when there is only one. The short-run curves are taken as proxies for the long-run curves in those locations for which data covered plants of under 120,000 tons annual output.[10]

In the context of the linearized programming model, the high Mexican pulp costs and the low value added to pulp in paper production might be expected to result in Mexican importation of cheap pulp to be made into paper. This apparently erroneous combination probably results in underestimation of the total cost of paper production in the region and of the cost of paper consumed in Mexico. In the case of both pulp and paper produced in Mexico, however, the probable net error is greatly reduced since the bias resulting from the overestimate of pulp cost would be offset by that from the underestimate of paper costs net of pulp input.

Optimum Location of Production

The cost curves estimated from Table 8-8, along with transportation costs, are used in determining a geographical pattern of production that

---

9. ECLA, *Chile—Potential Pulp and Paper Exporter*, E/CN.12/424/Rev. 1 (1957). The reason for the difference may lie in the moisture content of the wood input. The Chilean estimate (5.8 cubic meters per ton) is for wood at 10 percent water content. The U.N. and Mexican estimates, however, refer to completely dry wood, which makes them equivalent.

10. For a comparison of these estimates with those resulting from other studies, see App. F.

Table 8-8. Cost Structure of Kraft Cellulose and Kraft Paper Production[a] in LAFTA, 1975

Percent of total costs

Producing country and plant capacity in tons	Materials	Direct labor	Utilities	Maintenance	Depreciation	Insurance	Opportunity cost of capital	Other	Total	Cost per ton in national currency
				Kraft cellulose						
Brazil										
9,000	55.0	5.8	11.2	7.3[b]	[b]	°	12.4	8.3	100.0	282,020
63,600[d]	27.2	2.9	20.1	°	15.2	°	18.4	16.2	100.0	268,300
Chile										
35,000	32.4	6.6	9.7	°	13.8	1.1	26.2	10.2	100.0	588.2
105,000	42.5	4.0	12.7	°	11.6	0.9	22.0	6.3	100.0	533.1
Mexico										
120,000	40.5	3.5	6.7	°	°	°	18.8	30.4	100.0	1,771.7
120,000[e]	44.2	3.4	8.4	°	°	°	16.7	27.3	100.0	1,992.9
Peru										
30,000[f]	38.0	3.6	10.9	2.4	20.3	°	20.7	4.1	100.0	4,594.1
				Kraft paper						
Brazil										
300	53.2	5.4	14.4	4.5	5.1	°	13.1	4.3	100.0	657,900
9,000	65.8	6.1	12.0	6.4[b]	[b]	°	6.8	2.9	100.0	509,903

Chile										
35,000	27.7	7.4	8.3	°	15.8	1.2	30.0	9.6	100.0	653.7
105,000	41.9	4.5	12.0	°	11.6	0.9	22.0	7.1	100.0	968.7
										435.6
Colombia										
40,000	33.0	2.4	16.8	7.7	12.8	°	16.7	10.6	100.0	4,562
80,000	35.1	2.4	17.9	7.1	11.8	°	15.3	10.3	100.0	4,290
120,000	36.2	2.2	18.5	6.8	11.4	°	15.0	9.8	100.0	4,157
Ecuador										
6,600	33.2	5.2	12.5	6.1	10.8	3.1	16.1	12.9	100.0	4,000
Peru										
50,000	40.5	8.3	26.1	8.9	4.8	°	4.8	6.6	100.0	5,898
75,000	46.3	6.4	26.3	7.5	4.3	°	4.3	4.9	100.0	5,161
Mexico										
66,000	83.8	0.6	5.5	°	°	°	3.6	6.4	100.0	2,297

Source: ECIEL, Martin Carnoy (ed.), *The Optimum Location of Specific Industries in the Latin American Free Trade Association (including Venezuela)*, Vol. 4: *Pulp and Paper* (Brookings Institution, 1966; processed).
a. Includes cost of pulp.
b. Percentage listed for maintenance includes depreciation.
c. Included in other.
d. Bleached cellulose.
e. Undried cellulose.
f. Bagasse input.

would minimize the total cost to the area of meeting 1975 demand for pulp and kraft paper.

The linear programming model yields solutions whose total costs show considerable spread (see Table 8-9). Unlike the solutions to the fertilizer model, there are only one or two distributions of production that are not significantly below the optimum. The optimum location in the minimum cost case is Chile for all cellulose production for both newsprint production and kraft paper, as well as for all kraft paper except for plants in Mexico producing for its market. In the maximum cost case, the optimum locations are the United States for all cellulose production and Mexico for all kraft paper production for the area, except that Brazil produces all its own pulp and paper. As can be seen from the list of sample solutions, the deviations from the optima can be quite large. One of the more favorable solutions is national production, in which every potential producer supplies its own market, and Chile produces for all the others. The absolute cost of this solution is $59 million annually in both the minimum and the maximum cost cases.[11]

The most important assumption in the analysis of optimum location is that both the kraft cellulose and kraft paper plants are limited to 120,000 tons capacity. This is equivalent to about 363 tons per day, which is higher than the maximum capacity of both the Chilean plant shown in this study and the plants considered in the original ECLA Latin American pulp and paper study,[12] but lower than the maximum for developed countries.[13]

In the minimum cost optimum solution (Solution 1) Chile has thirteen plants producing kraft pulp and eight plants producing kraft paper, and Mexico, four plants producing kraft paper. In the maximum cost case (Solution 4) the cellulose price from the United States is not affected by changes in size of the Latin American market. Mexico has nine plants

11. As noted on pp. 192–93, the cost to the region of solutions in which Mexico imports pulp and produces paper are probably underestimated. Therefore, in the minimum cost case, Solution 3 may be the optimum, and the national production solution would deviate from it by less than 15 percent. In the maximum cost case, Solution 13 may be the true optimum, and national production would deviate from it by only 5 percent.

12. ECLA, *Pulp and Paper Prospects in Latin America*, Pt. 2, E/CN.12/370/Rev. 1 (1955).

13. U.S. Bureau of the Census, *U.S. Census of Manufactures*, Vol. 2, *Industry Statistics*, Pt. 1, *Major Groups 20 to 28* (1961). In 1958, there were fifteen pulp mills (establishments) in the western United States, producing an average of about 248,000 metric tons per establishment.

Table 8-9. Optimum Location of Production of Pulp and Paper in LAFTA, and Selected Alternatives, and their Costs, 1975

Thousands of metric tons

Producing country	Pulp		Kraft paper	
	Amount produced	*Consuming countries*	*Amount produced*	*Consuming countries*
Solution 1: Ŝ291.7 million (minimum);[a] *Ŝ408.4 million (maximum)*[b]— optimum solution under minimum cost assumptions				
Chile	1,500.1	All	859.2	All but Mexico
Mexico	...	...	424.2	Mexico
Solution 2: Ŝ294.4 million (minimum)[a]				
Chile	1,500.1	All	...	...
Mexico	...	...	1,283.4	All
Solution 3: Ŝ305.7 million (minimum);[a] *Ŝ432.8 million (maximum)*[b]				
Chile	1,500.1	All	1,283.4	All
Solution 4: Ŝ308.1 million (minimum);[a] *Ŝ321.3 million (maximum)*[b]— optimum solution under maximum cost assumptions				
Brazil	400.6	Brazil	267.2	Brazil
Mexico	...	...	1,016.2[c]	All but Brazil
United States	1,099.5	All but Brazil	...	...
Solution 5: Ŝ362.2 million (maximum)[b]				
Brazil	400.6	Brazil	267.2	Brazil
Chile	52.7	Argentina, Chile[d]	...	...
Mexico	...	...	1,016.2	All but Brazil
United States	1,046.8	Mexico	...	...
Solution 6: Ŝ326.0 million (maximum)[b]				
Brazil	400.6	Brazil	267.2	Brazil
Chile	162.6	Argentina,[e] Chile[f]	109.9	Argentina, Chile, Paraguay, Uruguay
Mexico	...	...	906.3	All others
United States	936.9	Mexico	...	...
Solution 7: Ŝ313.7 million (minimum);[a] *Ŝ334.6 million (maximum)*[b]				
Mexico	...	...	1,283.4	All
United States	1,500.1	All	...	...
Solution 8: Ŝ351.1 million (minimum);[a] *Ŝ380.6 million (maximum)*[b]— national solution under both sets of cost assumptions				
Brazil	400.6	Brazil	267.2	Brazil
Chile	351.7	Argentina, Chile, Colombia, Peru	109.9	Argentina, Chile, Paraguay, Uruguay

Table 8-9. (*continued*)

Producing country	Pulp		Kraft paper	
	Amount produced	*Consuming countries*	*Amount produced*	*Consuming countries*
Colombia	...	...	127.6	Colombia[g]
Ecuador	293.0	Ecuador	293.0	Ecuador
Mexico	454.8	Mexico	242.2	Mexico
Peru	...	...	61.5	Peru[g]

Solution 9: Ŝ351.7 million (minimum)[a]

Brazil	1,207.1	All but Ecuador	322.3	Argentina, Brazil, Paraguay, Uruguay
Ecuador	293.0	Ecuador	293.0	Ecuador
Mexico	...	...	668.1	Chile, Colombia, Mexico, Peru

Solution 10: Ŝ372.8 million (minimum),[a] *Ŝ397.0 million (maximum)*[b]

| Mexico | 1,500.1 | All | 1,283.4 | All |

Solution 11: Ŝ375.8 million (minimum),[a] *Ŝ377.0 million (maximum)*[b]— *import solution under both sets of cost assumptions*

| United States | 1,500.1 | All | 1,283.4 | All |

Solution 12: Ŝ381.5 million (minimum),[a] *Ŝ406.9 millio ʿmaximum)*[b]

| Brazil | 1,500.1 | All | 1,283.4 | All |

Solution 13: Ŝ362.8 million (maximum)[b]

Brazil	400.6	Brazil	267.2	Brazil
Chile	52.7	Argentina, Chile	...	...
Mexico	1,046.8	Mexico	1,016.2	All others

Solution 14: Ŝ368.3 million (maximum)[b]

| Brazil | 400.6 | Brazil | 267.2 | Brazil |
| Mexico | 1,099.5 | All but Brazil | 1,016.2 | All but Brazil |

Solution 15: Ŝ377.4 million (maximum)[b]

Brazil	400.6	Brazil	267.2	Brazil
Chile	1,099.5	All but Brazil	592.0	All but Brazil and Mexico
Mexico	...	...	424.2	Mexico[g]

Note: Venezuela presented no study of kraft paper or pulp demand, and is therefore not included in these solutions. Argentina, Brazil, Chile, and Mexico are the only countries with demand for pulp for newsprint.
a. Minimum transport costs and free exchange rates.
b. Current transport costs and official exchange rates.
c. Pulp imported from the United States.
d. For newsprint production in both countries.
e. Argentina imports pulp from Chile for newsprint production.
f. Chile produces pulp for its own newsprint production.
g. Pulp for kraft paper production is imported from Chile.

producing kraft paper with pulp imported from the United States, and Brazil has four pulp plants and three kraft paper plants. In all cases, the constraints on plant size are included by adding in fixed costs for the approximate number of plants. Importing both pulp and paper costs about $376.0 million annually, or 28 percent over the minimum cost optimum solution and 18 percent over the maximum cost optimum solution.

The prices of kraft paper and pulp in LAFTA in 1975, based on these solutions, are shown in Table 8-10.

The Exchange Rate Influence

Besides transport costs, a key variable in determining prices is the rate of exchange used between the various national currencies and the unit of account, the simón. To differentiate between minimum and maximum costs, two rates of exchange are altered: the Chilean escudo, from 5 to 3.5 escudos per simón, and the Colombian peso, from 17.5 pesos to 13.5 pesos per simón. These rates are varied as a response to the uncertainty about the "true" rate for the period in which costs were estimated. The variation affects both the configuration of optimum locations and the combinations of sources of supply and consumption points. The size of this effect can be seen clearly in the figures for the total cost of production and transportation when Chile produces all pulp and paper for the area—Solution 3. The cost of this solution is $305.7 million when minimum costs are assumed, and $432.8 million under the maximum cost assumptions, compared with the cost of the optimum of $291.7 million under the minimum assumptions. Thus, from less than 5 percent, the deviation from the optimum increases to almost 48 percent when the exchange rate assumption is altered.

Since there are many combinations of exchange rates that could be tested, an approximation to the solution of the exchange rate problem is presented by comparing c.i.f. prices of the four products studied under the assumption that the total regional demand for them is supplied by one location. Table 8-11 shows the implicit indifference exchange rates between pesos, escudos, and cruzeiros, on the one hand, and simones, on the other, given the concentration of production in Mexico, Chile, Venezuela, or the United States.

In general, the farther a consumption point is from the production point, the less competitive the producer. Table 8-11 shows, for example,

Table 8-10. Prices of Kraft Pulp and Kraft Paper in LAFTA, 1975

Simones

Consuming country	Kraft pulp for newsprint production		Kraft paper	
	Minimum[a]	Maximum[b]	Minimum[a]	Maximum[b]
Optimum location[c]				
Argentina	129.8	164.5	200.3	247.2
Brazil	144.8	145.4	216.3	226.2
Chile	126.2	181.5	210.8	271.0
Colombia	...	...	213.1	248.8
Ecuador	...	...	213.4	241.2
Mexico	135.0	146.1	184.5	192.8
Paraguay	...	...	211.5	258.4
Peru	...	...	213.6	243.1
Uruguay	...	...	200.6	247.0
Imports from the United States[d]				
Argentina	164.5	164.5	264.7	264.7
Brazil	178.0	178.0	278.2	278.2
Chile	181.5	181.5	315.1	315.1
Colombia	...	...	277.4	287.4
Ecuador	...	...	282.4	282.4
Mexico	146.1	146.1	226.0	226.0
Paraguay	...	...	275.9	275.9
Peru	...	...	292.3	292.3
Uruguay	...	...	264.7	264.7
National production[e]				
Argentina	134.0	182.8	209.5	302.3
Brazil	145.4	145.4	226.2	226.2
Chile	137.5	198.5	220.0	293.5
Colombia	...	...	302.7	400.8
Ecuador	...	...	248.0	248.0
Mexico	195.6	195.6	233.0	233.0
Paraguay	...	...	220.7	313.5
Peru	...	...	325.5	385.9
Uruguay	...	...	209.8	302.9

a. Minimum transport costs and free exchange rate.
b. Maximum transport costs and official exchange rate.
c. Minimum cost—Solution 1; maximum cost—Solution 4 (see Table 8-9).
d. Minimum and maximum costs—Solution 11.
e. Minimum and maximum—Solution 8.

that Chile is competitive with the United States in all markets for both products at 5 escudos per simón, but in no market except Chilean kraft paper at the official trade rate of 3.37 escudos per simón in September 1965, the date for which Chilean costs were estimated.

Welfare Benefits and Costs

Table 8-12 gives the welfare benefits of producing at the optimum location versus importing from the United States and the welfare costs of national production versus buying from the optimum location, under both the minimum and the maximum cost assumptions. Benefits over importing are $51 million to $74 million for pulp for newsprint production and kraft paper, depending on cost assumptions; the benefits attributable to the minimum production effect are about 20 percent of the cost of production and transportation of the optimum pattern. The benefit falls considerably for the maximum cost case, since in this optimum all pulp is imported from the United States. The welfare cost of national production is also relatively high—$48 million (approximately the same for both minimum and maximum cost cases). The production element of welfare cost is therefore about 15 percent of the total cost of production and transportation.

Although the national solution would annually cost the area $60 million more than the optima to satisfy demand at the 1975 level (about $48 million in welfare cost), a less costly national solution can be envisaged. It would maintain production at present levels in all countries except those designated by the optimum solutions. This would be an "excess demand" solution, and would entail supplying the following demands in 1975:

Country	Pulp for newsprint	Kraft paper
	(thousands of tons)	
Argentina	5.4	3.7
Brazil	42.4	182.2
Chile	net exporter	24.8
Colombia	...	79.6
Ecuador	...	293.0
Mexico	18.6	264.2
Paraguay	...	0.6
Peru	...	39.5
Uruguay	...	5.8
Total	66.4	1,143.4

The ranking of the solutions in terms of cost is not altered by the changes in demand at each point; of course, the total cost to the area of supplying the two products is much lower—about $200.1 million for both Solution 1 and Solution 2.

Table 8-11. Prices and Implicit Indifference Rates for Chemical Pulp for Newsprint Production and for Kraft Paper in LAFTA, 1975

Producing country, product, price ratio, and currencies exchanged	Consuming country								
	Argentina	Brazil	Chile	Colombia	Ecuador	Mexico	Paraguay	Peru	Uruguay
Prices per metric ton in simones									
Brazil[a]									
Pulp for newsprint	174.43	145.03	192.23	...	...	184.63	...	...	...
Kraft paper	255.84	224.24	294.94	277.84	278.94	287.84	267.04	278.24	255.74
Chile[b]									
Pulp for newsprint	129.75	144.85	126.25	...	...	135.05	...	...	...
Kraft paper	198.37	214.37	208.87	211.17	211.47	221.47	209.57	211.67	198.67
Mexico[c]									
Pulp for newsprint	210.30	224.70	221.20	...	...	194.70	...	...	...
Kraft paper	256.70	270.80	280.50	259.20	260.90	230.80	267.90	262.30	256.50
United States									
Pulp for newsprint	164.50	178.00	181.50	...	...	146.10	...	...	...
Kraft paper	264.70	278.80	315.10	277.40	282.40	226.00	275.90	292.30	264.70
Price ratios									
Mexican to Chilean									
Pulp for newsprint	1.62	1.56	1.67	...	...	1.44	...	...	...
Kraft paper	1.29	1.26	1.34	1.23	1.24	1.04	1.28	1.24	1.29

					Indifference exchange rates				
Brazilian to Mexican									
Pulp for newsprint	0.83	0.64	0.87	...	...	0.95	...	...	...
Kraft paper	1.00	0.83	1.05	1.07	1.07	1.25	1.00	1.06	1.00
Chilean to U.S.									
Pulp for newsprint	0.79	0.81	0.70	...	...	0.92	...	...	...
Kraft paper	0.75	0.77	0.66	0.76	0.75	0.98	0.76	0.72	0.75
Mexican pesos to Chilean escudos[d]									
Pulp for newsprint	4.05	3.90	4.17	...	...	3.60	...	...	...
Kraft paper	3.22	3.15	3.35	3.08	3.10	2.60	3.20	3.10	3.22
Brazilian cruzeiros to Mexican pesos[e]									
Pulp for newsprint	146	113	153	...	...	167	176	186	...
Kraft paper	176	146	185	188	188	220	176	186	176
Chilean escudos to simones[f]									
Pulp for newsprint	3.95	4.05	3.50	...	...	4.60	...	...	...
Kraft paper	3.75	3.85	3.30	3.80	3.75	4.90	3.80	3.60	3.75

a. The exchange rate is 2,200 cruzeiros per simón.
b. The exchange rate is 5 escudos per simón.
c. The exchange rate is 12.5 pesos per simón.
d. Calculated as the ratio of Mexican to Chilean prices times 2.5 (the number of pesos per escudo).
e. Calculated as the ratio of Brazilian to Mexican prices times 176 (the number of cruzeiros per peso).
f. Calculated as the ratio of Chilean to U.S. prices times 5 (the number of escudos per simón, or dollar).

Table 8-12. Welfare Benefits and Costs of Selected Alternatives to Optimum Location of Production of Kraft Pulp for Newsprint Production and Kraft Paper, 1975

Thousands of simones

Consuming country	Pulp for newsprint Production effect	Total	Kraft paper Production effect	Total	Total, both products Production effect	Total
Minimum costs—optimum location[a] versus importing from U.S.[b]						
Argentina	319	360	2,197	2,548	2,516	2,908
Brazil	3,670	4,110	12,715	14,622	16,385	18,732
Chile	1,552	1,894	3,812	4,765	5,364	6,659
Colombia	...	...	6,254	7,192	6,254	7,192
Ecuador	...	...	15,006	17,407	15,006	17,407
Mexico	330	344	14,088	15,637	14,418	15,981
Paraguay	...	...	29	34	29	34
Peru	...	...	3,547	4,221	3,547	4,221
Uruguay	...	...	424	491	424	491
Total	5,871	6,708	58,072	66,917	63,943	73,625
Minimum costs—national production[c] versus optimum location[a]						
Argentina	−46	−46	−366	−377	−412	−423
Brazil	...	...	−2,312	−2,381	−2,312	−2,381
Chile	−414	−435	−462	−471	−876	−906
Colombia	...	...	−8,157	−9,870	−8,157	−9,870
Ecuador	...	...	−8,754	−9,454	−8,754	−9,454
Mexico	−1,281	−1,575	−16,436	−18,572	−17,717	−20,147
Paraguay	...	...	−5	−5	−5	−5
Peru	...	...	−4,466	−5,678	−4,466	−5,627
Uruguay	...	...	−70	−73	−70	−73
Total	−1,741	−2,056	−41,028	−46,881	−42,769	−48,887
Maximum costs—optimum location[d] versus importing from U.S.[b]						
Argentina	...	...	791	822	791	822
Brazil	2,327	2,584	11,484	12,862	13,811	15,446
Chile	...	...	2,079	2,245	2,079	2,245
Colombia	...	...	4,127	4,457	4,127	4,457
Ecuador	...	...	10,601	11,555	10,601	11,555
Mexico	...	...	12,268	13,372	12,268	13,372
Paraguay	...	...	9	10	9	10
Peru	...	...	2,542	2,796	2,542	2,796
Uruguay	...	...	152	158	152	158
Total	2,327	2,584	44,053	48,277	46,380	50,861

Table 8-12. *(continued)*

Consuming country	Pulp for newsprint		Kraft paper		Total, both products	
	Production effect	Total	Production effect	Total	Production effect	Total
	Maximum costs—national production[c] versus optimum location[d]					
Argentina	−192	−204	−2,033	−2,257	−2,226	−2,461
Brazil	...	...	...	...	...	...
Chile	−670	−703	−1,188	−1,236	−1,858	−1,939
Colombia	...	...	−12,064	−15,804	−12,064	−15,804
Ecuador	...	...	−2,120	−2,162	−2,120	−2,162
Mexico	−1,118	−1,308	−13,904	−15,433	−15,021	−16,740
Paraguay	...	...	−28	−31	−28	−31
Peru	...	...	−5,532	−7,191	−5,532	−7,191
Uruguay	...	...	−391	−438	−391	−438
Total	−1,980	−2,215	−37,260	−44,552	−39,240	−46,766

a. Solution 1, Table 8-9.
b. Solution 11.
c. Solution 8.
d. Solution 4.

The investment required to build the physical plant indicated by the various optima is shown in Table 8-13. All alternatives take account of 1963 production in the producing country. Alternative 1 represents the minimum cost optimum (Solution 1), to satisfy which would require between 1963 and 1975 total investment of $566.1 million in Chile plus $22 million in Mexico. Alternatives 2 and 3 represent the maximum cost optimum and the national solution, respectively. These show total required investment to be $203 million and $493.4 million, respectively, between 1963 and 1975. The relatively low investment indicated by Alternative 2 is the result partly of the importing of pulp from the United States and partly of the low investment estimated for kraft paper production in Mexico using already prepared pulp. In Alternative 4, all existing production is accounted for, and it is assumed that Chile and Mexico, in the "excess demand" optimum, produce only to meet the demand in excess of 1963 production. This also means subsidization of 1963 production of both products in all countries except Chile and of paper in Mexico. Required investment under Alternative 4 is $416.1 million. If Chile produces all the newsprint for the area, total investment between 1963 and 1975 would have to be $254.8 million.

Table 8-13. Investment Required for Pulp and Kraft Paper Production in LAFTA, 1963–75

Capacity in thousands of tons; simón amounts in millions

Alternative[a] and producing country	Pulp Plants Number	Pulp Plants Capacity per plant[b]	Pulp Simones	Kraft paper Plants Number	Kraft paper Plants Capacity per plant[b]	Kraft paper Simones
Alternative 1						
Chile	12	120	316.0	7	120	250.1
Mexico	...	...	...	2	120⎫	
				1	30⎭	22.0
Total	12	1,440	316.0	10	1,110	272.1
Alternative 2						
Brazil	2	120	72.0	1	120⎫	
				1	60⎭	54.0
Mexico	...	...	...	7	120⎫	
				1	60⎬	77.0
				1	20⎭	
Total	2	240	72.0	11	1,100	131.0
Alternative 3						
Brazil	2	120	72.0	1	120⎫	
				1	60⎭	54.0
Chile	1	120⎫		1	60⎫	
	1	40⎭	34.0	1	40⎭	22.9
Colombia	...	...	...	2	40	51.8
Ecuador[c]	...	...	...	2	120⎫	
				1[d]	30⎭	140.0
Mexico	2	120⎫		2	120⎫	
	1	40⎭	94.0	1	30⎭	22.0
Peru	...	...	...	1	40	2.7
Total	7	680	200.0	13	940	293.4
Alternative 4						
Chile	8	120	204.0	5	120⎫	
				1	30⎭	190.1
Mexico	...	...	...	2	120⎫	
				1	30⎭	22.0
Total	8	960	204.0	9	900	212.1
Alternative 5						
Chile	9	120⎫		...	...	...
	1	40⎭	254.8			
Total	10	1,120	254.8			

a. For definitions of alternatives, see p. 205.
b. Except for total.
c. Peruvian investment-per-ton estimate is used.
d. Produces own pulp.

Newsprint: Demand and Costs

Because the characteristics of demand for and supply of newsprint in Latin America differ sharply from those of the other paper products, it is useful to discuss it separately. The most significant difference is that, in contrast with the widely dispersed production of paper and pulp, described above, only four countries were producing newsprint in 1964, and of those, only Brazil and Chile came close to satisfying domestic demand (see Table 8-1). Mexico, one of the newsprint producers, provides a striking contrast: It met only 13.6 percent of its newsprint consumption with its own production in 1964, but used less than half of existing capacity for newsprint and free textbook paper production. Newsprint capacity, furthermore, was not expected to increase in Mexico before 1970.[14] Even though newsprint production increased, proportionately, more rapidly than consumption, owing largely to the expansion of Brazilian production, regional output was just a third of regional consumption in 1964.

Table 8-14 lists the minimum and maximum projections of demand in 1975, and the estimates of the manner in which it will be met by imports and domestic production. The totals do not reflect total production, since they do not include Chilean exports; in general, in fact, production figures are probably underestimated because of the apparent underestimate of Brazilian output. According to a Grace study, Brazilian output of newsprint was 117,000 tons in 1965.[15] This is only one-third less than its projected 1975 production shown in Table 8-14.

As cost data are estimated for only one location within LAFTA for the production of newsprint itself (see Table 8-15) that product is not included in the linear programming model. It is possible, however, to compare supply prices in LAFTA countries of newsprint from the Chilean plant and from the United States, assuming that either produces all newsprint for the area (see Table 8-16). The comparison is especially meaningful since Chile is the only exporter of newsprint in Latin America. The implied indifference exchange rate shows that Chile could not compete with U.S. imports in any LAFTA country at the official trade rate in September

14. Nacional Financiera, S.A., Gerencia de Programación Industrial, *Proyecciones de Demanda, Costos de Fabricación y Costos de Transporte de Papel y Celulosa* (Mexico, D.F.: 1965; processed), Table 9-9.

15. W. R. Grace & Co., "The Outlook for the Paper and Paperboard Industries of Latin America, 1972 and 1977" (July 6, 1967; processed), p. 17-3.

Table 8-14. Projected Demand for and Supply of Newsprint in LAFTA, 1975

Thousands of metric tons

Consuming and producing country	Demand		Sources of supply		
	Minimum estimate	*Maximum estimate*	*Total*[a]	*Imports*	*Domestic production*
Argentina	157.0	222.0	189.5	174.3	15.2
Brazil	471.9	561.2	515.6	342.4	173.2
Chile	47.7	58.8	53.2	0	53.2
Colombia	76.0	97.0	86.5	86.5	0
Ecuador	17.8	29.6	23.7	23.7	0
Mexico	233.5	233.5	233.5	193.8	39.7
Paraguay	1.9	2.2	2.0	2.0	0
Peru	53.6	64.8	59.2	59.2	0
Uruguay	n.a.	n.a.	n.a.	n.a.	n.a.
Venezuela	95.0	102.0	98.5	98.5	0
Total	1,154.3	1,371.2	1,261.7	980.4	281.3

Source: ECIEL, *Demand for Chemical Fertilizers.*
n.a. Not available.
a. Midpoint of maximum and minimum projections. Allocation of total projected consumption between imports and domestic production is calculated by using the average percentage distribution between the two sources of supply observed in each country during the period 1959–63.

1965 of 3.37 escudos per simón, but is competitive in all LAFTA countries at the free rate of 5 escudos per simón.

Some Conclusions

This discussion has taken no account of existing and potential natural resources in producing countries. This appears to be no problem in the national solution for pulp and paper except in Ecuador, whose relatively large projected demand is based on packing bananas in cartons for export. If each ton of kraft paper is assumed to require 1.25 tons of cane bagasse, Ecuador would need 368,000 tons of cane bagasse a year to fill 1975 demand for kraft paper by domestic production. Whether Ecuador sugar cane production could supply this much bagasse was not explored. In the minimum cost optimum solution, Chile would produce 1.5 million metric tons of pulp annually, not including any pulp production for newsprint exports. Using the wood-unbleached pulp ratio of 5.3 cubic meters to 1 ton,[16] the quantity of wood required annually in 1975 is 8 million cubic

16. ECLA, *Programming Data and Criteria for the Pulp and Paper Industry*, E/CN. 12/702 (1964).

Table 8-15. Cost Structure of Newsprint Production

Percent

Category of cost	Chile, 105,000 ton plant
Materials	59.6[a]
Direct labor	3.9
Utilities	[a]
Depreciation	8.6
Insurance	0.6
Opportunity cost of capital	16.4
Other[b]	10.8
Total	100.0
Cost per ton in escudos	512.3

Source: Carnoy (ed.), *Optimum Location of Specific Industries*, Vol. 4.
a. Percentage listed for raw materials includes utilities.
b. Includes maintenance.

Table 8-16. Projected Cost of Production and Transportation of Newsprint in LAFTA, 1975

Simones[a]

Consuming country	Producing country		Implied indifference exchange rate of escudos per simón
	Chile	United States	
Argentina	147.5	178.7	4.1
Brazil	166.0	195.3	4.2
Chile	158.4	195.4	4.0
Colombia	171.8	198.6	4.3
Ecuador	160.7	196.4	4.1
Mexico	158.0	165.2	4.8
Paraguay	158.7	189.9	4.2
Peru	152.1	188.3	4.0
Uruguay	157.7	178.7	4.4
Venezuela	149.2	171.0	4.4

a. Assumes all newsprint is produced at one location or the other (twelve plants in San Pedro, Chile), and an exchange rate of 5 escudos per simón; cost at plant is $122 per ton. The cost f.o.b., New York or San Francisco, is $148 per ton.

meters. The United Nations, using data of the Corporación de Fomento de la Producción (CORFO), estimates that Chile has only 3.3 million cubic meters of pulpwood available for production in 1970, implying a potential output of 620,000 tons of pulp in that year. This would fall short of projected demand in the area,[17] and could place a restriction on the optimum indicated by the model. Once newsprint production for the area is introduced, the restriction on pulp production obviously becomes critical. It would necessitate a shift in the optimum location, even in the minimum transport cost case, to other countries, like Mexico and Brazil, that are already large pulp and paper producers.

17. ECLA, *Chile—Potential Pulp and Paper Exporter*, p. 87.

PART THREE

Methodology

CHAPTER NINE

The Model and Its Applications

THIS CHAPTER SETS OUT the general model for finding the lowest cost location for each product, on which the estimates in the earlier chapters were based. The model is described in greater detail in Appendix A. The first section deals with the model itself. The next describes how the data on demand and costs were estimated, while the third treats the measurement of welfare costs and benefits of alternative production patterns. The last section of the chapter deals with the problem of exchange rates, and how various relationships among the currencies of the area can affect the patterns of industrial location.

The Linearized Programming Model

The method of determining the minimum cost location of industry in a given market has been well developed.[1] In all of the products studied here (with the exception of powdered milk and cheese), economies of scale dictate an optimum output beyond that required to meet the demand of the individual Latin American national markets. This characteristic means

1. See esp. Thomas Vietorisz and Alan S. Manne, "Chemical Processes, Plant Location, and Economies of Scale," in Alan S. Manne and Harry M. Markowitz (eds.), *Studies in Process Analysis: Economy-Wide Production Capabilities* (John Wiley & Sons, 1963), Chap. 6 and its bibliography.

that a free trade area affords opportunities for expansion to plants producing these products. The constraint on the expansion—and hence on the location of all production at one low cost point—is transport costs between the production site and additional markets. The model used here weighs both types of costs in order to determine how industries characterized by decreasing costs should be distributed.

The objective of the model is to find the combination of plants to supply, at a minimum cost to the Latin American Free Trade Association (LAFTA), the fixed demands for a given product at specified locations in the area. The cost minimization depends on the quantity demanded at each consumption point, the cost of production at each production point, and the cost of transportation between each production point and each consumption point. In multistage production processes, the costs of transportation between successive stages are also taken into account. The generalized form of the model can be thought of in terms of production points, consumption points, and production-consumption points that consume the output of earlier stages and produce both for the next stage of production and for final consumption. This study treats only single- and two-stage production processes, largely because of data limitations. Nevertheless, both the theoretical model and the algorithm written for the computer are capable of handling a product produced in three or more stages.

As explained more fully in the detailed description of the model given in Appendix A, a maximum plant size is assumed for the production of each good. With three exceptions, the size chosen equals approximately the maximum size of similar plants in the United States in 1965 (which was taken as a proxy for the maximum technically feasible plant size). The first two exceptions are lathes and dairy products, for which maximum size was held to that of the largest Latin American plant observed in this study, because single-plant, short-run cost curves are used for cost comparisons rather than curves derived from several different size plants in each country.[2] Lathes were assumed to be produced in a plant limited only by total demand in 1975 and also in a plant limited to annual production of 500 units. The best locations for tractor production are also found for

2. For some industries, such as nitrogenous fertilizers, the maximum technically feasible plant size has increased markedly since 1965. No attempt was made to forecast technological change for the industries studied, since in most cases that would amount to speculation. The model, however, can utilize information on more up-to-date plant sizes and production processes.

two cases: plants limited to 20,000 units annually (the largest plants in the United States are about 25,000 units) and plants with output equal to total regional demand in 1975 (62,000 units). Since the upper limit on plant size is rather high in the four groups in which estimates of long-run costs are used, the constraint on plant size has little effect on optimum location and raises unit costs only slightly.[3]

Demand and Cost Estimates

In applying the linear programming model to industrial location in LAFTA, severe data problems were faced: Availability of data varied greatly among the countries concerned, and data had to be "constructed" in many cases rather than simply collected. In order to obtain the projections of demand in the area for a product, and of unit production costs in the alternative locations, it was decided that each participating institute should attain the best projections permitted by the available data, rather than follow a uniform system applicable to all countries. Common definitions of products and costs and other elements were, however, adopted by all the participating institutes (see Appendix B).

Demand Projections

For every product, demand is projected to 1975 to provide a guide to the expansion of production over time, and to test the possibility of changes in the location of production in response to changes in the geographical composition of final consumption.[4] As has been noted, consumption is spatially fixed.

3. The biases in the optimum solutions and shadow prices resulting from the different kinds of cost curve estimates for all products are discussed below.
4. In the study all projections were made for 1970 and 1975, but only those for the latter year are presented and analyzed in this book.
The minimum cost location and most alternatives to it are particularly insensitive to changes in demand because the regional demand for most products studied is far above the maximum efficient plant size. The smaller the maximum size of the plant, the less sensitive the optimum, since economies of scale are confined to a much smaller range of output, and therefore price is less affected by changes in output beyond very low levels. The minimum cost solution does not change for any product between 1970 and 1975 despite quite large increases in total consumption projected for those years. In addition to optimum location based on total future consumption, we could estimate the optimum loca-

Projections of consumption to 1975 in each of the countries under study, while differing in the choice of explanatory variables, are based on linear regression equations. The types of regression used by the institutes to estimate the relationships between consumption and projectable factors that affect it fall into three categories: (1) multivariate time series regression analysis of consumption of the product itself; (2) cross-section regression analysis, both international and national (interregional within one country);[5] and (3) derived demand of inputs based on projections of final output and technical relationships between inputs and outputs.[6]

Once the relationship between the independent variable and consumption of a product has been established, demand for the product in 1975 can be estimated if projections of the independent variables are available. The difficulties in making demand projections are well known. The statistically computed error in the relationship between the consumption of a good and the independent variables chosen, found by one of the above methods, ideally should be quite small, say, no more than 10 to 15 percent. That ideal is seldom fulfilled for Latin American economies, largely because of the crudity of the data. Besides the error in the estimated relation and in the input-output coefficients themselves, an additional, and perhaps more important, source of error enters from the projection of the independent variables. In this study, an attempt was made to increase the reliability of the results of the demand projections by specifying the error in the regression equations and projecting the independent variables in such a way as to yield "maximum" and "minimum" estimates of consumption of the product in 1975. These estimates are obtained by esti-

---

tion of *new* plants to fill the increase in demand net of existing capacity in a specified product. Such "additional" production would be less than total future consumption. For one product (tractors), practically no new capacity is necessary to fill 1975 projected demand, but for the others, estimating the optimum location on the basis of net *additional* capacity needed to fulfill projected demand does not change the optimum location from that estimated on the basis of total demand in 1970 and 1975. The optimum locations shown, therefore, are applicable (except for tractors) either to the construction of "new" plants alone or the construction of both "new" plants and plants to displace existing production at nonoptimum locations.

5. Such regression equations usually use gross national product or the consumption of an important final use product as the independent variable.

6. The input-output coefficients are determined on the basis of either factory data in the country itself or other studies such as ECLA's of the chemical industry in Latin America; see UN, Economic Commission for Latin America (ECLA), *La Industria Química en América Latina*, E/CN.12/628 (1962).

mating demand under "extreme" assumptions: The projection of gross national product, for example, may use the national plan as a maximum and, as a minimum, a figure based on the projected rate of increase in population. While these types of assumptions obviously do not cover the entire range of possibilities for the independent variables, they narrow the range of plant sizes that has to be examined in the analysis of cost differentials.[7]

The total demand for a product—the aggregate of the projections for each country—yields an approximation of the maximum and minimum market size provided by LAFTA in 1975. The most significant difficulty in aggregating the national projections for each product is in finding a regional common denominator for goods of different quality and size. Because of the strict technical definitions under which they are produced, chemicals, powdered milk, newsprint, and cellulose generally pose a quality problem only in the sense of adherence to the standards. On the other hand, tractors and lathes can vary considerably in size, kraft paper in chemical content, and cheese because of its type or its aging process.[8]

In these cases, the projections here express all products within the category in terms of a standard type or size, as follows:

Tractors	50 pulley horsepower
Lathes	1,500 millimeters between points
Kraft paper	100 percent sulfur kraft paper
Cheese	Hard, semihard, or bland batter

To express projected demand in terms of the standard units, the ratio between the prices of nonstandard and standard products in a base year is multiplied by the projected quantity of the product demanded. These calculations are set out in Appendix D. This method assumes a high elasticity of substitution among sizes and types within the category and a

---

7. For those interested in total demand as a result in itself, the relationships found for each country permit a determination of future demand based on their own assumptions for the independent variables. See ECIEL, *The Demand for Chemical Fertilizers, Tractors, Paper and Pulp, Milk Concentrates, and Lathes in the Latin American Free Trade Association* (*including Venezuela*) (Brookings Institution, 1966; processed).

8. Semihard cheeses include cacciocavallo, cheddar, fontina, gruyere, and Holland pategras. Hard cheeses include goya, moliterno, pepato, provolone, reggiano, romano, saldo, briuy and reggionito, and tafi. Bland paste cheeses include ricotta, minas, jaive, Colombian "white cheese," and others.

selection by the consumer that depends largely on the relative prices within the group in each country.

Cost Projections

The cost studies are intended to provide data and analysis that would be useful for the formulation of policy with respect to industry expansion. The production cost per unit of output is related to plant size at a given point in time and the relation projected into the future, given historical tendencies in input prices.

Like the demand projections, cost studies vary considerably in sophistication and reliability among the products and countries.[9] When data were available, the institutes estimated cost curves from actual operating plant costs by cross-sectional analysis. Costs for plants that could supply the potential regional markets were projected from these curves. Some institutes were severely limited because some of the products under consideration were not being produced in their countries. Even where the product was being manufactured, the producers in most cases would not release cost data. It is therefore difficult to avoid projecting costs for some products, such as chemicals, on the basis of factor combinations used in developed countries. While the error in transferring United States or European production functions to Latin America may not be great, especially with respect to the location of new industries, one of the more important purposes of a study of this type becomes difficult to achieve: to test differences in production technique, and to determine whether they arise from rational allocation of resources in a reasonably free market.

One of three methods is used to arrive at unit costs for plants of various sizes. The goal in every case is to reach an estimate of long-run average and marginal costs of production for each product in each country concerned. Unlike demand, which is projected for each product by all the institutes, cost projections are not made by all institutes. To assure consistency of estimates of unit costs among the countries dealing with each product no matter which method was used, the breakdown and treatment of the costs of production are defined uniformly for all product categories (see Appen-

---

9. The original cost studies are presented in detail in a series of compilations (four volumes): ECIEL, Martin Carnoy (ed.), *The Optimum Location of Specific Industries in the Latin American Free Trade Area* (*including Venezuela*) (Brookings Institution, 1966; processed).

dix B). Unit costs for all products used in intercountry comparisons include estimates of sales and packaging costs. Where it was not measured directly, estimates for such overhead are based on its average percentage in observed plants making the same product. The three methods are presented here in declining order of preference.

Long-run costs derived from cross-section studies of plants operating within the country. Because of the limited number of observations available, it was impossible to use multivariate regression analysis in any form to estimate production functions. Instead, where cross-section studies were made, total and average costs were plotted against plant size to obtain long-run curves based on current input prices. The curves obtained were then adjusted for projected changes in input prices.[10] Cross-section data on operating plants are used to estimate costs for tractors in Brazil and Argentina, paper and pulp in Brazil, and semihard and hard paste cheese in Uruguay. Costs of some operating plants are used in cost curves for Mexican and Colombian production of nitrogenous fertilizers and for Mexican methanol.

Long-run costs derived from hypothetical plants of various capacities. Hypothetical plants were designed by local engineers familiar with the industry under study. This method was used to estimate costs for nitrogenous fertilizers and methanol-formaldehyde (except in Mexico), and for Chilean, Colombian, and Peruvian pulp and paper.

The principal shortcoming of this technique is that it usually merely duplicates plants in developed countries, and differs little from a simple application of production functions for the industry in more advanced economies. The first and the second methods differ in that the plants that are designed by engineers generally use the most advanced techniques, while estimated production functions present some sort of average of old and new plants in a developed economy. A strong argument can be made for basing cost comparisons on the most efficient plants, since any expansion of production should, and probably would, be made with the latest machinery. It is not at all clear, however, that, given factor costs and market size in Latin America, minimum unit cost for all industries would be achieved through techniques employed in countries with different input costs.

10. This method of estimation is carefully detailed in José Maria Dagnino Pastore, *La Industria del Tractor en la Argentina* (Buenos Aires: Centro de Investigaciones Economicas, Instituto Torcuato di Tella, 1966).

Short-run costs based on a single plant. In this method, fixed costs and total costs at capacity are estimated in annual terms. Annual fixed costs equal total costs of production at zero output. A short-run cost curve is constructed between zero and capacity output. This linear approximation to short-run costs is used as a proxy to long-run costs in the pulp and paper industry. In the production of powdered milk, cheese, and lathes, the short-run curves are also taken as proxies for long-run curves, but the size of the plant permitted in the estimates of optimum location is limited to the maximum output of the plants studied. Cost curves for all dairy products (except Uruguayan semihard and hard paste cheese), as well as for lathes, are estimated with cost data from a single plant. Chilean lathe costs are for a hypothetical plant but the estimates for lathes for other countries and for all dairy products are for operating plants.

Bias Introduced by Linear Approximation

In order to establish the minimum cost location with the linearized programming model, both long- and short-run curves are represented by linear approximations made by cutting through the total cost curve at two points.[11] The bias in estimating marginal cost from a straight-line total cost curve is probably small, since the upper ranges of output are weighted

---

11. Ana M. Martirena-Mantel (Centro de Estudios Economicos, Instituto Torcuato di Tella), in commenting on this methodological exposition, defines three ways of linearly approximating the cost curves: "a) A tangent to the total cost function at a technologically justifiable fixed level of production. This approximation is poor on the one hand because it underestimates economies of scale at levels of production higher than the fixed point, but on the other hand it gives an advantage to smaller countries by overestimating economies at lower capacity levels. b) A straight line that cuts the total cost function. This implies justifying the selection of two levels of production, a minimum and a maximum for each possible location. It has the advantage of a better approximation of the theoretical function, but the disadvantage of not revealing the degree of bias of real costs (used by Vietorisz and Manne). c) A number of straight-line segments. This method has the advantage of a very close approximation to actual cost functions, but the disadvantage of multiplying the number of local optima that must be calculated. Each segment added has an effect equivalent to increasing the number of plants at each location." (Author's translation of correspondence.) See also Ana M. Martirena-Mantel, "Integración y Economías de Escala," *El Trimestre Económico*, Vol. 31 (July–September 1964.)

The approximations implicit in Chaps. 3–8 are of type (b), but since many of the cost curves involve only two points or are close to linear if they involve three or more points, the bias from the approximation itself is small.

more heavily than the lower ranges. However, greater weighting of the upper ranges of output means that the line does not pass through zero, and the approximation results in an intercept term, the cost at zero production. This represents "fixed" costs and generates economies of scale.[12]

Since the approximation to the total cost curve used here is linear and does not go through the origin, marginal costs are constant and average costs decline. For the purpose of the welfare analysis, resource costs should be taken equal to marginal costs, as the welfare gain model below shows. However, marginal costs estimated from straight line total cost curves do not reflect economies of scale, while average costs do. Resource costs are therefore set equal to average costs to represent changes in costs due to increases in market size. This biases upward actual resource costs of a given output. At large outputs, however, differences between marginal and average costs derived from the linear total cost curves are not large. For example, in the case of production of methanol in Venezuela (which is the optimum location) under the low cost assumption, the assumed technically maximum output of a plant is 33,000 metric tons annually. At that output, the estimated marginal cost to Venezuela of production and transportation of methanol is $74 per ton. The estimated average cost is $85 per ton, or 15 percent more. The use of average cost results in an underestimate of the welfare gain of buying from the optimum location versus importing from the United States.

In addition to linearization of the total cost curve, several other factors could bias the estimates of production costs:

(1) If the range of output of plants entering into the estimates of long-run total costs is lower for one country than another, the linear approximation of the cost curve for the lower range would bias upward estimates for both marginal and average cost for that country relative to the other producing countries. This upward bias may have occurred in estimating ammonia production costs in Colombia and Peru, methanol costs in Mexico and Chile, tractor costs in Brazil, and paper costs in Brazil and Peru. In all of these cases but Brazilian paper, however, the range of output observed is close enough to those of the other countries to make the probability of bias small.

(2) If a long-run curve is used for some countries producing a product

---

12. In the long run, there should be no fixed costs, that is, all elements of cost become variable. The long-run total cost curve should therefore start at the origin.

and a short-run curve for others, the short-run marginal cost would be biased upward relative to the long-run marginal cost and short-run average cost would also be greater than long-run average cost when the plant chosen for the short-run estimate is smaller than the long-run optimum for the region (or the maximum size used in the long-run curves). If the capacity of the plant for which short-run costs are estimated is close to the long-run optimum, short- and long-run average costs would tend to be equal as would short- and long-run marginal costs. Short- and long-run cost curves are compared for the paper and pulp group, but the plants chosen for the short-run estimates for kraft paper produced in Ecuador and Mexico are smaller than the maximum size used in the long-run case for Brazil, Chile, Colombia, and Peru.

(3) If short-run cost comparisons are used to determine minimum cost locations, even if plants observed have approximately the same capacity, there is the possibility of error in estimating the optimum location of production and the likelihood of overestimating the shadow price of output. Assuming that costs observed in the chosen plants are for short-run optimum output, differences in linear estimates of short-run marginal costs between countries would be unbiased estimates of differences in long-run marginal costs *at that level of output.* However, the differences between long-run marginal costs may be very different at other levels of output. Relative and absolute advantage in production could reverse itself. Long-run average and marginal costs are, in any case, lower than short-run costs at levels of output higher than capacity in the estimated short-run curves.

Short-run curves are used to estimate costs for the powdered milk and cheese group and for lathes. The relatively small size of the observed lathe plants makes it likely that the estimated short-run average and marginal costs are upward-biased estimates of costs at output levels closer to the long-run optimum. Conversely, the nature of cheese and dry milk production puts an upper limit on the size of plants that is much closer to the output of the plants observed in the study; therefore, the bias in cost estimates for this product group may not be large.

(4) Since new plants will embody more modern technology than existing plants do, the engineering estimates of future costs are more accurate than those based on plants already in operation. Engineers tend, however, to underestimate the real interest cost of capital, installation costs, contingencies, and other costs, and thus to understate the "true" cost in plants with newer technology. On the other hand, estimates based solely on existing plants will overstate costs whenever the technology they embody has

been superseded by newer, more efficient techniques. In products for which all countries use engineering estimates, or a combination of engineering estimates with present operating costs, such as nitrogenous fertilizers and methanol-formaldehyde, the minimum cost location is probably not biased, but the shadow price derived from the optimum location may be underestimated. For paper and pulp and lathes, engineering estimates are compared with costs in existing plants, thus favoring countries that make engineering estimates. The shadow prices derived from the minimum cost solution are also probably underestimated.

(5) Although the cost curves are based on present costs in most cases, they are the best available means of estimating costs in 1975. A host of assumptions underlies these projections. In some cases, they assume changes in input prices, or factor prices and proportions, or both; in others—particularly lathes, tractors, powdered milk, and cheese—production processes are assumed to remain unchanged. The possible error in projection is compounded by changes in factor proportions that may result from general reductions in tariffs. The analysis is particularly tenuous in industries such as tractors whose imported parts are subject to heavy duties and whose production is subject to complex and varied requirements regarding the contents that must be produced nationally. Estimates of production costs may vary from country to country for other reasons as well, so it should be recognized that a margin of error exists in all the estimates, which may be widened in the projections.

There may be an additional source of bias, which does not reflect an error resulting from linearizing the cost curves or from the methods of cost estimation. As has been explained, the price of the goods studied is assumed to equal average costs of production plus marketing and transport costs. Since the production of most of the goods considered is characterized by economies of scale in the relevant output range, the organization of industry producing these goods in a customs union would probably tend to be monopolistic or oligopolistic. Hence, prices could be set considerably above average cost in order to capture monopoly rent. If regional planning included some means of taxing away monopoly rent, then welfare estimates would not be affected by such pricing policies.

Transportation Costs

Transportation costs are estimated in three parts: (1) costs from the production point to the nearest port or frontier; (2) costs from the port or frontier to the port or frontier of the consuming country (including both port charges); and (3) costs from the latter port or frontier to a representative consumption point, which might be (a) costs to a typical consumption point or (b) average costs to a number of consumption points within the country. Transportation costs per unit are considered to be constant between any two points. Where maritime rates figure in transportation between two points, a set of maximum and minimum transport costs are estimated to cope with the difficulties of predicting future ocean freight rates between LAFTA countries. The maximum rates reflect current published rates between countries, and the minimum rates are estimates of future costs provided by shipping companies. A detailed explanation of transport cost estimates is set out in Appendix B.

The calculation of overland transport costs between countries also poses problems because rail rates are subsidized in differing amounts and freight movements are often subject to taxes within each country. It was not possible to make corrections for these factors, but the effect of taxes may be especially relevant for tractors and lathes because their transport is assumed to involve considerable overland movement among southern cone countries (Argentina, Brazil, Chile, Uruguay, and Paraguay). A downward bias also stems from the omission of minor customs taxes from port costs.

Distributing Gains and Losses from Locating Optimally

The linearized programming model used in this study permits the estimation of the cost to LAFTA of producing the products studied at nonoptimum locations. Distributing production in a nonoptimum manner would raise the delivered price of a good to some or, in an extreme case, all markets. The program itself estimates for each good production and transportation costs for various combinations of production locations. This calculation implicitly assumes that demand for a good is fixed and not responsive to price change, that is, a demand curve with zero elasticity. The difference in cost to the region of a nonoptimum location over the minimum cost, or optimum, location represents the economic loss to the region, under the assumptions of the model, of not locating production at the optimum.

The second way of estimating the loss to the region of nonoptimum locations is the application of welfare analysis to alternative consumption-production decisions. It is useful to know the effects on individual members of policies that do not adhere to these locations, or to free trade within LAFTA and between LAFTA and the rest of the world. More specifically, estimates are made of the welfare benefits in 1975 to each member of buying from the optimum location designated by the minimization-of-cost model rather than (a) producing the good domestically or (b) importing from sources outside the area. On the other hand, where importing is the optimum, the welfare costs for a country of buying the product within the area must also be estimated. As these estimates of welfare benefits and costs assume for convenience demand curves with constant unitary elasticities, while the linear programming model implicitly assumes demand curves with zero elasticity, the *total cost* differences between alternatives derived from the linear programming model are not directly comparable to their respective welfare gains and costs.[13] The optimum location model is concerned with the difference in absolute monetary outlay of two alternatives under an assumption of fixed demands, not with how much better or worse off consumers are under the various production alternatives, considering the possibility of substitution in consumption.

The welfare benefit-cost estimates address two alternatives. The first is the increase or decrease in the average cost of a product bought from the optimal location relative to the average cost of imports from outside Latin America. The second is the increase in average cost when a country elects to produce for itself rather than import from the lowest cost regional source. The formal model and the assumptions used in the product-by-product estimates are presented in Appendix C.

This model shows that the welfare gains to a country from buying the product in the region rather than importing (the "gain" may be negative in some cases) can be separated into a "production effect," or the resource saving on the amount of the product purchased in the base year, and a "consumption effect," which results from the increased quantity consumed when the price falls. This division is made in order to compare, for the fourteen products, the production effect with the total value of output and to estimate the contribution of economies of scale to economic efficiency.

---

13. The unitary elasticity assumption is arbitrary but reasonable. Other elasticities can be assumed and different estimates of welfare gains made by the interested reader.

Welfare effects are also estimated for two sets of transport costs—the minimum and maximum estimates discussed above—and, where they differ, for "free" (curb) and official rates of exchange. The minimum transport cost is combined with the free rate of exchange to determine one estimate of benefits and losses, and the official rate is combined with the maximum transport cost to obtain a different set of shadow prices and therefore of welfare benefits.

Rates of Exchange

The costs of production are estimated in terms of local currency. The cost of imported inputs is expressed in dollars (or other foreign currencies) and converted to the national currency at the rate of exchange prevailing at a specific date.[14] To compare production costs among various locations, some specified rates of exchange must be used to convert the national currencies involved. The role of exchange rates in determining comparative advantage and the lowest cost production points is important in almost all the products analyzed in the study.

Rather than setting a "correct" exchange rate for each country, two other approaches are taken: (1) In the estimates of the optimum location and alternatives to it, the free rate of exchange at the date costs were measured is used to convert costs in national currency to simones; where the free rate differs from the official rate (Argentina, Chile, and Colombia), the official (low) rate for simones is used in the maximum cost estimate, and the free (high) rate, in the minimum cost estimate. (2) Once the optimum (lowest total cost) location is found for both minimum and maximum sets of transport costs and rates of exchange, another calculation is made in which indifference rates of exchange between the c.i.f. (cost plus insurance plus freight) prices of the specific product originating at different production points are estimated at every consumption point.[15]

To estimate indifference rates in each market for various production locations, it is assumed that all production takes place at a single location. Thus all delivered costs that are compared with one another have the full advantages offered by economies of scale. Because of the fixed element of costs, concentrating production at one point may reduce average cost. In

14. Where possible, these dollar costs are separated out again in making cost comparisons between countries.
15. See example of indifference rate calculation on pp. 35–36.

some cases, like nitrogenous fertilizers and paper and pulp, the single-location assumption is only an approximation to the size of the market that would face any one production point; but even in those industries, plant size constraints mean that average costs, and hence the estimated indifference rates, are quite close to those that would prevail under a more complicated distribution of plants.

A second source of bias is that ocean transport and imported capital costs, because they enter costs in simones originally, *could* distort the estimates of indifference exchange rates. This problem is probably not serious: The cost of a given product at a given consumption point consists of a production cost in national currency and the portion of capital and other input costs and transportation costs paid in foreign currency. The greater the fraction that transport plus imported capital costs is of total costs of production, and the larger the difference between the rate of exchange used to convert these simón costs into the national currency and the rate implied by the estimated indifference rate, the greater the bias in the estimated indifference rate.[16]

The extreme case of ammonia production in Chile can serve as an example. Assume that the exchange rate used to convert to national currency

16. The calculated indifference rates shown in Table 2-8 can be expressed as the ratio of the sums of the two costs (costs in simones have been converted to national currency at given exchange rates):

$$R_{12} = \frac{c_1 + t_1 x'}{c_2 + t_2 y'},$$

where c is production costs in national currency and t transportation plus capital import costs, converted at exchange rates x' and y' to national currency.

If a_1 and a_2 represent t_1/c_1 and t_2/c_2, respectively, then:

$$R_{12} = \frac{c_1(1 + a_1 x')}{c_2(1 + a_2 y')}.$$

Ideally, R_{12} estimated with the exchange rate used to convert t_1 and t_2 to national currency (x'/y') would equal R_{12} estimated with the exchange rate implied by $R_{12}(x/y)$. The bias in the estimate of R_{12} can be expressed as the ratio of the indifference rate calculated with the exchange rates used to the indifference rate calculated with the implied rates:

$$B = \frac{(1 + a_1 x')/(1 + a_1 x)}{(1 + a_2 y')/(1 + a_2 y)} = R_{12} \text{ (estimated)}/R_{12} \text{ (actual)}.$$

If it is assumed that $y = y'$ (only x is varied), the estimated indifference rate as a fraction of the actual rate equals

$$B = \frac{(1 + a_1 x')}{(1 + a_1 x)}.$$

is 3.5 escudos per simón and that transport and imported capital account for 40 percent of the total cost of production. Further assume that the escudo-simón rate implied by the indifference rates of exchange, holding the rate of country 2 constant, is 5.0 escudos per simón. These assumptions yield an estimated indifference rate that is 80 percent of the "actual" indifference rate. This bias results in part from the very high ratio of costs of transport and imported capital to total cost—the highest proportion of any of the products studied. The difference in exchange rates—5.0 versus 3.5— is also the largest of any of the countries studied.

The indifference rate concept then, is a supply price rather than a resource cost approach to comparative advantage; it is assumed that in decreasing cost industries, average cost pricing will occur if firms are not subsidized. As a practical matter average cost at the high outputs used in these estimates is close to marginal cost. With the indifference rates of exchange, the sensitivity of an optimum location based on official rates to changes in them can be determined. In industries where the international differences in costs are small, this sensitivity is greater than it is in industries where the advantage of one country over others is large.

Appendixes

APPENDIX A

The Linearized Programming Model

THE MATHEMATICAL FORM of the generalized programming model is the following:

Minimize
$$\sum_i a_i w_i + \sum_j b_j u_j + \sum_k f_k t_k + \ldots + \sum_m h_m s_m$$
$$+ \sum_i \sum_j c_{ij} x_{ij} + \sum_j \sum_k d_{jk} y_{jk}$$
$$+ \sum_k \sum_l e_{kl} v_{kl} + \ldots + \sum_m \sum_n g_{mn} z_{mn} \qquad (1)$$

subject to

$$\sum_i \frac{x_{ij}}{\alpha_{ij}} = \sum_k y_{jk} \qquad \text{(over all } j\text{)};$$

$$\sum_j \frac{y_{jk}}{\beta_{jk}} = \sum_l v_{kl} \qquad \text{(over all } k\text{)}; \ldots$$

$$\vdots$$

$$\sum_o \frac{p_{om}}{\pi_{om}} = \sum_m z_{mn} \qquad \text{(over all } m\text{)}; \qquad (2)$$

$$\sum_m z_{mn} = R_n \qquad \text{(over all } n\text{)}. \qquad (3)$$

If $\qquad w_i \begin{Bmatrix} = 1 \\ = 0 \end{Bmatrix}$, then $\sum_j x_{ij} \begin{Bmatrix} \geq 0 \\ = 0 \end{Bmatrix} \qquad$ (all i).

231

If $\qquad u_j \begin{Bmatrix} =1 \\ =0 \end{Bmatrix}$, then $\sum_k y_{ik} \begin{Bmatrix} \geq 0 \\ =0 \end{Bmatrix}$ (all j).

If $\qquad t_k \begin{Bmatrix} =1 \\ =0 \end{Bmatrix}$, then $\sum_l v_{kl} \begin{Bmatrix} \geq 0 \\ =0 \end{Bmatrix}$ (all k).

.
.
.

If $\qquad s_m \begin{Bmatrix} =1 \\ =0 \end{Bmatrix}$, then $\sum_n z_{mn} \begin{Bmatrix} \geq 0 \\ =0 \end{Bmatrix}$ (all m).   (4)

$$x_{ij}, y_{jk}, v_{kl}, \ldots, z_{mn} \geq 0; \tag{5}$$

$$w_i, u_j, t_k, \ldots; s_m = 0 \text{ or } 1. \tag{6}$$

$$\sum_j x_{ij} \leq Q_1$$

$$\sum_k y_{jk} \leq Q_2$$

.
.
.

$$\sum_n z_{mn} \leq Q_N \tag{7}$$

a_i = fixed annual cost of a "first stage" plant at i
b_j = fixed annual cost of a "second stage" plant at j
.
.
.

h_m = fixed annual cost of a "final stage" plant at m
c_{ij} = variable annual cost per unit of production of a "first stage" plant at i, plus the cost of transportation from i to j
d_{jk} = variable annual cost per unit of production of a "second stage" plant at j, excluding the cost of the product input from stage one to avoid double counting, plus the cost of transportation from j to k
.
.
.

g_{mn} = variable annual cost per unit of production of a "final stage" plant at m, excluding the cost of the product input from the previous stage to avoid double counting, plus the cost of transportation from m to n

w_i = dichotomous variable (0 or 1); equals unity when plant exists at i
u_j = dichotomous variable; equals unity when plant exists at j
.
.
.

s_m = dichotomous variable; equals unity when plant exists at m
x_{ij} = units of stage one products produced at location i and shipped to second stage production location j
y_{jk} = units of stage two products produced at location j and shipped to third stage production location k
.
.
.

z_{mn} = units of final stage products produced at location m and shipped to markets n
α_{ij} = inverse of input-output coefficient relating output of plant i to plant j
.
.
.

π_{om} = inverse of input-output coefficient relating output of plant o to plant m
Q_N = output restriction on each plant producing stage N products
R_n = units of final stage products consumed at market n.

Equation (1) represents the objective function; it defines the sum of the costs to be minimized. These are the fixed and variable costs of production at all stages and the transportation costs between stages and between each stage and final markets. Imports from the United States are accounted for by a plant with constant marginal and average costs (since the Latin American demand is small relative to total output, it can be assumed that the U.S. price to Latin American markets is given).

Equations (2) state that the output from stage m divided by the reciprocal of the input-output coefficient between stage m output and stage $(m + 1)$ output equals the output of stage $(m + 1)$. If one unit of second-stage output requires 0.5 unit of first-stage output, then, for example,

$1/0.5_{12} = 2$. In the even more generalized model, where each stage is also allowed to ship to final markets as well as to other plants, equations (2) would be of the form:

$$\sum_o \frac{p_{om}}{\pi_{om}} + \sum_o q_{op} = \sum_n z_{mn} \qquad \text{(over all } m\text{)},$$

where q_{op} is the quantity shipped from plants o to final markets.

Equation (3) is the condition for fulfillment of final demand. Again, where several sets of plants ship to final markets as well as to other plants, a series of equations here would relate the output of each set of plants to the final demand for that output.

Because of the intercept term in the production cost curve, the solution to the relatively simple problem of minimizing total variable costs does not necessarily represent the minimum of variable plus "fixed" costs. To minimize total costs, economies of scale must be accounted for. This makes it necessary to enumerate all solutions to the linear programming model shown above. The computation of the complete set of solutions follows the "brute force" method worked out by Vietorisz and Manne:

Once a particular pattern of zeros and ones is assigned to the . . . zero-one variables, the remaining unknowns . . . are related to each other via a "transshipment" problem—one of the easiest of all linear programming structures.

The computational approach may be summarized as follows: Enumerate all possible combinations of the zero-one variables, finding a *local* optimum to each of the . . . transshipment problems. Variable costs are calculated for each local optimum and added to the fixed costs associated with that particular combination of zero-one variables. The combinations are then ranked in ascending order to total costs, thereby determining not only a minimum-cost solution, but also a cumulative distribution of all local optima.[1]

For many of the products, the algorithm assumes a maximum plant size[2] that is below the total production specified by the solution (see equation

1. Thomas Vietorisz and Alan S. Manne, "Chemical Processes, Plant Location, and Economies of Scale," in Alan S. Manne and Harry M. Markowitz (eds.), *Studies in Process Analysis: Economy-Wide Production Capabilities* (John Wiley & Sons, 1963), p. 151. The "local optimum" is the minimum cost of production location for each possible combination of plants. More specifically, the optimum location is estimated with all plants allowed and then for combinations of plants with one or more plants not allowed. The lowest cost solution for each of these combinations is called the "local optimum." Since there is a fixed cost component at each location, and the local optimum is estimated by minimizing only variable cost (that associated with changes in output), the *total* cost associated with all local optima must be listed to determine their order, and to find the lowest *total* cost local optimum.

2. The maximum plant size chosen approximately equals the maximum size (output) of plants producing the same product in the United States in 1965, except in the case of

7). In these cases, the fixed cost or intercept term is added in as many times as there are plants at each location. This process reaches an extreme for powdered milk and cheese, where maximum plant size is 1 percent or less of total area demand. For products that have so many local optima that it is not feasible to calculate all of them, only some key locations alternative to the optimum are shown in the product studies. These are chosen for their relevance to policies in which political considerations are paramount (for example, autarky, where there would be production in each country rather than at the minimum cost location).

---

lathes and dairy products, where the maximum equals the maximum plant size observed in this study. The latter constraint is imposed because short-run cost curves are used for cost comparisons rather than long-run curves.

Cost of Production and Transportation

So that the measurement of production and transport costs would be as consistent as possible, considerable time was spent at several semiannual seminars to reach accord among the various institutes on a set of definitions. The definitions and agreements set forth below exceeded what most institutes could achieve with the data, and therefore must be considered an ideal that could be met in only a few of the case studies.[1]

Costs of production are divided into three general categories: (1) materials, (2) direct production labor, and (3) general costs of production, each of which in turn is divided into a number of subcategories.

Materials

The materials category contains raw materials, semifinished materials, parts and components, and auxiliary materials.

Raw materials are defined as all the materials acquired for processing within the plant, or for incorporation in the product, and processed by third parties.

Semifinished materials are elements or pieces that have undergone some process previous to acquisition but that require additional processing

---

1. See José Maria Dagnino Pastore, *La Industria del Tractor en la Argentina* (Buenos Aires: Centro de Investigaciones Económicas, Instituto Torcuato di Tella, 1966).

before utilization in further operations or incorporation into the product. For example, gears that must be filed and finished before mounting fall into this category.

Parts and components are finished pieces that require only assembly to enter into the final product.

For continuous process industries, a general subcategory defined as *auxiliary materials* is included; these are elements that are used in the process of production itself. One example is catalysts in chemical processes, if they can be quantified directly and assigned (in whole or in part) to a single final product. Another example is steam consumed in the production of powdered milk. It is possible to include fuel and lubricants if the input per unit of final product is known.

Each of the subcategories of materials is divided into imported or domestically produced materials. For imported goods the division is made between the net cost of the material and the tariff charges. For nationally produced materials, an attempt is made to determine the proportions of domestic and imported inputs. In calculations involving imported goods, the rate (and its date) used in converting their price in foreign currency into the national monetary unit is specified. Any government subsidy on the production of materials is designated and calculated in their unit costs.

Direct Production Labor

The cost of direct production labor is separated into three parts: net salaries paid to workers; required social payments; and all other benefits, such as salaries in kind, housing, or meals.

Labor payments are broken down and described to the maximum possible extent. An attempt is made to identify *direct labor costs* according to the types of workers and the processes in which they are engaged; *social charges*, according to whether they are legally imposed; and *all other benefits*, according to whether they are automatically received or awarded under special circumstances.

The sum of the costs of materials and direct production labor is the "primary cost," or the "cost of direct production." Primary cost plus the general costs of production, described next, equals the total cost of production.

General Costs of Production

General costs of production comprise the following subcategories:

Services and supplies, which include, among other things, electric power, maintenance, fuel, lubricants, and insurance. In continuous process industries, some of the general costs included here are relegated instead to the category of auxiliary materials.

Depreciation charges on factory buildings, machinery, and other durables that enter into the production process. Straight-line depreciation is used, based, for all countries, on average production life of fixed assets computed for Argentina by the Instituto Torcuato di Tella. These estimates were checked against average life computed from engineering estimates for the United States.

Taxes used directly for services that enter into the production process: property taxes, municipal taxes for street lighting and street cleaning, taxes for sewage systems. All of these are approximated on the basis of the proportion of the taxable base entering into production. The method of estimating the proportion was presented in every case. Profits tax, where it exists, was not included; however, its legal aspects were described for each country in order to determine its influence on a firm's operation.

Labor indirectly involved in production, in storage and maintenance, and in plant administration. The breakdown of costs is identical to that of direct labor costs, but the type of labor is stressed to reflect the greater range of skills.

Costs of administration. These include all administrative costs of the plant other than those for personnel.

Other general costs of administration not included in the previous categories. This category picks up costs that cannot be fitted into the other groups.

Interest. Interest payments are conceived in terms of the opportunity cost of capital and are expressed in real terms (net of changes in the value of the monetary unit).[2] The interest on fixed assets is taken as 8 percent on assets owned by the firm, and at the market real rate of interest (taking

2. In the case of engineering estimates, the current market value of the asset is used. If the assets are imported, the dollar value is translated into local currency at current rates of exchange. The effect of this is discussed on pp. 226–28. In the case of existing plant and equipment, replacement cost estimates are used. For the details of the methodology employed in estimating replacement cost of capital see Pastore. *La Industria del Tractor.*

account of length of term of the credit) on the liabilities to third parties. Where hypothetical plants or production functions are used, the 8 percent rate applies to all fixed assets. The rate of interest on working capital is taken as the market rate in each country.

Joint Costs

A general problem in determining the cost of production of a good is that some plants in the countries studied produce products other than that under study. Where the data were obtainable from existing plants, the companies surveyed were asked to supply, where they were applicable, an allocation of costs to the product class, and to a particular product model and type. General costs of running the plant are allocated proportionately to the value of the various outputs, or by another, specified method.

In the design of hypothetical plants to produce several final products, joint costs are assigned according to the proportion of value added accounted for by each product. It is also possible, for many products, to design an alternative set of plants that produce each of the products separately, usually with the product of one of the plants used as an input for the others. In the case of nitrogenous fertilizers, for example, joint costs are allocated among ammonia, ammonium nitrate, urea, and ammonium sulphate in plants producing them all; alternatively, joint costs can be allocated among these four products by designing plants to produce the last three, each of which uses the output of the ammonia plant as input.

Historical Analysis and Cost Projections

The long-run cost curves derived from cross-sectional plant studies in a given recent year yield information about costs in relation to plant size based on input prices at that point in time. The projection of costs derived from such studies requires "the determination of trends in unit costs and the cost-structure, and in the productivity ratios (and other significant relationships), which can be compared as among plants and countries (and related to other significant characteristics, such as size of firm or plant), and which serve as a background for projections into the future."[3]

3. John W. Kendrick, "The Study of Costs for Selected Project Classes" (Buenos Aires: Centro de Investigaciones Economicas, Instituto Torcuato di Tella, Project No. 15, Progress Report No. 3, Annex No. 1; processed).

Trends in production techniques and in the prices of factors of production affect the long-run cost curves estimated by cross-section studies: The former changes the shape of the curves, and the latter the level of costs, if no change is made in the production function.

In the studies using curves derived from engineering estimates of unit costs associated with new plants of various sizes, the implicit assumption is that the shape of the curves does not change over time with the costs of inputs. Future changes in input prices projected on the basis of time series analysis alter only the level of costs. The real difficulty of projecting the level of costs lies in predicting changes in prices of inputs acquired by the plant under monopsonistic conditions. Given that situation, the historical trend in the prices of inputs would underestimate future prices when the plant expands or a new plant is constructed. Strictly speaking, the supply curve of these inputs should be known in order to predict their future prices under alternative assumptions of plant size. However, without going into such detail, it is possible to anticipate bottlenecks in the supply of certain inputs with plant expansion. These could occur in electric power, skilled labor, management, or other specialized inputs. Where actual or potential monopsonistic conditions prevail, the studies attempt to deal with them in projecting input prices and long-run cost curves.

Transport Costs[4]

The measurement of transport costs for the determination of optimal plant location presents few conceptual difficulties. The principal problem is to assure that the classification of the elements and components of the cost is complete. For the purposes of this study, the transport cost of inputs used in fabricating the final product are assumed to be reflected in the price of inputs at the factory.[5] This does not rule out the possibility of alternative plant sites; differences in input prices at various sites would reflect differences in transport costs of the inputs.

4. This section is based on a short paper presented by Robert Brown at the Second ECIEL Seminar in Montevideo, May 1964.

5. In the case of chemicals, some of the products studied serve as inputs for other products studied. Allowance is made for the case in which plants produce only the input chemical, while others (in the same or other countries) produce only the final product. In the chemical study, therefore, transport costs of certain inputs are separated out.

To collect information on transport costs, three questionnaires were sent to the institutes. They concentrated on intranational transportation. The major part of transport among the countries of the Latin American Free Trade Association (LAFTA) is by sea; and the costs between ports were estimated separately by the Brookings Institution. The data collected highlight the fact that the actual movement of the cargo, as opposed to its loading and unloading, is only a small part of the total cost of transport. Each institute determined this total cost for every product. In the case of overland international transport between two LAFTA countries (Questionnaire No. 3), the institutes computed costs to the border, including the cost of cargo handling during any customs inspection on the near side. The transport cost from the border to the market in the adjoining country is calculated on the basis of the cost of transporting the good from the consumption center in the adjoining country to the same border point. Since consumption centers and factory sites usually coincide and the number of border crossings is limited, these estimates present little problem.

In order to determine transport costs on seaborne trade, each institute calculated the cost of moving the product from the factory (there may be alternative sites) to the nearest port and on board ship (Questionnaire No. 1). The cost includes the overland transport charges and the charges within the port, separated into the various components. Shipping rates are figured on the basis of both existing maritime transportation facilities between LAFTA countries,[6] and the possibility that rates may drop by 1975. In the first case, published rates are used where available; but, because of extremely limited service between some countries, present published rates may not reflect rates in the future, if tariff reduction stimulates trade between those countries. Shipping rates depend in part on the volume of trade, the type of service, the restriction on ships from outside the zone, and the competition of shipping companies based within LAFTA. These factors could all change greatly by 1975, perhaps substantially lowering rates on the routes under consideration. Changes in overland transport that lead to a net rise in trade could affect maritime rates in a similar way. Published rates therefore represent a maximum estimate of transportation costs. In the present study, the possibility that transport costs will drop through an effective LAFTA is incorporated by estimating a "minimum"

6. Robert Brown, *Transport and the Economic Integration of South America* (Brookings Institution, 1966).

set of maritime freight rates. The estimate is made by means of a general formula that yields rates independent of published rates. When the rates calculated by formula are approximately equal to published rates, only one set of transport costs is used.

The formulas are as follows:

Product type	1,000 miles	3,000 miles	12,000 miles
Bulk (solid fertilizers, newsprint kraft paper, cellulose, powdered milk, cheese)	9%	10%	20%
Dangerous (formaldehyde, methanol, ammonia, ammonium nitrate)	20.25	22.5	45
Machinery (tractors, lathes)	3.5	5	10

The percentages represent the approximate rate as a percent of product value according to distance carried. The 3,000 mile haul is the base, and the 1,000 and 12,000 mile hauls should be read as 90 percent and 200 percent, respectively, of the base. While rates are not proportional to distance (for example, the 1,000 mile haul is 90 percent, rather than one-third, of the 3,000 mile haul), a fair estimate of ruling rates can be derived by interpolating *between* rate factors. Thus, from Acapulco to São Paulo the distance is 8,400 miles (around the Horn) so that the rate for, say, tractors would be approximately 8 percent ad valorem, or, put another way, the surcharge on the haul in excess of 3,000 miles would be

$$0.05 \left(\frac{5,400}{9,000} \right) = 0.03.$$

or 3 percent.

If the percentages were used in the linear programming model directly, taking the value of the product (price times quantity shipped) as the unknown, then all the programming models would be nonlinear, since both prices (cost) and quantity would be variable. Rather than incur the extra cost involved in that type of problem, the percentage from the formula is multiplied by the price of the good in the United States. Although U.S. prices are higher than those in the world market in some products, the resulting rates per ton are low enough to serve the purposes of the study.

Benefits and Costs to Individual Countries of Buying from Optimum Locations

THE SOLUTIONS TO THE linearized programming model yield delivered prices of each product at each market from the minimum cost locations and from alternative patterns of production. These prices can be used to find the welfare costs or benefits to a country of buying from the minimum cost location in the Latin American Free Trade Association (LAFTA) rather than importing from third countries or producing domestically.

The estimation of welfare benefits (or costs) is shown geometrically in Figure C-1. Country A initially produces product X domestically. Its supply curve of X is S_A,[1] and its demand curve is D_A. The incremental resource cost of producing X_0 is $OECX_0$. Country B's supply curve of X is S_B; in order to protect its producers from B's exports, A levies a tariff equal to $P_A - P_B$. With union, A imports X from B, increasing A's consumption to X_1, and lowering the price of X from P_A in A and P_B in B to P'_A in both countries. The resource cost to A of consuming X_1 is P'_AQX_1O. The net welfare gain to A of buying from B rather than producing domestically equals $ECRQP'_A$.

If it is assumed that country B represents the integrated region with the exception of country A, the addition of country A's demand would probably have a small effect on the price of X to the region $(P_B - P'_A)$

---

1. The supply curve is taken as the marginal cost curve for the purpose of this analysis. As will be seen, where the marginal cost curve is almost flat over the relevant range, the supply curve can be taken as the average cost curve, which is closer to reality.

Figure C-1. Welfare Benefits of Importing from Optimum Regional Location Compared with Autarkic Production

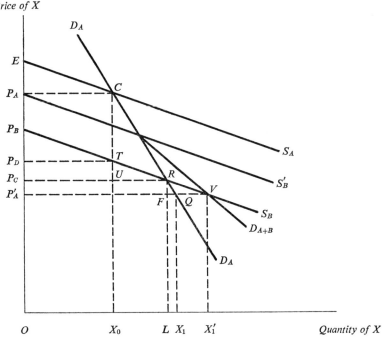

Note: the origin represents $X = 0$ for S_A and D_A, but for S_B and D_{A+B} the origin represents $X =$ regional consumption and production at P_B.

relative to the fall in price due to switching from a domestic to regional source of production $(P_A - P_C)$. If $P_B - P'_A$ can be assumed to be small relative to $P_A - P_C$, then $P_C - P'_A$ may, for purposes of measurement, be considered negligible. Based on this assumption, and the assumption that X_1 is the measured 1975 projected demand at P'_A (taken as equal to P_C),[2] the welfare gain to A can be expressed as $ECRP_C$, which equals $P_A CRP_C$ plus ECP_A, which equals $P_B TP_D$.

Based on Figure C-1, the calculation of the welfare gain (WG) is as follows:

$$P_A CRP_C = P_A CUP_C + CRU \text{ and } P_B TP_D = \tfrac{1}{2}(P_B - P_D)X_0.$$

2. This assumes that demand projections are based on prices lower than those that prevail currently.

The difference $P_B - P_D$ is the slope of $S_B(\dot{Y})$ times X_0. Since P_C approximately equals P'_A, the welfare gain may be expressed as:

(1) $\quad WG = X_0(P_A - P'_A) + \frac{1}{2}(X_1 - X_0)(P_A - P_A') + \frac{1}{2}\dot{Y}X^2_0$

(2) $\quad WG = X_1Z(P_A - P'_A) + \frac{1}{2}X_1(1 - Z)(P_A - P'_A) + \frac{1}{2}\dot{Y}X^2Z^2,$

where

$$\eta = \text{arc elasticity of demand for } X \text{ in country } A = \dfrac{\dfrac{X_0 - X_1}{X_0 + X_1}}{\dfrac{P_A - P'_A}{P_A + P'_A}}$$

and $\qquad X_0 = X_1\dfrac{P_A(1 + \eta) + P'_A(1 - \eta)}{P_A(1 - \eta) + P'_A(1 + \eta)} = X_1Z.$

Since country A's additional demand is usually small relative to regional demand, $\dot{y}$—the slope of the minimum cost location supply curve—is assumed equal to zero (it is very close to zero) between X_0 and X_1 in Figure C-1. Therefore,

(3) $\qquad WG = X_1Z(P_A - P'_A) + \frac{1}{2}X_1(1 - Z)(P_A - P'_A).$

If η is taken equal to -1, $Z = P_A'/P_A$ and the expression becomes

(4) $\qquad WG = X_1P'_A\left(1 - \dfrac{P'_A}{P_A}\right)\left[1 + \frac{1}{2}\left(\dfrac{P_A}{P'_A} - 1\right)\right]^3$

There is a special case of Figure C-1 that shows the welfare gain to country A from supplying to the region instead of undertaking autarkic production. In that case, A is the minimum cost location of production in the region and S_A and S_B represent different sections of A's supply curve of X; S_A represents the section when only A's demand for X is included, and S_B the section when total regional demand is used. The calculations of welfare benefits of producing for the region rather than solely for domestic demand are essentially the same as above. The principal difference is that the welfare gain to A would be less by the triangle P'_AVP_B, or,

---

3. This expression probably underestimates the welfare benefits to A of importing from the regional optimum rather than producing nationally. Besides eliminating FRQ by the assumptions made here, Figure C-1 has depicted S_B and S_A as having the same slope in the region OX_0. Since S_B is the portion of the minimum cost supply curve with the origin representing regional demand at P_B, and S_A is A's supply curve, it is likely that the latter will have a greater slope than S_B between 0 and X_0. This would increase the welfare gain to A.

assuming $P'_A = P_C, P_C R P_B$. If the slope of the S_B is taken as zero, the welfare gains in the two cases are equivalent.

Figure C-2 represents a situation in which A initially imports X from outside the region. S_F is the supply curve of imports and S_B is the supply curve of the minimum cost location in the region. Before A joins the union, it is shown as facing a supply curve from the partners that equals the import price of X at the origin. As noted, the origin is defined for S_B as regional consumption (production) of X at a price of P_A.

It should also be remembered that S_B represents the supply curve of the minimum cost location with all countries joined in union except A. S_C is the cost curve of the minimum cost location when that country is producing for domestic consumption only. Expansion of the markets facing the optimum location producer drives the price of X down to the point

Figure C-2. Welfare Benefits of Importing from Optimum Regional Location Compared with Extraregional Importing

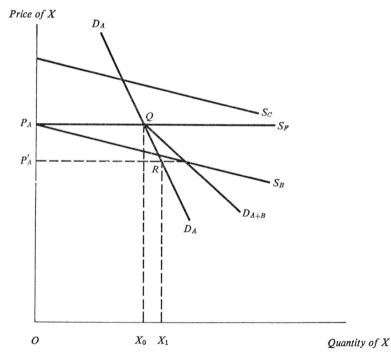

Note: the origin represents $X = 0$ for S_F and D_A, but for S_B and D_{A+B}, the origin represents $X = $ regional consumption and production at P_A.

where it is competitive with third country imports. The welfare gain to A over importing from F (again assuming $\dot{y} = 0$) equals $P_A QRP'_A$, which is expressed the same as equation (3).[4] The most important possible bias in estimating the gains of importing from the minimum cost location in the region rather than from third countries lies in the assumed 1975 world market price of products studied. In each case but fertilizers, the price used is the 1965 world price, which may be much higher than the price in 1975 for some products. In addition, the stability of location optima in the face of increased or decreased demand (resulting from price changes) must be determined. To do this, projections were all decreased and increased by 20 percent, and the optima calculated, but no change occurs in them. This means that demand can be varied within this range without a change in the location of production.

4. Equation (4) probably overestimates the welfare benefits to A of buying from the optimum location in the region rather than importing from outside the region. Figure C-2 has depicted S_F and S_B as having different slopes, but the estimate from equation (1) assumes that they are parallel. The latter assumption would tend to overestimate gains to shifting from foreign to partner-country suppliers.

Standardization of Tractor Size

EVEN THOUGH THE RELATIONSHIP between size of tractor (in horse-power) and price would be expected to vary among countries—especially in the Latin American Free Trade Association (LAFTA) region, where conditions of agriculture differ greatly—the importation of tractors to fill the entire demand in most of the economies studied would have a homog-enizing effect on it. Since the countries under study are all marginal buyers in the world tractor market, the particular demand conditions for different size tractors would have little influence on prices f.o.b. in the exporting countries. On the other hand, in countries like Brazil, Argentina, and Mexico, which produce or assemble a large fraction of their own annual tractor demand and protect domestic producers, differentials in the horsepower-price relation can be expected.

Lack of data precludes establishing country-by-country schedules of the horsepower-price relationship. In addition, several studies (for Paraguay, Peru, Uruguay) do not present the current structure of consumption by tractor size; without it, conversion to a standard size cannot be made even if the horsepower-price relationship is known. Fortunately, data that are available for Argentina[1] can be used to approximate tractor proportions in Paraguay and Uruguay. Tractor proportions in Peru are approximated by using Colombian percentages. The percentages by tractor size and country are shown in Table D-1.

1. *Review of the River Plate*, Nov. 21, 1966, p. 277.

Table D-1. Percent Distribution of Tractor Sales by Size in Horsepower, in Selected LAFTA Countries, Selected Years

	Argentina 1956–63		Brazil 1963		Chile 1957–61		Colombia 1963		Ecuador 1964	
	Horse-power[a]	Percent of total sales	Horse-power[a]	Percent of total sales	Horse-power[a]	Percent of total sales	Horse-power[a]	Percent of total sales	Horse-power[a]	Percent of total sales
	0–29	5.7			0–19	1.7	0–30	2.6		
	30–35	10.6	25–35	40.3	20–30	4.3	30–35	12.5	0–35	22.2
	36–40	7.6	36–45	42.2	31–40	13.5	36–40	27.2	40	37.5
	41–45	12.4	Over 45	17.5			41–45	20.0		
	46–50	12.7			41–50	24.8	46–50	10.2	50	22.2
	51–55	11.4			51–60	41.6	51–55	20.4		
	Over 55	39.6			61–70	4.7	Over 55	7.0	55–70	12.5
					71–100	0.9			Over 70	5.6
					101–150	0.8				
					Over 150	1.1				

Source: ECIEL, *The Demand for Chemical Fertilizers, Tractors, Paper and Pulp, Milk Concentrates, and Lathes in the Latin American Free Trade Association (including Venezuela)* (Brookings Institution, 1966; processed).

a. The differences in horsepower ranges among countries reflect the manner in which they were reported by the various institutes.

249

In order to convert demand for various tractor sizes to demand for a single, equivalent size, a relation was found between the retail tractor price and tractor horsepower, holding constant the type of fuel used (diesel or gasoline) and the tractor model (standard or tricycle). The data used are from the *Official Tractor and Farm Equipment Guide* (Fall 1965), compiled by the National Farm and Power Equipment Dealers Association, St. Louis, Missouri. The sample, which includes 300 observations, takes only new tractors, standard and tricycle, diesel and gasoline models, in each model series; options are not included.

Several estimates were made of the relation for the United States by regression analysis; the best is presented below:

$$\log P_t = 1.9617 + 0.9460 \log T + 0.0983\ D - 0.0050\ M_t, \qquad (1)$$
$$ (0.0251) (0.0079) (0.0077)$$
$$R^2 = 0.863$$

where

$T =$ pulley horsepower
$D =$ dummy variable for diesel ($D = 1$ for diesel, 0 for gas)
$M_t =$ dummy variable for tricycle ($M_t = 1$ for tricycle, 0 for standard).

Figures in parentheses are standard errors of the coefficients.

The conversion rate from equation (1) can be calculated by finding the ratio of the price of each size tractor included in Table D-1 to the price of a 50-horsepower tractor (as estimated from the equation). Since equation (1) yields a constant slope in percentage terms, a more direct estimator can be derived for the conversion rate, P_x/P_{50}.

Let $\qquad \log P_t = a + b \log t$

$$\frac{dP_t}{P} = b\,\frac{dt}{t}$$

$$\frac{P_{50} - P_x}{P_x} = b\,\frac{t_{50} - t_x}{t_x}$$

$$\frac{P_x}{P_{50}} = \frac{t_x}{bt_{50} + (1 - b)t_x} = \text{conversion rate.}$$

$$t_{50} = 50,\ b = 0.9460,\ \text{and}\ (1 - b) = 0.0540$$

$$\frac{P_x}{P_{50}} = \frac{t_x}{47.300 + 0.0540t_x}. \qquad (2)$$

With the inclusion of the horsepower of the given size tractor, the conversion rate is found. This conversion rate is multiplied by the corresponding

Table D-2. Percentage Equivalents of Tractors of Selected Horsepower to 50-Horsepower Tractors Derived from U.S. Conversion Equation, Selected LAFTA Countries

Argentina[a]		Brazil[b]		Chile		Colombia		Ecuador	
Horse-power	Fraction	Horse-power	Fraction	Horse-power	Fraction	Horse-power	Fraction	Horse-power	Fraction
0–29	0.018	25–35	0.247	0–20	0.004	0–29[c]	0.011	35	0.160
30–35	0.069	36–45	0.341	21–30	0.022	30–35	0.083	40	0.304
36–40	0.058	Over 45[d]	0.191	31–40	0.097	36–40	0.208	50	0.222
41–45	0.106			41–50	0.224	41–45	0.172	55–70	0.153
46–50	0.121			51–60	0.455	46–50	0.097	Over 70[e]	0.086
51–55	0.119			61–70	0.060	51–55	0.214		
Over 55[f]	0.470			71–100	0.014	Over 55[g]	0.095		
				100–150	0.018				
				Over 150[h]	0.031				
Total	0.961		0.779		0.925		0.880		0.925

Source: Conversion rates of equation (2) multiplied by percentages in Table D-1. The Argentine equivalent derived from the Argentine equation is used for Argentina and Paraguay. The Brazil equivalent derived from the Argentine equation is used for Brazil. All other equivalents are derived from the U.S. equation.

a. With the Argentine equation, described on p. 252, the fractions, in order, are as follows: 0.039, 0.087, 0.067, 0.117, 0.128, 0.121, 0.442; total—1.001.
b. With the Argentine equation, the fractions, in order, are as follows: 0.310, 0.373, 0.184; total—0.867.
c. Midpoint taken as 20 horsepower.
d. Midpoint taken as 55 horsepower.
e. Midpoint taken as 80 horsepower.
f. Midpoint taken as 60 horsepower.
g. Midpoint taken as 70 horsepower.
h. Midpoint taken as 165 horsepower.

percentages to obtain percentage equivalents of 50-horsepower tractors. In each case, the midpoint of the range shown in the table is used. The new percentages (see Table D-2) are added, and the total is an approximation to the 50-horsepower equivalent of projected demand in 1975. The total percentages are used in converting the original projected demand in the country studies[2] to 50-horsepower-equivalent demand.

To keep demand projections for Paraguay and Brazil consistent with supply cost projections, an alternative conversion is made using the Argentine equation of horsepower-price relation. This results in a higher 50-horsepower-equivalent demand than the U.S. equation does.[3]

This equation yields the following conversion ratio:

$$P_x/P_{50} = \frac{2514.62 + 68.204t_x}{5924.82}. \tag{3}$$

2. See ECIEL, *The Demand for Chemical Fertilizers, Tractors, Paper and Pulp, Milk Concentrates, and Lathes in the Latin American Free Trade Association* (*including Venezuela*) (Brookings Institution, 1966; processed).

3. See José Maria Dagnino Pastore, *La Industria del Tractor en la Argentina* (Buenos Aires: Centro de Investigaciones Economicas, Instituto Torcuato di Tella, 1966), p. 2.22. The Argentine equation is derived using weights of quantity sold, which are not included in the U.S. equation.

APPENDIX E

Calculation of Powdered Milk and Cheese Production Costs

THE MODEL[1] ASSUMES that the appearance of a powdered milk producer in the region does not affect the price of milk at the farm, because the producer would consume only a small proportion of milk in the region. As production of powdered dairy products expands, of course, the price of milk at the farm could rise. Other factors not accounted for in this study also affect the price of milk. If beef prices rise, for example, farmers will use grassland for beef production instead of milk production, so milk prices will rise. Therefore, milk prices should be positively correlated with beef prices. The powdered milk producer may be a monopsonist or large buyer of milk in the region. In that case, since the producer pays a fixed price at the plant for milk, the price at the farm gate will be lower, land prices lower, and transport costs higher the farther the farm from the plant. The model also assumes no geographical overlap of sources of supply among dairy processors. Figure E-1 therefore represents a typical milk supply area for a processor that is independent of the supply areas of all other processors.

---

1. The model was developed by Mario Brodersohn, J. M. Dagnino Pastore, Antonio Delfim Netto, Juan Carlos de Pablo, and Raúl Vigorito at the seminar of ECIEL held in São Paulo, Brazil, November 1965. It is presented in Juan Carlos de Pablo and Fernando Arturo Ibarra, *Industria del Queso en la Argentina* (Buenos Aires: Fundación de Investigaciones Económicas Latinoamericanos, 1966), pp. 73–75.

The total cost function expresses the increasing fresh milk price the processor faces as he attempts to expand production:

$$C_t(x) = C_p(x) + g(x), \qquad (1)$$

where

    $C_t(x)$ = total cost of fluid milk (x units) at the factory
    $C_p(x)$ = total cost of "production" of milk at the farm
    $g(x)$ = nonlinear transport cost of milk from farm to factory.

Figure E-1. Fluid Milk Production of Uniform Density in a Circular Area Centered on a Milk Processing Plant

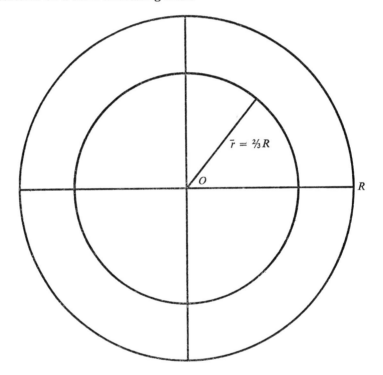

Assuming a circular and uniform expansion of the milk-producing area around the plant, the total cost of transportation would equal:

$$g(x) = c\bar{r}x, \qquad (2)$$

where

    c = cost of transport per unit of fluid milk per unit of distance
    $\bar{r}$ = the average distance between farm and factory (see Figure E-1)
    x = number of units of fluid milk.

The average distance $\bar{r}$ is found by taking the first moment of the function describing the circumference of a circle of radius r over the range O to R, the maximum radius, and dividing by the integral of that function over the same range:

$$\bar{r} = \frac{\int_o^R r\, 2\pi r\, dr}{\int_o^R 2\pi r\, dr} = \tfrac{2}{3}R. \tag{3}$$

Since, under an assumption of the full utilization of land and constant technology, the area grows as a function of the quantity of milk needed, R is a function of fluid milk demanded at the factory. Assuming a *constant yield* of land,[2]

$$x = b\pi R^2 \text{ and}$$
$$R = (x/b\pi)^{\frac{1}{2}}, \tag{4}$$

where

    b = the yield of milk per unit area,

so that

$$\bar{r} = \tfrac{2}{3}(x/b\pi)^{\frac{1}{2}}$$

and
$$C_t(x) = C_p(x) + \tfrac{2}{3}c(b\pi)^{-\frac{1}{2}}x^{\frac{3}{2}}. \tag{5}$$

Marginal cost of milk at the factory is

$$C'_t(x) = c(b\pi)^{-\frac{1}{2}}x^{\frac{1}{2}}. \tag{6}$$

Assuming that the marginal cost of milk production at the farm equals milk price and is a fixed price from the point of view of the milk concentrates factory, the marginal cost of fluid milk at the factory increases with increased production and proportionately to the square root of fluid milk

---

2. Again, this assumes that powdered milk production uses only a small fraction of total milk production.

demanded. The higher the cost of transport from farm to factory, the higher the total cost of fluid milk, and the higher the yield per unit of area, the lower the total cost of production.

Since cost of transport in Latin American countries tends to be higher, and the yields of fluid milk per unit of area lower, than in the United States, Argentine, Uruguayan, and Peruvian fluid milk "production" costs at the farm must be lower, or the final output of the plants smaller, than those in the United States if lower prices of delivered milk are to result. This hypothesis is borne out empirically. The Brazilian powdered milk plant, with an output comparable to that of larger U.S. manufacturers, also has a higher delivered milk price.

The production cost curves in the plant (net of fluid milk cost) for powdered milk and cheese have the following form:

$$C(y) = A + By, \tag{7}$$

where

y = output of milk concentrates
A = fixed cost of production, and
B = variable cost of production.

The total variable cost of production of milk concentrates is, in turn, a function of delivered fluid milk price. Assuming that yield per unit of area remains constant as production expands, and taking price at the farm of fluid milk equal to $C_p(x)$ in equation (5) and also assuming it to be constant (which again assumes only a small fraction of the milk going to the powdered milk plant), we can solve for the cost of milk concentrates as a function of the cost of milk at the factory and the output of concentrates.

The total cost of production of fluid milk at the farm, $C_f(x)$, can be expressed as a function of y, the output of milk concentrates plant since $x = ty$, where t is the number of liters of fluid milk required per unit of output.

$$C_f(y) = C_p(ty) + \tfrac{2}{3}c(b\pi)^{-\frac{1}{2}}(ty)^{\frac{3}{2}}. \tag{8}$$

Therefore, the new production cost curve for each country is

$$C(y) = A + By + C_p(ty) + \tfrac{2}{3}c(b\pi)^{-\frac{1}{2}}(ty)^{\frac{3}{2}}$$
$$C(y) = A + (B + C_p t)y + \tfrac{2}{3}c(b\pi)^{-\frac{1}{2}}t^{\frac{3}{2}}y^{\frac{3}{2}}, \tag{9}$$

where $C(y)$ is the total cost of milk concentrates at the processing plant and C'_p is the constant cost of milk at the farm.

The difficulty in estimating the parameters of this equation is that data are not available on the yield of milk per hectare (*b*) for any of the countries under study, and the cost of transport per kilometer of fluid milk at the farm is also available only in the Brazilian case. Nevertheless, using the Brazilian figures for C_p and *c*, and a rough figure for *b* derived for the United States, it is possible to approximate the parameters of equation (9), and hence, the cost functions for powdered milk and cheese in each location.

Brazil's production cost curve for powdered milk in the plant, net of fluid milk cost, estimated in the form of equation (7), is

$$C(y) = 409,000 + 0.167y, \tag{10}$$

where $C(y)$ is in dollars and *y*, in kilograms of powdered milk. In terms of equation (8), therefore, *A* equals 409,000 and *B* equals 0.167.

The cost of milk at the farm in Brazil in 1964 was $0.086 per liter and the transport cost per liter-kilometer, approximately 0.034×10^{-2}. The requirement of fluid milk per unit of output (*t*) equals 8.6 liters per kilogram of powdered milk. In the United States, approximate figures for the amount of pasturage required per dairy cow (2–2.5 acres) and the average yield of milk per cow in 1963–66 (3,154 pounds annually) indicate that *b* is equal to about 3,700 liters per hectare, or 370,000 liters per square kilometer. Equation (8) therefore has the following form for Brazil:

$$C_t(y) = 0.740y + 4.730 \times 10^{-6}y^{\frac{3}{2}}. \tag{11}$$

Equation (9) is

$$C(y) = 409,000 + 0.907y + 4.730 \times 10^{-6}y^{\frac{3}{2}}. \tag{12}$$

Corrected for marketing of the final product, equation (12) is multiplied by 1.25.

Since the cost function that includes the cost of transportation of milk from farm to factory is nonlinear, a linear approximation to this curve must be estimated to use in the linear programming model. The calculation is made by estimating the slope and intercept of a line that connects points on the nonlinear function at two chosen levels of output. The two output levels correspond to (a) the "turning point" of the *average* cost curve (where the slope of the average cost curve goes from negative to positive), and (b) the point of zero production.

Taking the total cost function as

$$C = k_1 + k_2 y + k_3 y^{\frac{3}{2}},$$

and the average cost function as

$$C/y = \frac{k_1}{y} + k_2 + k_3 y^{\frac{1}{2}},$$

the turning point comes at

$$y = \left(\frac{2k_1}{k_3}\right)^{\frac{2}{3}}.$$

The slope and intercept of the line connecting these points are easily estimated in terms of the k_1's and yield the linear approximation to the total
cost function.

For powdered milk in Brazil, the turning point comes at about 37 million
kilograms of annual output. Assuming that yield per cow is one-half, and
pasturage required per cow double, that of the United States, k_3 would be
doubled and the turning point output reduced to 23 million kilograms.
Using this latter figure yields a slope of 1.117 and a final cost curve of

$$C(y) = 511{,}000 + 1.117y.$$

The high output turning point casts some doubt on the relevancy of the
transport cost of fluid milk given for Brazil. The important constraint
not reflected in transportation cost is the cost of time in milk spoilage.
Given the condition of roads in rural Brazil, time spent on the road would
severely limit the distance fluid milk could be carried, and hence the size
of the plant. If the turning point output is taken as 3.4 million kilograms
(the output of the Brazilian powdered milk plant shown in Table 7-5)
and the yield per cow half and pasturage per cow twice that of the United
States, the implicit transport cost would be $0.0081, or about twenty
times the reported transport rate. The total cost function (adjusted for
marketing cost) becomes

$$C(y) = 511{,}000 + 1.14y + 1.63 \times 10^{-4} y^{\frac{3}{2}},$$

and the linear approximation to the function becomes

$$C(y) = 511{,}000 + 1.592y.$$

Taking the same high transport cost and yield per hectare for fluid milk
in Uruguay, the total cost curve for powdered milk is

$$C(y) = 94{,}000 + 0.455y + 2.53 \times 10^{-4} y^{\frac{3}{2}};$$

the turning point is 820,000 kilograms annually, or almost the same as the output of the Uruguayan plant (900,000 kilograms). The linear approximation to the cost curve using 900,000 kilograms as the turning point is

$$C(y) = 94,000 + 0.797y. \tag{13}$$

However, if Uruguayan milk production were to expand to 3,400 tons of powdered milk annually, either in one plant or in several plants in the same location, the cost curve would be characterized by diseconomies of scale. The linear approximation to the Uruguayan total cost curve between the turning point and 3,400 tons of output is

$$C(y) = -166,000 + 0.999y, \tag{14}$$

where $C(y)$ is in simones and y in kilograms of output. The difference in marginal costs between equations (13) and (14) is about Š200 per ton, and represents the higher cost of raw material (milk) when output is expanded. The important distinction to be made is that many 900 ton plants could probably operate in various parts of the country without overlapping milk sources, and the cost of producing powdered milk would be lower in a plant of that size than in the 3,400 ton plant. Nevertheless, in order to make costs more comparable for each product, they are estimated for the same size plant in each country. The largest plant for which costs are estimated is taken as the norm.

APPENDIX F

Comparison of Estimates of Costs of Producing Pulp and Paper

As a check on the reasonableness of the estimates used here, Table F-1 compares cost curves calculated in a working paper by the U.N. Secretariat in *Pulp and Paper Prospects in Latin America* with those derived from costs in Table 8-8. In the case of unbleached pulp, there is a much larger variance in the ECIEL curves, and total costs in a 100,000 ton plant in Mexico are considerably higher than costs for the same size plant in other countries. For the nonintegrated kraft paper plants, the ECIEL cost curves again vary more, but Mexican costs, for a given size plant, are much lower than those in any other country. This comparison casts some doubt on the distribution of costs between pulp and paper in the Mexican estimates. Nevertheless, the cost of Mexican pulp and paper, taken together, at an output of 100,000 tons is much nearer to the estimates for other countries than are the costs of the two products considered separately.

For further comparison, a study of pulp and paper prospects in Chile published in 1957 presents cost figures that are very similar to those shown here. Capital investment requirements in plants that produce 35,000 and 105,000 tons of unbleached pulp annually are estimated as $390 per ton and $240 per ton, respectively.[1] The corresponding figures estimated for this study are $360 and $260 per ton.[2] The investment in the larger plant

1. ECLA, *Chile—Potential Pulp and Paper Exporter*, E/CN.12/424/Rev. 1 (1957).
2. ECIEL, Martin Carnoy (ed.), *The Optimum Location of Specific Industries in the Latin American Free Trade Association (including Venezuela)* (Brookings Institution, 1966; processed), Vol. 4.

260

Table F-1. Comparison of ECLA and ECIEL Estimates of Total Cost Curves for Unbleached Pulp and Kraft Paper[a]

Estimating organization and producing country	*Unbleached pulp*	*Kraft paper*
ECLA		
Sweden	$0.830 + 0.0754X$	$0.541 + 0.0418X$
Yucatan	$1.139 + 0.0571X$	$0.796 + 0.0464X$
Amaja	$1.420 + 0.0787X$	$0.945 + 0.0667X$
ECIEL		
Chile	$1.641 + 0.0648X$	$2.674 + 0.0382X$
Mexico	$6.084 + 0.0940X$	$1.229 + 0.0163X$
Brazil	$0.215 + 0.1096X$	$0.468 + 0.0560X$

Sources: ECLA, *Pulp and Paper Prospects in Latin America*, E/CN.12/370/Rev. 1 (1955), Pt. 2, p. 147; ECIEL, Martin Carnoy (ed.), *The Optimum Location of Specific Industries in the Latin American Free Trade Association (including Venezuela)*, Vol. 4: *Pulp and Paper* (Brookings Institution, 1966; processed), Table 12.
a. The first term of each equation is the fixed cost at the plant in millions of dollars. The second is the factor to be multiplied by the capacity of the plant, denoted here X, in thousands of metric tons annually.

Table F-2. Production Costs for Chilean Pulp and Paper Production

Dollars per ton

	Size of mill (tons per day)			
Product	*50*	*100*	*200*	*500*
Unbleached plup	127	96	77	73
Bleached pulp	157	118	96	91
Unbleached kraft papers	187	146	125	119
Bleached kraft papers	224	174	145	135
Newsprint	...	117	98	95

Source: ECLA, *Chile—Potential Pulp and Paper Exporter*, E/CN. 12/424/Rev. 1 (1957), p. 19.

is higher in this study than in the UN study because it is based on the production of bleached pulp, which requires an additional process. Production costs from the UN study are lower than the estimates made here. Table F-2 shows the cost estimated by the United Nations to be $96 per ton for bleached pulp produced in a plant of 70,000 tons annual output (200 tons per day). Bleached pulp costs in the plant producing 105,000 tons per year, shown in Table 8 8, are $107 per ton, using the free rate of exchange. For kraft paper made from unbleached pulp, the relative difference in price is greater: $125 versus $87 per ton. The estimates of newsprint cost of production are almost identical: $98 versus $102 per ton (see Table 8-15).

Index

Ammonia: anhydrous, 42; consumption, 75, 77–78; demand projection, 76–78; economies of scale, 40–41, 79; optimum location, 42–43; plant size, 88–89; production costs, 79–80, 84–85, 221; transport costs, 41–42; U.S. production, 42, 85. *See also* Nitrogenous fertilizer production

Ammonium nitrate: consumption, 75–76, 78; demand projection, 76, 78; economies of scale, 87; optimum location, 43; production costs, 82, 84–85, 98–99

Ammonium sulphate: consumption, 75, 78; demand projection, 75–76, 78; economies of scale, 87; optimum location, 42–43; production costs, 83–85, 98–99

Andean Development Corporation, 18

Argentina: cheese production, 47, 166–68, 170, 173, 178; formaldehyde production, 117–18; import substitution, 7; industrial growth, 4, 7, 18–20; integration attitude, 13, 26; intraregional trade, 24, kraft paper, 190; lathe production, 46–47, 151, 153–55, 160–64; meat production, 24; nitrogenous fertilizer production, 77, 97, 100; powdered milk production, 47, 169; tractor production, 45, 135–39, 141–50, 219; wheat production, 24

Autarkic production, *see* National production

Baer, Werner, 4n
Bagasse pulp, *see* Pulp and paper

Balance of payments, 7–8

Balassa, Bela, 5n, 12n, 31

Bolivia: industry in, 18–20, 35; integration role, 13, 17–18; subsidy needs, 35

Brazil: butter production, 171; cheese production, 170, 173, 178; import substitution, 7; industrial growth, 4, 7, 20; integration attitude, 13, 26; intraregional trade, 24; lathe production, 47, 151–54; methanol-formaldehyde production, 117–18, 129; newsprint production, 207; nitrogenous fertilizer production, 75–76, 78, 97, 100; powdered milk production, 169, 178, 183; pulp and paper production, 49, 186, 189, 221–22, 219; regional differences, 61, 64; regional production gain, 56; tractor production, 45, 135–39, 141–50, 219, 221

Butter production, 170–71

CABEI, *see* Central American Bank for Economic Integration

CACM, *see* Central American Common Market

Carnoy, Martin, 12n, 29n, 88n, 143n, 154n, 171n, 172n, 192n, 195n, 218n

Cellulose, *see* Pulp and paper

Central American Bank for Economic Integration (CABEI), 13, 25

Central American Common Market (CACM): foreign investment, 27; formation, 13; clearinghouse arrangement, 13, 15; industrial growth, 14, 19; intraregional trade, 14; membership, 13; ob-

262

stacles in, 18–21; Regime of Integration Industries, 13–14, 25

Cheese: consumption, 169; demand projection, 166–69; fluid milk cost, 173–74; optimum location, 47–48; production costs, 170, 172; study types, 217. *See also* Powdered milk and cheese

Chenery, Hollis B., 54n

Chile: ammonia production, 80, 82, 84, 86–87; cellulose production, 196; copper in, 24; industrial growth, 20; integration attitude, 13, 17; intraregional trade, 24; lathe production, 46, 153–55, 160–64, 220; methanol-formaldehyde production, 118–25, 127–29, 221; natural gas in, 41; natural nitrate in, 74; newsprint production, 207; nitrogenous fertilizer production, 77–78, 101–02, 104; pulp and paper production, 186, 189, 192–93, 196, 205, 219, 222; urea production, 81, 87; regional production gain, 56

Chilean Institute of Steel, 154

Coffee, 24

Coke oven gas, 97

Colombia: ammonia production, 80, 82, 86–87, 104–05, 221; cheese production, 168; coffee production, 24; integration attitude, 13, 17; intraregional trade, 24; lathe production, 153; methanol-formaldehyde production, 43, 117–19, 121–22; nitrogenous fertilizer production, 77–78; pulp and paper production, 189, 219, 222; urea production, 81, 87; regional production gain, 56

Common external tariff, *see* Tariff

Complementarity agreement: and foreign multinational corporations, 27; and integration, 59; in petrochemical industry, 18; v. regional international companies, 45

Cooper, C. A., 12n, 13n, 59n

Cordeen, W. M., 5n

Corporación de Fomento de la Producción (CORFO), 209

Cost projections, *see* Production costs

Costa Rica, 13, 18

Cuba, 8

Curaçao, 77

Currency, *see* Exchange rates

Customs union, 9–13. *See also* Integration

Dagnino Pastore, José Maria, 135n, 139n, 142n, 219n

Dairy products, *see* Powdered milk and cheese

de Pablo, Juan Carlos, 166n

Demand projection: cellulose, 190–92; kraft paper, 190–92; lathes, 152–55; methanol and formaldehyde, 117–18; newsprint, 190–92, 207–08; nitrogenous fertilizers, 109; powdered milk and cheese, 166–69; study definition, 32–33, 215–18; tractors, 137–42

Economic Commission for Latin America (ECLA): foreign exchange study, 5–6; industrialization study, 6–7; integration impetus, 29; lathe study, 152; methanol-formaldehyde study, 118; nitrogenous fertilizer study, 40, 76–77; pulp and paper study, 196

Economies of scale: in ammonia production, 40–41, 78, 87; integration effect, 69; and market size, 11–12; in methanol-formaldehyde production, 43–44, 119–22; in nitrogenous fertilizer production, 85–89; in powdered milk and cheese, 174–75; in processed food, 47; in tractor production, 45, 148–50

Ecuador: cheese production, 168; industrial growth, 19–20, 35; integration attitude, 13, 17–18; intraregional trade, 24; pulp and paper production, 49, 184, 189–90, 208, 221; regional production gain, 56; subsidy need, 35

Effective tariff, *see* Tariff

El Salvador, 13, 64

Esquenazi-Mayo, Roberto, 29n

Exchange rates: and currency evaluation, 5, 9, 34; lathe production effect, 46–47, 164; nitrogenous fertilizer production effect, 101–04; optimum location determinant, 64–68; pulp and paper production effect, 199–200, 202–03; study definition, 35–36, 226–28; tractor production effect, 144, 149–50. *See also* Indifference rates of exchange

Export subsidy: integration alternative, 9

Fertilizers, *see* Nitrogenous fertilizers

Ffrench-Davis, Ricardo, 12n

Fluid milk, 173–74. *See also* Powdered milk and cheese

Food processing, 4

Formaldehyde, *see* Methanol and formaldehyde

Frei, Eduardo, 16, 27

Gehrels, F., 9n
González del Valle, Jorge, 15n
Grace, J. P., Jr., 141n
Grace, W. R., & Co., 207
Great Britain, 142–43
Griffin, Keith, 12n
Gross domestic product (GDP): optimum location effect, 55, 58; uneven development of, 18–20
Grunwald, Joseph, 12n, 20n, 21n
Guano, 74
Guatemala, 13
Guayanas, 13
Guisinger, Stephen E., 5n

Haldi, John, 11n
Hansen, Roger D., 14n
Herrera, Felipe, 16
Hilton, Ronald, 14
Honduras: in CACM, 13; and El Salvador, 64; industrial growth, 14, 18; Regime of Integration Industries, 25
Hughlett, Lloyd, 151

Ibarra, Fernando Arturo, 166n
IDB, *see* Inter-American Development Bank
Import substitution, 4–7
Imports: lathes, 164; nitrogenous fertilizer, 97, 99, 111–13; v. optimum location, 50–57, 97, 143, 148–49, 225; powdered milk, 178; pulp and paper, 188, 199, 201; tractor, 135, 138, 141–43, 145–46, 148–49; welfare cost, 50–56, 111–13, 143, 148–49. *See also* Tariff; Trade
Indifference rate of exchange: defined, 64; lathe production effect, 160–61; methanol-formaldehyde effect, 127, 129–31; newsprint production effect, 207–08; nitrogenous fertilizer production effect, 101–04; optimum location determinant, 38, 68; powdered milk and cheese production effect, 178–81, 183; study definition, 35–36, 226–28; tractor production effect, 146–48. *See also* Exchange rates
Industrialization: balance - of - payments constraint, 7–8; concentration fear, 30; ECLA study, 6–7; growth, 4, 18–20; import-substitution, 4–7; Regime of Integration Industries, 13–14, 25. *See also* entry for specific industry
Instituto de Economía de la Universidad Nacional de Chile, 152

Instituto Torcuato di Tella (Argentina), 136
Integration: alternatives to, 8–9; benefits and costs, 50–59, 68–70; and complementarity agreements, 59; economies of scale, 69; and migration, 61, 64; obstacles to, 18–27; Regime of Integration Industries, 13–14, 25; regional investment programs, 69; study need, 29–31; theory, 6–13; trade effect, 58. *See also* Central American Common Market; Latin American Free Trade Association
Inter-American Development Bank (IDB), 29; funding, 104; and Regime of Integration Industries, 25
Investment projections: lathe production, 162, 164; methanol-formaldehyde production, 43, 129, 132; nitrogenous fertilizer production, 42, 106–10; pulp and paper production, 205–06
Isard, Walter, 31n

Johnson, Harry G., 10n; customs union theory, 11
Johnson, John J., 8

Kraft cellulose, *see* Pulp and paper
Kraft paper, *see* Pulp and paper

LACM, *see* Latin American Common Market
Lathes: current production, 151–52; demand, 152–55; exchange rate effect, 46–47, 65, 67, 164; imports, 164; and indifference rates of exchange, 160–61; investment projection, 162, 164; market orientation, 46; national production, 160–62, 164; optimum location, 46–47, 155–59; plant size, 160, 214; production costs, 153–55, 220, 222–23; regional production gain, 56; shadow prices, 160, 164; skilled labor, 46, 56; study size, 217; tariffs on, 162; transport costs, 155; welfare costs, 56, 163–64
Latin American Common Market, 16–17
Latin American Free Trade Association: Andean subgroup, 18; formation, 13; industrial growth, 19; LACM proposal, 16–17; Protocol of Caracas, 17; trade, intraregional, 15, 17; and U.S., 27; weaknesses, 15–16, 18–24. *See also* Integration
Lipsey, R. G., 9n
Little, I. M. D., 45n
Location, *see* Optimum location

Macario, Santiago, 7*n*
Managua Treaty (*1960*), 13; Integration Industries Scheme, 25
Manne, Alan S., 125, 213*n*, 220*n*
Markowitz, Harry M., 125*n*, 213*n*
Martirena-Mantel, Ana M., 220*n*
Massell, B. F., 12*n*, 13*n*, 59*n*
Massey-Ferguson, 142
Mayer, Michael, 29*n*
Mayobre, José Antonio, 16
McClelland, Donald, 14
McKinnon, Ronald I., 5*n*
Meade, J. E., 9*n*, 50*n*
Meat production, 24
Methanol and formaldehyde: consumption, 117; demand projection, 116–18; and indifference rates of exchange, 127, 129–31; investment projection, 43; natural gas use, 43; optimum location, 60–62, 122–25; production costs, 44, 219, 221; shadow prices, 125, 127; tariff on, 134; uses, 116
Mexico, 13; ammonia production, 80–84, 86–88; import substitution, 7; industrial growth, 20; lathe production, 151–52, 162–63; methanol-formaldehyde production, 117–24, 127–29, 221; natural gas production, 41; newsprint production, 207; nitrogenous fertilizer production, 75–76, 78, 101–02, 104; pulp and paper production, 49, 189–90, 192–93, 196, 205, 222; tractor production, 135–38; urea production, 81, 84, 87
Montevideo Treaty (*1961*), 13, 15; "reciprocity" principle, 24–25
Munk, Bernard, 135*n*
Musgrove, Philip, 21*n*

Nacional Financiera (Mexico), 136
National production: "excess demand" solution for paper and pulp, 201; lathes, 160–62, 164; methanol and formaldehyde, 127, 129, 132–34; "modified" national alternative for methanol and formaldehyde, 129, 132; nitrogenous fertilizers, 97, 99–100, 111–15; v. optimum location, 50, 56–59; powdered milk and cheese, 178, 183; pulp and paper, 196, 201; tractors, 144–46, 148–49; welfare cost, 56–59, 129, 132–34
Natural gas: in fertilizer production, 39–40, 43, 76–77; pricing, 40; and petroleum production, 40; transport costs, 41–42
Navarreta, Jorge, 29*n*

Nelson, Glen T., 171*n*
Newsprint: consumption, 207; demand projection, 190–92, 207–08; and indifference rates of exchange, 207–08; optimum location, 49, 208, 210; production costs, 209; transport costs, 209–10
Nicaragua: CACM member, 13; industrial growth, 14, 64; Regime of Integration Industries, 25
Nitrogenous fertilizers: consumption, 74–78; demand projection, 76–79, 109; economies of scale, 79, 85–89; exchange rate factor, 65–66, 101–04; imports, 98–99, 112–13; and indifference rates of exchange, 101–04; investment projection, 42, 106–10; optimum location, 42–43, 56, 60, 62, 88–104, 111–15; national production, 97, 99–101, 111–15; and natural gas, 39–40; production costs, 77, 79–85, 104–06, 219, 223; tariff need, 79. *See also* Ammonia; Ammonium nitrate; Ammonium sulphate; Urea

Optimum location: exchange rate variable, 64–68; general equilibrium analysis, 36–37; heavy industry, 37–38; import alternative, 50, 57, 97, 143, 148–49, 225; and indifference rates of exchange, 38; market orientation, 44–45; methanol and formaldehyde, 43, 122–25, 127; "modified" national alternative for methanol and formaldehyde, 129, 132; national production alternative, 50, 97, 111–15, 127; newsprint, 208, 210; nitrogenous fertilizers, 88–104, 111–15; political considerations, 50, 68–69; powdered milk and cheese, 174–78, 183; production effect, 52–56; pulp and paper, 193, 196–99; and raw materials, 37–38; study definition, 31, 222, 224–26; v. suboptimum location, 59–64; tractors, 143–48, 150; welfare gains, 34, 50–59, 143, 148–49, 201, 205

Panama: industrial growth, 19–20; subsidy needs, 35
Paraguay, 13; industrial growth, 19–20, 35; paper and paperboard, 184; regional production gain, 56
Peru: ammonia production, 80, 82–84, 86–87, 106, 221; cheese production, 170, 173, 178; copper in, 24; guano production, 74; integration role, 13, 17; powdered milk production, 166; natural gas,

41; nitrogenous fertilizer production, 77–78; pulp and paper production, 189, 219, 221–22; regional production gain, 56

Petrochemical industry, 18

Petroleum production, 24, 40

Plant size: dairy products, 214; formaldehyde production, 43; lathe production, 160, 214; nitrogenous fertilizer production, 40; powdered milk and cheese production, 166, 170, 175, 178, 214, 222; pulp and paper production, 196, 199; study assumptions, 214–15, 217; tractor production, 141–42, 144–45, 148, 150, 214–15. *See also* Economies of scale

Powdered milk and cheese: current production, 166, 168–69; demand projection, 166, 168; economies of scale, 174–75; imports, 178; indifference rates of exchange, 178–81, 183; national production costs, 178, 183; optimum location, 47–48, 60, 63, 174–78, 183; plant size, 166, 170, 175, 178, 214, 222; production costs, 169–74, 220, 222; "second best" solution, 178; shadow price, 48; tariffs, 166–67; transport costs, 174–75, 178; turning point output, 174–75

Prebisch, Raúl, 6–7, 16

Preferential tariff, *see* Tariff

Preston, Homer J., 171*n*

Production costs: ammonia, 221; cheese, 170, 172, 220; dairy products, 220; fluid milk, 173–74; lathes, 153–55, 220, 222–23; methanol and formaldehyde, 118–24, 127, 219, 221; newsprint, 209; nitrogenous fertilizers, 219, 223; paper, 221–22; and plant size, 218; powdered milk and cheese, 169–74, 220, 222; study definition, 33, 218–23; tractors, 138–42, 221

Protocol of Caracas, 17

Pulp and paper: bagasse pulp, 48; cellulose, 192–99; consumption, 185–86; demand projection, 190–92; economies of scale, 49; "excess demand" solution, 201; exchange rate variable, 199–200, 202–03; imports, 199, 201; investment projection, 205–06; national production, 49, 196, 201; optimum location, 48–49, 56, 61, 63, 193, 196–99, 201, 204–05; plant size, 196, 199; production costs, 192–95, 219–23; study definition, 217; subsidy, 205; tariff, 186, 188; transport cost, 48, 193, 199. *See also* Newsprint

Punta Arenas, Chile, 40, 84, 118, 122

Punta del Este Conference: foreign investment, 27; LACM agreement, 17

Quintanilla, Juan B. Rodriguez, 186*n*

Rate of exchange, *see* Exchange rate

Raw materials, 37, 39–40

"Reciprocity" principle, 25

Regime of Integration Industries, 13–14, 25

Regional integration, *see* Integration

Regional international companies, 45

Regional investment programs, 69

Roback, Stefan, 61, 64*n*

Sanz de Santamaria, Carlos, 16, 73*n*

Schydlowsky, Daniel M., 5*n*

Scitovsky, Tibor, 12

Shadow price: lathes, 160, 164; methanol and formaldehyde, 125, 127; study assumption, 222–23; tractors, 144

Soligo, Ronald, 5*n*

Stern, Joseph J., 5*n*

Suboptimum location: v. optimum location, 59–64; study definition, 35. *See also* Optimum location

Subregional Andean Integration Agreement, 17–18

Subsidy: pulp and paper production, 205; study assumption, 35

Tariff, 4; common external, 16, 18; effective, 111, 114, 134, 188; intraregional, 16–18; on lathes, 162; nominal, 111, 114, 134, 188; on nitrogenous fertilizers, 79; on powdered milk and cheese, 166–67; preferential, 9; on pulp and paper, 186, 188; on tractors, 150; U.S., 42. *See also* Trade

Teubal, Miguel, 8*n*

Textile industry, 4

Timber, 24

Tractor production: demand projection, 137–42; economies of scale, 45, 148–50; exchange rate variable, 144, 149–50; imports, 135, 138, 141–43; and indifference rates of exchange, 67–68, 147–48; market orientation, 44–45; middle-level countries, 45; national production, 144–46; optimum location, 44–45, 143–49; plant size, 141–42, 144–45, 148, 150, 214–15; production costs, 219, 221; study size, 136–37, 217; tariff, 150; transport cost, 44

Trade: CACM, 14; customs union theory, 9–12; free trade theory, 3–4; integration effect, 59; intraregional, 14–16, 22–24; LAFTA, 15–16; manufactured goods, 20–24. *See also* Tariff

Transport cost: ammonia, 42; fluid milk, 173–74; lathes, 155; location constraint, 214; methanol and formaldehyde, 127; natural gas, 39–42; newsprint, 209–10; nitrogenous fertilizer production, 42–43, 111–15; powdered milk and cheese, 174–75, 178; processed food, 47; pulp and paper, 193, 199; study definition, 34, 37, 223–24; tractor parts, 44, 144

United Nations, 209

United States: butter production, 171; cellulose production, 196; lathe production, 164; and LAFTA, 27; methanol-formaldehyde production, 122, 127, 129; newsprint production, 207; nitrogenous fertilizer production, 85, 102; powdered milk production, 170–71, 173, 178; pulp export, 201, 205; Regime of Integration Industries, 25; tractor production, 141–44

Urea: consumption, 75; demand projection, 76, 78; economies of scale, 87; optimum location, 42–43; production costs, 81, 84–85, 98–99

Urquidi, Victor, 25

Uruguay, 13; cheese production, 168, 170, 178, 220; dairy products, 61; powdered milk production, 169, 178–80, 183; processed food products, 47–48; regional production gain, 56; subsidy needs, 35

Used paper, 48

Venezuela: ammonia production, 80, 82–83, 86–87; industrial growth, 18–19; integration attitude, 13, 17–18; methanol-formaldehyde production, 43, 118–25; natural gas, 41; nitrogenous fertilizer production, 42, 77–78, 101–04; petroleum production, 24; powdered milk production, 166; urea production, 81, 87; regional production gain, 56

Vietorisz, Thomas, 125, 213n, 220n

Viner, Jacob, 9n; customs union model, 10

Walker, Scott H., 171n

Welfare cost: and complementarity agreements, 45; cheese industry, 166; imports, 50–56, 111–13, 143, 148–49; lathe production, 163–64; methanol-formaldehyde production, 129, 132–34; national production, 56–59, 129, 132–34; nitrogenous fertilizer production, 111–13; and optimum location, 34, 50–59, 143, 148–49, 201, 204–05; powdered milk and cheese production, 182–83; pulp and paper production, 201, 204–05; study definition, 34, 221, 225–26; suboptimum location, 60–61; tractor production, 143, 148–49

Wheat production, 24

Whitcomb, David, 11n

Wionczek, Miguel, 12n

Wood pulp, *see* Pulp and paper

093329